Ruminating on the relationship between law, memory and human rights, this impressive collection dazzles in content and scope. Its empirically rich and theoretically provocative contributions range from international law to literary studies, crossing an expanse of geographies and histories, all to remind readers that while wrongs cannot be righted, and memory cannot be trusted, the pursuit of justice in the present cannot be abandoned. A valuable collection for scholars – legal and otherwise – working in the areas of transitional justice, de-colonization, reconciliation and public memory.

Stacy Douglas, Assistant Professor of Law and Legal Studies, Carleton University, Ottawa, Canada

Injustice, Memory and Faith in Human Rights

This multi-disciplinary collection interrogates the role of human rights in addressing past injustices. The volume draws on legal scholars, political scientists, anthropologists and political philosophers grappling with the weight of the memory of historical injustices arising from conflicts in Europe, the Middle East and Australasia. It examines the role of human rights as legal doctrine, rhetoric and policy as developed by states, international organizations, regional groups and non-governmental bodies. The authors question whether faith in human rights is justified as balm to heal past injustice or whether such faith nourishes both victimhood and self-justification. These issues are explored through three discrete sections: moments of memory and injustice; addressing injustice; and questions of faith. In each of these sections, authors address the manner in which memory of past conflicts and injustice haunt our contemporary understanding of human rights. The volume questions whether the expectation that human rights law can deal with past injustice has undermined the development of an emancipatory politics of human rights for our current world.

Kalliopi Chainoglou is a Lecturer in International and European Institutions at the University of Macedonia, Thessaloniki (Greece) and visiting Research Fellow at the Centre on Human Rights in Conflict, at the University of East London. She completed her PhD in International Law at King's College London and is an Associate Fellow of the British Higher Education Academy. She works in the areas of human rights law, cultural rights and policies, and international peace and security. She is an expert of the Council of Europe/ERICarts Compendium of Cultural Policies and Trends in Europe and has published extensively on human rights and international law. Her most recent publication is *Culture and Human Rights: The Wroclaw Commentaries* (de Gruyter, 2016).

Barry Collins is a Senior Lecturer at the University of East London, where he is a member of the Centre on Human Rights in Conflict. His research deals with themes of legal theory, international law, human rights and memory in post-conflict societies, with a particular focus on Ireland and the Middle East.

Michael Phillips is a banking lawyer and independent researcher. He has had an interest in the relationship between religion, politics and transitional justice since doing his PhD on the Aboriginal reconciliation process at the University of Sydney. He was formerly Senior Lecturer in Law at the University of East London.

John Strawson is honorary Professor of Law at the University of East London, where he is a member of the Centre on Human Rights in Conflict and a fellow of the Terrorism and Extremism Research Centre. He works in the areas of Law and Middle East Studies focusing on colonial legal history and Islamic law. His publications include *Partitioning Palestine: Legal Fundamentalism in the Palestinian–Israeli Conflict* (2010) and he is the editor of *Law after Ground Zero*, re-issued in hardback by Routledge in 2016.

Injustice, Memory and Faith in Human Rights

Edited by
Kalliopi Chainoglou,
Barry Collins, Michael Phillips
and John Strawson

Routledge
Taylor & Francis Group
LONDON AND NEW YORK

First published 2018
by Routledge

2 Park Square, Milton Park, Abingdon, Oxfordshire OX14 4RN
52 Vanderbilt Avenue, New York, NY 10017

Routledge is an imprint of the Taylor & Francis Group, an informa business

First issued in paperback 2019

British Library Cataloguing-in-Publication Data
A catalogue record for this book is available from the British Library

Library of Congress Cataloging-in-Publication Data
A catalog record for this book has been requested

ISBN: 978-1-4724-6232-9 (hbk)
ISBN: 978-0-367-26704-9 (pbk)

Typeset in Galliard
by Florence Production Ltd, Stoodleigh, Devon, UK

Contents

Acknowledgements

This book would not have been possible without the invaluable work of the Centre on Human Rights in Conflict at the University of East London, which provided the administrative support for the workshop which initiated the project. We owe a debt to Fiona Fairweather who, as then Dean of the School of Law and Social Sciences, agreed to fund the workshop. We also thank our contributors who have demonstrated such creative commitment to the book. We are grateful for the generous comments which participants at various academic conferences have made on aspects of the project – especially at the Law and Society Association and the Association for the Study of Law, Culture and the Humanities. We must also thank Alison Kirk and Ruth Noble at Routledge for their support for this project and their patience in seeing it through to fruition.

Notes on contributors

Mireno Berrettini is a researcher at the Università Cattolica (Milan). He is interested in issues related to the Spanish Church and Catholicism and is part of the Catolicismo y secularización en la España del siglo XX research group (Spain). Among his publications are *From Accomplice to Victim: Catholic Church, Spanish Civil War and Collective Memory* (2016); *Tarancón, Obispo de Solsona* (2015); and *The Spanish Catholic Church from the Zapatero Era to the Rajoy Government* (2013).

Georgina Blakeley is a Senior Lecturer in Politics at the Open University. She has published widely on various aspects of Spanish politics including the 15M movement, citizen participation, urban governance and historical memory. Her editorial work includes three co-edited books on political concepts with Valerie Bryson. These include *Marx and Other Four-Letter Words* (Pluto Press, 2005) and *The Impact of Feminism on Political Concepts and Debates* (Manchester University Press, 2007).

Kalliopi Chainoglou is a Lecturer in International and European Institutions at the University of Macedonia, Thessaloniki (Greece) and visiting Research Fellow at the Centre on Human Rights in Conflict, at the University of East London. She completed her PhD in International Law at King's College London and is an Associate Fellow of the British Higher Education Academy. She works in the areas of human rights law, cultural rights and policies, and international peace and security. She is an expert of the Council of Europe/ERICarts Compendium of Cultural Policies and Trends in Europe and has published extensively on human rights and international law. Her most recent publication is *Culture and Human Rights: The Wroclaw Commentaries* (de Gruyter, 2016).

Barry Collins is a Senior Lecturer at the University of East London, where he is a member of the Centre on Human Rights in Conflict. His research deals with themes of legal theory, international law, human rights and memory in post-conflict societies, with a particular focus on Ireland and the Middle East.

Ignacio Fernández de Mata (PhD in History, PhD in Social Anthropology) has conducted research on topics ranging from history of cultural anthropology to contemporary ethnographic analyses of identity and memory conflicts; the cultural representation of violence; and the social management of the past. His relevant publications include 'Rude Awakening. Franco's Mass Graves and the Decomposition of the Spanish Transition Dream', in *Legacies of Violence in Contemporary Spain. Exhuming the Past, Understanding the Present*, Ofelia Ferrán and Lisa Hilbink, eds. (New York: Routledge, 2017); and *Lloros vueltos puños. El conflicto de los 'desaparecidos' y vencidos de la Guerra Civil Española* (Granada: Comares, 2016).

Nasia Hadjigeorgiou holds degrees from University College London (LL.B), the University of Cambridge (LL.M) and King's College, London (PhD) and is currently a Lecturer on Human Rights at the University of Central Lancashire. Her research interests focus on the protection of human rights and peace building in transitional societies. She has published on the conflicts in Bosnia and Herzegovina, Cyprus, Northern Ireland and South Africa.

Mertkan Hamit is a member of the Centre on Human Rights in Conflict at the University of East London where is completing a PhD on the Cyprus conflict. He also works with various NGOs in Northern Cyprus.

Eric Heinze is Professor of Law and Humanities at Queen Mary, University of London. His books include *Hate Speech and Democratic Citizenship* (OUP, 2016); *The Concept of Equality* (Routledge, 2013); *The Logic of Constitutional Rights* (Ashgate, 2005); *The Logic of Equality* (Ashgate, 2003); *The Logic of Liberal Rights* (Routledge, 2003); *Of Innocence and Autonomy: Children, Sex and Human Rights* (Ashgate, 1999); and *Sexual Orientation: A Human Right* (Nijhoff, 1995).

Cillian McGrattan lectures in politics at Ulster University. He is the author of *The Politics of Trauma and Peace-Building: Lessons from Northern Ireland* (Routledge, 2016) and *Haunted by History: Memory, Politics, Identity* (Palgrave Macmillan, 2012).

Wayne Morrison is Professor of Law, Queen Mary University of London and a barrister and solicitor of the High Court of New Zealand. At Queen Mary he teaches courses on criminology, jurisprudence and has developed the only undergraduate course in the world on Law and the Holocaust. His writings span criminology, legal theory and the Holocaust and have been translated into Chinese, Spanish, Portuguese and Russian. He was Director of the University of London's external programs for law (1999–2009) and has traveled and lectured globally. Recently he has worked towards a more global criminology that includes topics traditionally excluded from the canon, such as genocide, war and methods of representation and remembrance. He first visited Bangladesh in 1997 and has been a frequent visitor and keen observer since (see for example, 'Looking into the Abyss: Bangladesh, Critical Criminology and Globalisation,' in *Green Harms and Crimes*, Ragnhild Sollund (ed.), Palgrave Macmillan, 2015).

Paul Muldoon teaches political theory in the School of Social Sciences at Monash University, Australia. His research focuses on the way societies come to terms with the past, paying particular attention to the role of the emotions in post-colonial and post-conflict societies. He is also a member of a multi-disciplinary research team funded by the Australian Research Council investigating resistance to reconciliation in South Africa, Northern Ireland and Australia.

Dominic O'Sullivan is an Associate Professor in political science at Charles Sturt University. He is the author of four books: *Faith, Politics and Reconciliation: Catholicism and the Politics of Indigeneity* (Wellington: Huia Publishers and Adelaide: the Australasian Theological Forum, 2005); *Beyond Biculturalism: The Politics of an Indigenous Minority* (Huia Publishers, 2007); *Indigenous Health: Power, Politics and Citizenship* (Australian Scholarly Publishing, 2015); and, with Russell Bishop and Mere Berryman, *Scaling up Education Reform: Addressing the Politics of Disparity* (NZCER Press, 2010).

Michael Phillips is a banking lawyer and independent researcher. He has had an interest in the relationship between religion, politics and transitional justice since doing his PhD on the Aboriginal reconciliation process at the University of Sydney. He was formerly Senior Lecturer in Law at the University of East London.

John Strawson is honorary Professor of Law at the University of East London, where he is a member of the Centre on Human Rights in Conflict and a fellow of the Terrorism and Extremism Research Centre. He works in the areas of Law and Middle East Studies focusing on colonial legal history and Islamic law. His publications include *Partitioning Palestine: Legal Fundamentalism in the Palestinian–Israeli Conflict* (2010) and he is the editor of *Law after Ground Zero*, re-issued in hardback by Routledge in 2016.

Introduction

Injustice, memory and faith in human rights

Kalliopi Chainoglou, Barry Collins, Michael Phillips and John Strawson

This book surveys difficult but uncomfortably familiar themes. Injustice seems imprinted on the planet that we inhabit. Major catastrophes have shaped our societies and cultures. At the same time systemic inequalities and discrimination plague everyday life. The last hundred years have seen grotesque inhumanities, but also the first attempts to hold those responsible to account.

The Nuremberg trials were emblematic of this development. This has, of course, spawned a consciousness that political and military leaders can be subject to the law. The past three decades have witnessed a growth in international criminal tribunals, most obviously the International Criminal Court, and a series of domestic arrangements to deal with past atrocities. The birth of international criminal justice in Nuremberg[1] was also entwined with the development of the human rights movement.[2] This grew out of the references to human rights in article 1 of the United Nations Charter and their subsequent elaboration in the 1948 Universal Declaration of Human Rights. As a result, the link between the two has become common and human rights are usually associated with their breach. This has created human rights as a locational discourse for reviewing past injustice. Rather than articulating human rights as an emancipatory political program which aims at empowering present and future generations, the reverse has been true. Human rights have been mainly presented as a way of dealing with past injustice, creating a common perception that past wrongs can indeed be righted. This volume sets out to examine the challenges of addressing injustice from this viewpoint.

The seam that links the chapters is the role of memory.[3] In his incomparable work *Landscapes of the Metropolis of Death*, Otto Dov Kulka,[4] the historian of the

1 See: Ann Tusa and John Tusa, *The Nuremberg Trials* (London: Cooper Square Press, 2003).

2 See: Mark Mazower, 'The End of Civilization and Rise of Human Rights: The mid-twentieth century disjuncture,' in *Human Rights in the Twentieth Century*, edited by Stefan-Ludwig Hoffman (New York: Cambridge University Press, 2011), 29–44.

3 See: Kerwin Lee Klein, 'On the Emergence of Memory in Historical Discourse,' *Representations*, Vol 69, Winter (2000), 127–150.

4 Otto Dov Kulka, *Landscapes of the Metropolis of Death: Reflections on Memory and Imagination*, translated by Raphael Mendel (London: Allen Lane, 2013).

Holocaust, offers a searing distinction between his work as a historian and his text of personal remembrance of Auschwitz. He first explains the nature of the book, which is based on tape-recorded recollections and diaries. 'These recordings were neither historical testimony nor autobiographical memoir,' he says, but the reflections of a person in his late fifties and sixties 'turning over in his mind those fragments of memory and imagination that have remained from the world of the wondering child of ten to eleven that I had once been.'[5] He continues:

> I am aware that, beyond the dichotomy that looms between scholarly work and my reflective memory, this present book in itself reveals immanent tensions; a confrontation between images of memory and the representation of historical research.[6]

His book, 'though anchored in concrete historical events, transcends the sphere of history.' The reader then engages in a privileged but painful encounter with an experience of Auschwitz and the realization that the past horror continues in the present. For Kulka there is no escape from the 'images of memory.' The tensions between memory and history so well addressed at the beginning of the book strike the reader as more problematic by the end. Our necessarily superficial encounters with Kulka's remembrances are so strong that most readers probably think they have grasped the reality of Auschwitz more firmly than through reading a host of scholarly accounts. This paradox underlines the complexities of the relationship between memory and history that emerge within this volume.

In his discussion of the relationship between history and memory, Yosef Hayim Jerushalmi says that 'memory is always problematic, usually deceptive, sometimes treacherous.'[7] The conditionalities that he deploys are perhaps significant. We can all agree that memory is problematic. It suffers from human frailty, from its fragmentary and partial nature. These features are not confined to the individual memory but also to the collective memory of nations and communities. However, it is questionable whether it is 'usually deceptive.' That suggests there is an element of memory that is in some senses false. But this may miss the point, as the belief in a particular memory, even if historically erroneous, can become a material factor in nourishing conflicts and refreshing old wounds. In a sense, even an erroneous historical memory can become a sort of truth. It is, of course, quite true that memory can be treacherous. Indeed, this volume is replete with such examples from Bangladesh, Ireland, Australia, Spain and Cyprus. However, history also has its pitfalls. As Ian Cobain has demonstrated, the destruction of documents by the British in their retreat from Empire was precisely aimed to recraft the historical record.[8]

5 Ibid, xi.
6 Ibid.
7 Yosef Hayim Yerushalmi, *Zakhor: Jewish History and Jewish Memory* (Seattle and London: University of Washington Press, 1982), 5.
8 Ian Cobain, *The History Thieves: Secrets, Lies and the Shaping of a Modern Nation* (London: Portobello Books, 2016).

Maintaining a strict delimitation between history and memory is thus a challenge. Indeed, as Barry Collins argues in this volume in connection to Spain's Law of Historical Memory, history can become malleable. All the while the archive of the historian is undergoing a vast technological change. While documents will continue to be significant, they are being supplemented by a vast array of radio recordings, television and social and digital media. The latter bring the witness to history to a new location. The relationship between memory and history is in a state of flux.

Kulka has brought remembrance, with all its particularities, as a critical aid to understand a historical event. Its fragmentary nature is part of its power. By its nature it cannot address the whole event, but neither can history as scholarly discipline. History is selective, but there is a consciousness of this which takes the form of certain conventions of method. History is open for the gaps to be filled in. Memory operates differently. Both individual and collective memory are constructed through partial reflection. Its very subjectivity defines the boundaries. Memory is episodic, fragmentary and exclusory. There are things left unsaid, prevarications, circumlocutions. However, each individual as part of a shared community of memory becomes attuned to these silences and obfuscations. Momik, the child in David Grossman's *See Under Love*,[9] picks up on the silences and the coded way in which the Holocaust is referred to by his parents. He tries to overcome this by studying the Holocaust at the local library but has difficulty making sense of it all. In overhearing adults talking about the 'Nazi beast' he believes it must be his duty to hunt and destroy it. Thus he begins to trap a series of actual beasts and then tries to identify the Nazi among them. The murmurs and silences of his parents and relatives are part, no doubt, of their attempt to protect a young child from the horrors of the past. Equally for the adults, the trauma of the experience of surviving the Holocaust produces a degree of disorientation that makes reflection highly problematic. Speaking about such experience is fraught. The child is caught in a web of the unsettled memory of others. Grossman shows us the complexity and the pain of translating codes and silences. Momik makes his own sense of what is said and what is not. The silences become a reference point to be addressed. As Jacques Derrida enigmatically says, this 'silence is thus also that of a speech or word that is given.'[10] *Injustice, Memory and Faith in Human Rights* is much concerned with this 'given' as the starting point for a search for justice.

Grossman also demonstrates that the transmission of memory imposes a burden on the next generation. Momik feels impelled to act to rectify the past disaster but also to prevent its recurrence. International society has not been so very different in its approach to past injustice. The UN and the development of the concept of human rights emerged as a global code for future generations to

9 David Grossman, *See Under Love*, translated by Betsy Rosenberg (London: Jonathan Cape, 1900), 3–86.

10 Jacques Derrida, *Adeiu to Emmanuel Levinas*, translated by Pascalle-Anne Brault and Michelle Naas (Stanford: Stanford University Press, 1997), 117.

decipher the horrors of the Second World War.[11] The Charter is imprinted with the course and consequences of the war despite only oblique references to the events themselves. It is as if by articulating an image of a peaceful international society, based on humanitarian values, that the past tragedy has been recognized. The intergenerational references in the preamble also impose the burden of the past on the future.

The UN Charter is replete with elliptical and sometimes circular constructions. This is exemplified by the references to human rights. In the preamble, 'we the people' of the UN reaffirm 'faith in fundamental human rights.' In article 1(3) a purpose of the UN is 'promoting and encouraging respect for human rights and fundamental freedoms.' There is silence on the content apart from the clue that these rights are 'for all without distinction as to race, sex, language or religion.' The Charter implies that human rights must already exist as we are 'reaffirming our faith' in them. And yet in the words of article 1 it appears that this reaffirmation might be problematic, as the same UN has the obligation of 'promoting and encouraging' human rights. We are, it appears, left with not so much the recognition of what human rights are as faith in what they might be. If faith in human rights is merely being reaffirmed, there is an implication that such faith precedes the UN. The adoption the Charter thus does not mark the birth of human rights but rather it is a moment of renewal of faith in human rights. This collection examines what this faith might mean.

The human rights discourse is thus articulated through the UN as a universal truth devoid of temporality. Yet, in the first phase of the UN, human rights became an ideological battlefield in the Cold War. The west posed as the patron of human rights, claiming the concept as a logical outcome of western history. When the Cold War ended and the communist regimes collapsed, this narrative was reinforced. Significantly, however, many of the staunchest defenders of the universality of human rights have come from outside the Cold War dichotomy. Abdullahi An-Na'im argues that human rights offer the possibility of 'imagining the unimaginable and retrieving the irretrievable.'[12] He is particularly generous in the way in which he sees the western claims to human rights 'as part of a continuous narrative of global humanity, rather than a chauvinistic intellectual hegemony.'[13] The discursive location for universal claims for human rights shifts with each articulation of it. As we shall see in the chapters that follow, the universal is quickly patriated by municipal jurisdictions. In Chapter 1, as Wayne Morrison so subtly demonstrates, the Bangladesh War Crimes Tribunal's claims to be 'international' are problematic. The paradox is that universal human rights require the will of the state to recognize and then define them. However, as can be seen

11 See: Connor Gearty, 'Spoils for the Victor? Human Rights within the Democratic State,' in *The Cambridge Companion to Human Rights Law*, edited by Conor Gaerty and Costas Douzinas (Cambridge: Cambridge University Press, 2012), 214–230.

12 Abdullahi Ahmed An-Na'im, 'The interdisciplinarity of human rights,' in *The Cambridge Companion of Human Rights Law*, 95–113, 99.

13 Ibid.

in the case of Bangladesh, such assertions of universality can become self-serving to national interests. Faith in human rights can take many forms. Since the 1990s we have witnessed a series of attempts to test this faith with a plethora of international, regional and national projects mobilizing human rights as a standard to deal with past atrocities.

This book originated with an interest in one such project, the Spanish historical memory law of 2007. The Human Rights and Historical Memory research group at the University of East London, located in the Centre on Human Rights in Conflict, organized a workshop to examine its implications in 2013. This law offered a tantalizing path to create a register of justice through which to view the many tragedies and atrocities of the Spanish Civil War (1936–1939). It also provoked us to consider how to address conflicting narratives in which victims or martyrs on one side of a conflict are perpetrators and abusers to the other. Such acute issues confront many societies. In a world that has been constructed through imperial enterprise (and not just European), slavery and wars (civil and international), the debates on the Spanish law have a wider significance. The workshop thus drew scholars from Spain but also those working on different regions with interests in the relationship between memory and justice. The conversation it started has been joined by others and this book is the result. This volume brings together authors from various disciplines, including anthropology, political science, theology, law and the humanities. As is the case with many such conversations it begins, as the philosopher Willard van Orman Quine says, 'in the middle.'[14] There is much being written on the topics of international criminal law, transitional justice, memory studies and human rights. We think this book offers some helpful insights to an ongoing conversation.

Injustice, Memory and Faith in Human Rights is organized into three parts. The first deals with moments of memory and injustice. The five chapters in this part cover such moments in radically different ways. Wayne Morrison interrogates the Bangladesh War Crimes Tribunal by placing the researcher in the midst of the many dilemmas of addressing past catastrophes. Throughout his chapter he invites us to see through this prism of his experience. He gently weaves between an international criminal law conference in Nuremberg to the handing down of death sentences by the Bangladesh tribunal. The move between the academic setting and the stark realities of a society addressing its past is gripping. But it also underlines the importance of academic endeavor in making sense of atrocities – in this case the conditions that have given birth to a nation. John Strawson's chapter deals with the current crimes of ISIS. Rather than focusing on past crimes, he attempts to show how memory of past events can be mobilized to justify contemporary ones. The chapter plots the way in which the Indian Khilafat movement helped shape the modern conception of the caliph that ISIS uses to such deadly effect. Cillian McGrattan also discusses the use of history, this time in connection to Northern Ireland. He points out that since the Good Friday

14 See: Peter Hylton, *Quine* (New York: Routledge, 2007), 7.

agreement in 1998 there is less segregation in everyday life but political leaders have become increasingly deadlocked in attempting to move from stability to a better future. Part of the reason lies in the ways in which loyalist and republican leaders have clung to particular narratives of history that have largely been unchallenged by the peace agreement. As a result, Northern Ireland has reached a level of stability but its leaders and people struggle to imagine a new dispensation that is genuinely rooted in democracy and justice.

With Eric Heinze's chapter we are neatly reminded that these issues are not new. In his rich account of early modern drama, drawing on Shakespeare and Racine, he demonstrates a critical link between myth and memory that has crafted our modern conceptions of justice. This historical perspective helps us consider that the starting point for addressing injustice is not merely a desire brought about by the articulation of human rights but that it lies deep within the human condition. In the final chapter in this part, Ignacio Fernández de Mata explores the theme of justice and memory of the Spanish Civil War. In striking and sometimes disturbing examples drawn from interviews carried out with the relatives of those assassinated by the Franco regime during and after the war, he demonstrates the fragility of remembering. This chapter, influenced by the work of the Spanish Movement for the Recovery of Historical Memory, examines the way in which particular narratives of guilt and responsibility for the atrocities committed by the Franco regime have come to form part of popular memory in the country.

The second part of the book examines the way in which states, the UN and other international organizations have responded to past injustices. The contributors examine radically different approaches to achieving reconciliation and justice. Paul Muldoon sets out the array of possibilities, ranging from criminal trials to apologies. As we have noted, the era began with the Nuremberg trials. Muldoon perceptively comments that Nuremberg remains a paradox. He writes 'that Nuremberg, perhaps one of the greatest tributes that has ever been paid to law, should have done so much to expose its frailties remains one of the great ironies of history.' This deftly identifies the elusive character of justice and the problem of law's claim to deliver it. The relationship between law and justice in post-conflict situations is much discussed in this part of the book and is to the fore in Nasia Hadjigeorgiou's chapter, which teases out the relationship between reconciliation and human rights in UN peace building policy. This is an interrogation of the proposition that reconciliation can only be achieved in post-conflict societies on the basis of human rights. Hadjigeorgiou challenges the superficiality of human rights rhetoric and asks what the realization of human rights might mean and whether specifically legal institutions can or should enforce them. She argues that the condition for reconciliation is what she calls the 'rehumanization' of the 'other.'

Barry Collins turns his attention to the role of universal jurisdiction as a human rights mechanism. The doctrine which provides states with jurisdiction over the commission of extra-territorial international crimes has always been controversial. Collins focuses on the Spanish version of the doctrine, which he contrasts with the Law on Historical Memory. It is a case, he suggests, of law facing two ways. The Spanish universal jurisdiction law wraps the Spanish state in the embrace of international human rights standards while the historical memory law converts those principles into a contingent policy. He questions whether faith in human rights is too often an abstract humanism. Kalliopi Chainoglou ends this part with a discussion of how historical memory is mediated through the human rights judicial path; in particular, the way in which denial of historical crimes has been dealt with through international and regional systems. Much of the chapter focuses on the jurisprudence of the European Court of Human Rights. Chainoglou illuminates the way in which the court confronts the issue of denialism head on – as with Holocaust denial – and yet engages in the concern for the human rights of the denier. In such situations the court is reluctantly forced into being an arbiter of both history and freedom of expression.

The third part of the book focuses on whether we are justified to place our faith in human rights. The chapters consider the situations in Spain, and in Australia and New Zealand. Georgina Blakeley returns to the Spanish historical memory law and suggests there are problems both with the law and its implementation. She is concerned that the way the law works is to construct memory as an individual or, at best, a family phenomenon. Perhaps this is connected to the way in which human rights laws address individual claims. As she argues, this can undermine the capacity of society to repair itself. In an interesting twist, she suggests that Benedict Anderson's conception of the nation as an 'imagined community' should imply the right for all to participate in that very constitution of historical memory. In Dominic O'Sullivan's chapter, the issue of public memory takes center stage. This is a special type of public memory developed by the Catholic Church, which reminds us that civil society plays a critical role in forming and mobilizing memory. O'Sullivan shows how the Catholic churches in Australia and New Zealand have enabled a doctrinal outlook that takes responsibility for colonial practices to pursue contemporary reconciliation. He offers an illuminating discussion of the way in which the public memory is neither singular nor fixed.

Mireno Berrettini continues this theme in his discussion of the role of the Catholic bishops in Spain during the socialist government of 2004–2011, which introduced the historical memory law. He points out that the role of the church in the beatification and canonization of innocents and martyrs can become highly problematic. It reconstructs the past in religious metaphors which memorialize martyrs and which become entangled with contemporary politics. It shows us that faith which asks us to accept transcendent beliefs, whether religious or in human rights, is indelibly marked by temporal concerns. This part ends with Michael Phillips reworking similar themes, but more broadly, with the way in which the Australian Christian churches have engaged with reconciliation. Again faith plays a central role in the commitment to recognizing past injustice. In this case, unlike in Spain, the churches were not critical to the construction of the state. While they were implicated in colonial practices against the Aboriginal population that continued long into the twentieth century, they did not form a pillar of power. As Phillips argues, the churches overall played a progressive role in creating an ethical basis for reconciliation. However, the religious contribution to the idea of apology and forgiveness rarely translates to the political sphere.

The book ends with a reflection on the Cypriot neighborhood of Varosha which, emptied of its Greek Cypriot population in 1974, stands as a memorial to the Cyprus conflict. Mertkan Hamit and John Strawson suggest Varosha is a memorial to all conflict. By listening to the way in which former residents and their descendants talk about their memories of the past we are faced with the incommensurability of loss, the fickleness of memory and the limitations of human rights.

The past is always with us; trauma, loss and suffering cannot be erased. However, the past should not ensnare the future. This book offers glimpses into the problem of addressing our unjust past. Like memory itself our text is partial and the situations reviewed arbitrary. None the less, it provides a basis for considering the future of human rights in our unstable world. The UN formula reaffirming 'faith in human rights' appears quaint in the light of the Syrian civil war, the rise of ISIS and the refugee crisis. Long-standing conflicts over Israel-Palestine, Kashmir and the Western Sahara nourish human rights abuses daily. The Russian-Ukrainian war merely demonstrates that conflicts are born with ease. At the same time, inequality stalks the globalization that is transforming the world we live in. As the contributors to this book indicate, there is an uneasy relationship between human rights and law. Perhaps the rush to colonize human rights into treaties and legal institutions took place before an emancipatory politics of human rights could be articulated. Human rights law, however attractive as a project, has proved to be limited and problematic. If we are to reaffirm our faith in human rights we need political programs that can tame power. *Injustice, Memory and Faith in Human Rights* is a tentative contribution toward that end.

Part I

Moments of memory and injustice

1 Ghosts of war crimes past

An account from the frontline in Bangladesh

Wayne Morrison

Living in a divided past, fractured present

> Bangladesh still has not dealt with its past and the past has never left her. For any society, traumatized by serious crimes and widespread victimizations, dealing definitively with the past is critical, or else it will haunt the present and future. . . . In nearly four decades, Bangladesh has failed to reconcile with its past, an 'original sin'.[1]
>
> The first phone call that we received post-execution of Salahuddin Quader Chowdhury was from a brother living abroad: 'Are you all OK? What about *hartals*? Reactions? Vandalism? Violence?' It took us a while to calm him and tell him that we were all fine and all was well with the world and that nothing would ever go wrong again like before, and that the whole nation had stood in silence, steeped in memory, watching the news till about 1:00am of November 22, 2015 [when the news confirmed that the two men found guilty of war crimes had been hung shortly after midnight]. Many tweeted, failing the Facebooking option. Many placed regular calls to loved ones in place of Viber and WhatsApp. Many even blogged. I just tweeted ['Done, SQC. Done, Mujahid'] and rested.
>
> At around noon on the 22nd, a bright young lady, in response to my tweet, wrote: 'Where has all your compassion gone?' I . . . wondered if I should explain to the young lady that I had lived through 1971 as a young kid and had watched friends, brothers, fathers, cousins leave for war never to return.[2]

To transfer from Christianity the language of 'original sin' to label the burden Bangladesh carries from a failure to deal with its past, and in particular the events of 1971, itself displays the difficulty of finding a concept and vocabulary for a very real existential legacy. Rubana Huq, managing director of Mohammadi Group, a large garment manufacturing company, and occasional opinion columnist for one of Bangladesh's leading English-language newspapers, is but one of many who feel the memories of the past and a lack of justice as something inscribed in their own being. Thus she described her relation towards the final dismissal

1 Ahmed Ziauddin, Ahmed, 'The original sin: justice for 1971 crimes,' *The Daily Star*, March, 2008.
2 Rubana Huq, 'No Tears,' *The Daily Star*, 25 November 2015.

of appeals against the decision of the Bangladesh International War Crimes Tribunal[3] (WCT) by the Supreme Court and subsequent execution of Ali Ahsan Mohammad Mujahid, Jamaat-e-Islami Secretary General, and Salahuddin Quader Chowdhury, Bangladesh Nationalist Party (BNP) leader. As she states, failing the Facebook option she tweeted; the government on 18 November had shut down Facebook and messaging and voicecall services Viber and WhatsApp fearing violence by supporters.

Who were these men? As with all the defendants on trial by the WCT, set up in 2010 based on 1973 legislation (seen in 1973 as path-breaking and world leading[4]), they were political leaders either of the main Islamic party, Jamaat-e-Islami, or the main opposition party, the BNP. Chowdhury was a six-times MP and senior member of the BNP executive council, yet prosecutors had during the trial described him in 1971 as a young but merciless killer responsible for the deaths of more than 200 Hindus. All the defendants were said to have been youthful fanatics; not just students unmoved by the Bengali language movement or resistant to claims that the national government, located 1,600km away in West Pakistan (itself renamed simply Pakistan by executive order in 1970), treated East Pakistan as a neo-colonial dominion, but so pro-Pakistan that they abandoned student politics to set up paramilitary groups assisting the occupying Pakistan military.[5] Charges faced included abetting the Pakistani military, assisting and engaging in genocide and crimes against humanity, murder, abduction and rape. For many of the public there was little doubt as to their guilt: positioned in a narrative recall, steeped in pride mixed with bitterness, of the founding moment of Bangladesh – 'the 1971 war of liberation' – these were identified as men who had betrayed a tolerant and self-determining Muslim Bengali identity for a simplistic Islamic one and who showed ruthless determination to preserve their image of the Muslim nation.

And where was I as Rubana waited for and then celebrated their executions? I was in Germany, first giving a lecture on law in the social constitution of the Holocaust at the University of Passau and then going to Nuremberg to participate in the Nuremberg Forum. It was the seventieth anniversary of the Nuremberg trials and this was the first conference of a new institution, the Nuremberg Academy, which is dedicated to the dissemination of the Nuremberg principles as the foundational principles of international criminal law.

3 For all the reference to international, this is a domestic tribunal trying Bangladesh nationals for 'international crimes.'

4 But by 2009 many would say they needed radical upgrading and rephrasing in light of the subsequent development of the jurisprudence of international criminal law. For example, Bina D'Costa, 9 July 2009, 'Frozen in Time? The War Crimes Trial in Bangladesh,' www.asiapacific.anu.edu.au/blogs/southasiamasala/2009/07/09/frozen-in-time-the-war-crimes-trial-in-ban [accessed 17 June 2016].

5 See for example Jalal Uddin, 5 February 2009, 'Not Just Collaborators, Baksalite and the Rakhkhi-Bahini Elements Too,' News Forum Bangladesh at www.Bangladesh-web.com/view.php?hidRecord= 186352 [accessed 22 March 2017].

The opening took place in a hushed but cramped Courtroom 600 at the Nuremberg Palace of Justice. I knew it from those black and white images, newsreels and documentaries I show to my Law and Holocaust class. I had not been in person before, but now as Professor Thomas Buergenthal – President of the Academy's advisory board, Auschwitz survivor and former judge of the International Court of Justice – opened proceedings I felt in the presence of something more than a mere set of participants at a conference. Professor Leila Sadat's keynote address began by evoking a martyr-like image of Justice Jackson, who had put together the prosecution strategy for the original trials. Here was a man who faced huge odds to have a successful trial (and many would have preferred executions or a Soviet-style show trial) but was unshakable in his passion, commitment and desire to bring about the rule of law.[6] Sadat might also have referred to the language used in the trial of the Nazi justices where it was said that the Temple of Justice had been desecrated and needed to be rebuilt. I felt a new faith at work. But I was also slightly distracted, for the reality of the WCT in Bangladesh was my constant reference point as I listened, questioned and intervened, a duality of presence all the more acute as I knew that death sentences were about to be carried out at any moment.

I spoke with Stephen Rapp, former US Ambassador-at-Large and head of the Office of Global Criminal Justice in the US State Department for six years from September 2009 to August 2015 (he visited Bangladesh five times in that period). He had just sent off his personal retort to a newspaper article by one of the lead prosecutors, in which she had asserted that during his last visit, in August 2014, he had pronounced himself satisfied with the fairness of the proceedings. 'No! No!' he exclaimed to me. 'I am emailing the major newspapers and the Prime Minister expressing my deep disquiet and asking for suspension of the sentences of these men and expressly stating my concerns with the trial of S.Q. Chowdhury and the failure to allow his alibi claims to be properly presented.'

I appreciated that the WCT fell short of compliance with the Nuremberg principles (particularly in respect of equality of arms). But as I sat and listened to a former lead prosecutor at the *ad hoc* Tribunal for Rwanda (ICTR) explain that their adherence to the principle of equality of arms had meant that, when a lead defense counsel had suddenly resigned, the trial was suspended for six months to allow the new defense lawyer to come up to speed, I succumbed to existential vertigo. I passed back and forth from conversations in Dhaka, the Bangladesh capital, where I have been a frequent visitor since 1997, and in particular to a meeting with a prosecution witness and the son of an intellectual who had been taken from his family home and murdered by collaborators in the final few days leading to the victory of the pro-Bangladesh forces (and now celebrated as Martyr's Day). 'Why,' he had said with considerable fervor, 'do people outside of Bangladesh question the fairness of the trials? They are our trials! They

6 Available at www.nurembergacademy.org/events/nuremberg-forum-2015/ [accessed 17 June 2016].

are bringing justice for us, for the families that had had to put up with constant failure by government after government to deliver. Are they [the critics] corrupt? Are they bought by the money of the Islamists?' And another interview where my subject exclaimed: 'They want us to be of international standard but they give us examples of pure luxury! How many millions of dollars do international criminal courts spend to get one conviction?'[7]

It was as well that there was a polite queuing system to speak on Rwanda, as I would have been tempted to say: 'Madam, during that time when you delayed, more than ten people were dying a day in jails awaiting trials, and many more were developing gangrene in limbs from the terribly cramped conditions. In 1996 some 80,000 were in jail awaiting trial, by 2000 the figure was 130,000. Thousands died awaiting trial in terrible conditions, ultimately only 93 were indicted and 61 convicted by the ICTR; seeking solutions, local justice in the form of *Gacaca* courts dealt with hundreds of thousands (at a total cost of only $4m).[8] But that was a justice without lawyers, where only Hutu actions against Tutsi could be tried and commentators gave these processes "mixed" reviews at best. In 2014, 20 years after the genocide, *The Guardian* newspaper could report that "after almost 20 years of legal argument and an estimated bill of $1.7bn (£1.2bn) [for the ICTR], only a tiny proportion" of the Rwandan malefactors had been brought to internationally recognized justice.'

But I did not. Instead I phrased my interjections solely about Bangladesh: for as Osiel had written: 'The raging disagreements within humanitarian law today do not simply reflect diverging ideals of international order for competing normative visions of a better world. . . . They also disclose a new and shifting vocational field – international criminal law – within which various professionals struggle to establish and defend their expertise and, in so doing, secure commodious place for themselves at the high table.'[9] And I had dined, at least for lunch, quite peaceably. But my mind kept wandering. It returned to those days of my youth when, as an altar boy, I had served in Catholic services at the time when Latin was being replaced by English, never fully extinguishing the ritualistic and often simply mystifying language of miracles, saints and sinners. Now the language was of transitional justice, commitment to the Nuremberg principles, memory, hope, betrayal, victimhood. I felt guilt for my doubting; but confronting empirical reality, to engage in this new field of 'atrocity, punishment and international law,' is to move in existential circles. Aryeh Neier categorizes the International Criminal Tribunal for the former Yugoslavia and the ICTR as right deeds done for the wrong reasons, tribunals that were 'substitutes for effective action [by the United Nations or major powers] to halt Serb [or Hutu]

7 Morrison, interview notes, Dhaka, April 2014 (copy retained by author).
8 Philip Clark, *The Gacaca Courts and Post-Genocide Justice and Reconciliation in Rwanda: Justice without Lawyers* (Cambridge: Cambridge University Press, 2010).
9 Mark Osiel, *Making Sense of Mass Atrocity* (Cambridge: Cambridge University Press, 2009), p vii.

depredations in BiH [or Rwanda].'[10] But put in the context of subsequent events in Democratic Republic of the Congo and Central African Republic, Philip Lancaster is scathing. 'Twenty years after Rwanda, the world has learned nothing,' he writes, echoing Linda Melvern's 'Twenty years after the genocide, we have learnt nothing from Rwanda.' [11]

If the relevant agencies of the international community are now quick to criticize the WCT, they were absent or slow to protest the original atrocities. Bangladesh was created in a nomos dominated by Cold War politics and Westphalian sovereignty and was called a basket case by Henry Kissinger, US Secretary of State. The conflict was viewed as an internal matter, although the word 'genocide' resounded in contemporary articles in the *Sunday Times* of London.[12] Most governments appeared to hope that the situation would be soon over; New Zealand was the sole voice at the UN arguing that the breaches of human rights were so grave that intervention was required. Otherwise it was left to artists (George Harrison's concert for Bangladesh), and eccentric journalists (John Pilger) and politicians (Edward Kennedy) to bring the suffering to the world's attention. Today, with a population of 160 million, Bangladesh is regarded as an emerging market with approximately 6 per cent annual growth. Dhaka is polluted, with endless traffic jams, but it is also vibrant with coffee bars, art galleries and an ever-changing restaurant scene. Faced with innumerable problems the resilience of the people and their ingenuity stand out, causing many to now see it as a 'laboratory for innovative solutions in the developing world' and as a place where the future of an overpopulated and climate-changed world has in some ways arrived.[13] This creativity occurs alongside great corruption and an elitist, patronage-driven State. While Bangladesh is said to be the beneficiary of globalization, this has come at the cost of tremendous social upheaval, including the mass movement from the countryside to cities. The rising middle class increasingly globalizes, looks to the latest Indian or Pakistani fashions and communicates via Facebook and other social media while, by contrast, hundreds of thousands of young men are educated in madrasas financed by Saudi money, feeling shut out from the advances of modernization and prey to conservative narratives of Islam. Given a narrative of a Bangladesh born amidst global scheming and the subsequent betrayal of human dignity by immunity from prosecution, the desire for ownership of the war crimes trials aimed at local collaborators is understandable.

10 Aryeh Neier, *War Crimes: Brutality, Genocide, Terror, and the Struggle for Justice* (New York: Times Books, 1998), 112.
11 Linda Melvern, 'Twenty years after the genocide, we have learnt nothing from Rwanda,' *The Guardian*, 4 April 2014; Philip Lancaster, 'Twenty years after Rwanda, the world has learned nothing,' *The Globe and Mail*, 7 April 2014.
12 See for example Anthony Mascarenhas, 'Genocide' and 'Why the Refugees Fled,' *Sunday Times* (London), 13 June 1971.
13 For Don Beit, The Coming Storm, *National Geographic Magazine*, June 2011, 'Bangladesh *is* the future that many of us will later experience.'

On 21 January 2013 Abul Kalam Azad was sentenced to death *in absentia* charged with rape and killing 12 Hindus. On 4 February the second man to be convicted was Abdul Quader Mollah, Assistant Secretary General of Jamaati-e-Islami, who was sentenced to life imprisonment. As he was led from the tribunal he held his fingers out in a V for victory sign, implying, many understood, that if the BNP (traditional election allies of Jamaat) won polls due by year's end they would quash the tribunal's work and release him. Within hours, tens of thousands of messages were texted or read on Facebook and thousands of mostly young people gathered in Shahbagh Square to demand the highest possible sentence, that of capital punishment. The Shahbagh movement, also known as *Gonojagaran Mancha*, literally national awakening stage, became a domestic and international sensation, with similar protests being taken up in cities where the Bangladeshi diaspora reside, particularly London and Toronto. The western commentator David Lewis of the LSE found it a paradoxical 'watershed moment'[14] that liberals were demanding the unliberal death sentence. Suzannah Linton, who had edited the Criminal Law Forum's *Special Edition on Bangladesh* in 2010, simply labelled it 'bloodlust' and concluded that, 'instead of delivering justice, [the WTC] will likely go down in history for some of the most egregious irregularities in modern international criminal proceedings.'[15] On 27 February Delwar Hossain Sayeedi was sentenced to death, resulting in scenes of joy in Shahbagh Square. This led to the Jamaat groups organizing *hartals* and marches on Dhaka, which resulted in 60 people killed (by the end of 2013 the death toll from political violence was put at 300, with 4,000 injured).

The protests became embroiled in claim and counter claim, either a 'defining moment in the struggle for the soul of Bangladesh'[16] or 'a vindication of the present government's commitment' to 'build a secular, democratic polity that cherishes its multi-religious, multi-ethnic and multicultural character,'[17] or simply 'government inspired mob justice' (as several pro-Jamaat critics indicated to me personally). The government amended the ICT Act, allowing the government, informants and complainants to appeal against any verdict of the tribunal and clearing the way for a political party that had worked against the liberation of Bangladesh to be tried on the same charges as individuals. During the same

14 David Lewis, 'The paradoxes of Bangladesh's Shahbagh protests,' LSE Blogs SouthAsia, 21 March 2013, http://blogs.lse.ac.uk/southasia/2013/03/21/the-paradoxes-of-bangladeshs-shahbag-protests/ [accessed 22 March 2017].

15 Suzannah Linton, 'Bloodlust in Bangladesh: A Search for Justice Gone Wrong,' *Fletcher Forum of World Affairs*, 27 February 2013 at www.fletcherforum.org/2013/02/27/linton [accessed 30 September 2016]. Her views were shared by a number of expatriate Bangladeshis, for example Serajul Islam and Saidul Islam. 'War Crimes Tribunal in Bangladesh: A Miscarriage of Justice,' *JUST Commentary: International Movement for a Just World*, Vol 10, No 4 (2010), 3.

16 Mozammel Khan, 'International War Crimes Tribunal: A performance review,' Dhaka: *The Daily Star*, 1 January 2014.

17 Muhammad Zamir, 'Our war crimes trial: beyond politics,' *The Independent*, 1 March 2013.

period the Electoral Commission ruled that Jamaat-e-Islami was anti-democratic and unable to participate in the then forthcoming elections. Some saw this as a victory for the people (a living example of Durhkeim's collective conscience); for others the protesters at Shahbagh were either 'lynch law'[18] or did not reflect 'the Muslims of Bangladesh.' They were rather, it was claimed, part of a conspiracy to remove Islam from the politics of Bangladesh, organized by 'prominent atheists' and bloggers who had insulted the Prophet. Supporters of the Jamaat movement deflected criticism and the calls for justice by claiming that the new measures were directed at Islam itself and were part of a global war on Islam. Hefazot-e-Islam, a protest group formed in 2010 from teachers in the many madrasas of Chittagong, came up with a wide set of demands, including new anti-blasphemy laws and the destruction of any images or statutes celebrating the 'liberation war.' On 5 and 6 May its protesters, aided by Jamaat-e-Islami and its youth wing Chatra Shibir, were reported to be chanting: 'One point. One demand. Atheists must be hanged.' The same protesters moved into Dhaka, occupying and setting fire to parts of the commercial district and then facing off with the notorious Rapid Action Battalion (RAB) and police. When the RAB and police cleared the areas, video images circulated of extreme violence, mostly by the RAB and police. The government reported an official death toll of 11, but the Islamic groups claimed 3,500 had died and this figure circulated widely.[19]

The Shahbagh movement reflected, at least, the potential emergence of a new class of politically aware youth demanding justice in forms that a corrupt system could not deliver and relying on technologies that the government could not contain. But this reflects a crucial social division; while the emerging middle-class urban youth are, in part, products of lives shaped by access to information technology and social media, many Bangladeshis are barely literate and live in villages and rural situations in which traditional cultural and religious authorities carry great weight. Facebook and Twitter face off against the sermons of the Friday mosque.

Bangladesh in 2015 was a place of great contrasts. Those who might otherwise be seen as progressive liberals cheered the death penalty and recoiled in distaste at reports from internal and international human rights organizations and the UN that criticized the trials for breaches of due process, weak judicial oversight and implied political interference. On the streets, expressions of joy and hope that justice was being done faced explosions of rage at perceived injustice and cries that these were political trials and acts of revenge. Judicial executions of those found guilty led to a backlash of targeted killings of secular bloggers. Numerous political and

18 Geoffrey Robertson, 'Report on the international crimes tribunal of Bangladesh,' International Forum for Democracy and Human Rights, Sarajevo, Bosnia and Herzegovina, 2015, 11.

19 See: Human Rights Watch, 'Blood on the streets: the use of excessive force during Bangladesh protests,' 1 August 2013 at www.hrw.org/report/2013/08/01/blood-streets/use-excessive-force-during-bangladesh-protests [accessed 30 September 2016].

other opponents of the government disappeared while others were killed by police in 'cross-fire' incidents; pro-Jamaat bloggers went as far as labelling the Prime Minister 'a Lady Hitler.'[20] Even supporters of the government feared a loss of freedom for the press and noted attacks on free expression, while the fear of rising Islamic fanaticism played off against the belief that Islam was under attack. This was yet again a time of crisis, a reflection of processes in which the foundations of the State, of civil society and of identity were undercut and the future left uncertain. How does one begin to explain the impact of the WCT?

The trial of the birth of a nation: searching for truth or lost in circles of memories and indeterminate justice?

The Economist called the war crimes trials 'the trial of the birth of the nation.'[21] It offered hope in the outcome but soon ran a further story – 'Another kind of crime'[22] – arguing that 'Bangladesh's war crimes tribunal is sullying its judicial and political systems.' *The Economist* did not enter into the complex, interwoven memories and narratives that would need to be interrogated if this truly was to be a trial of the birth of a nation, which also would be a trial of the 'ultimate measure of the failure of governance in Pakistan.'[23] Instead in 2012 it focused on what appeared incontestable evidence of lack of due process when evidence appeared of hours of recorded Skype conversations between the tribunal's Chair and an adviser in Brussels whose role was denied; by 2013 *The Economist*, as we noted, labelled the proceedings 'another kind of crime.'

Few overseas observers appear to appreciate the existential depth of the memories from 1971. For example, Geoffrey Robertson, the leading British international criminal law advocate and first President of the Tribunal for Sierra Leone, rather crassly states in his 2015 'report' on the tribunal that 'these 1971 atrocities are remembered for not being remembered.'[24] It is rather that, outside Bangladesh, there is little memory. Inside Bangladesh, ghosts haunt; a multitude of small and often unkempt shrines and monuments to killing fields feature in almost every town and many villages. Rickshaw art often portrays events from 1971, while the privately financed Museum of the War of Liberation sends mobile

20 Pathik Rasel, CNN report, 'A Lady Hitler, Crimes against Humanity and Kamaruzzam,' 13 April 2015.

21 'Trying war crimes in Bangladesh: the trial of the birth of the nation,' *The Economist*, 15 December 2012, at www.economist.com/news/briefing/21568349-week-chairman-bangladeshs-international-crimes-tribunal-resigned-we-explain [accessed 30 September 2016].

22 'Justice in Bangladesh: another kind of crime,' *The Economist*, 23 March 2013 at www.economist.com/news/leaders/21573990-bangladeshs-war-crimes-tribunal-sullying-its-judicial-and-political-systems-another-kind [accessed 30 September 2016].

23 Rehman Sobhan, *Bangladesh: Problems of Governance* (New Delhi: Konvark Publishers, 1993), 149.

24 Robertson, 9.

exhibitions to schools and towns and is seen as more authoritative than the politically changeable representations located in the national museum.[25]

To re-emphasize, the burden of Bangladesh's birth and the legacy of blood are imbedded into the very heart of the body politic. For example, the current Prime Minister is Sheikh Hasina Wazed, daughter of Sheikh Mujibur Rahman, the 'father of the nation' who along with most of his family was assassinated in 1975. Abroad at the time, she was orphaned, exiled and shocked. She remembered that her father 'never thought about himself, only for people. How he can ensure to free people from exploitation, oppression. He was always ready to sacrifice his life for the sake of people.'[26]

In 1981 she returned, was at first arrested repeatedly and over time survived 19 attempts on her life, including on 21 August 2004 at a party rally when she was injured in a bomb attack that killed 22 people and injured 500. She reflected: 'I know my father sacrificed his life and I'm ready to sacrifice my life because I have to fulfil my father's unfinished job.' [27]

Such family issues seem to have generated deep hatred toward the leader of the opposition, Begum Klaleda Zia, who has led the BNP since the assassination of its founder, her husband Zinur Rahman, in 1983. Hasina rejects this as simplistic: 'We have deep ideological differences, because our party was established to ensure people's rights, every election to be free and fair, because we believe in democracy. But if you look at the BNP every time in the elections there is killing and manipulations.'[28]

On those now on trial she says: 'They are war criminals, they must be punished. . . . I don't understand how anyone could be against the trials. Sometimes I can hear the hue and cry that I'm taking revenge against opponents, but this is not true. Law will take its own course.'[29]

The fate of the collaborators continually appears. In his incisive 2001 account entitled *Freedom Unfinished*, Jeremy Seabrook recounts the narrative of Harun, who in 1971 was 17 and 'not at all political.' Harun had some basic training as a member of the Pakistani cadet force but after the crackdown he went to India to join the liberation army. He was involved in fighting alongside Indian forces, and then came the surrender.

> Tens of thousands of people came from the villages with armfuls of flowers, which they gave to the fighters; they wept tears of joy and relief.

25 Wayne Morrison, *Criminology, Civilisation and the New World Order* (Abingdon: Routledge/Cavendish, 2006) 286–290.

26 The Frost Interview – Sheikh Hasina: 'They should be punished,' 47 minutes, published 23 September 2013, available at www.aljazeera.com/programmes/frostinterview/2013/09/2013920103532114976.html [accessed 24 March 2017].

27 Ibid.

28 Ibid.

29 Ibid.

> I thought after liberation would be like the Garden of Eden. The reality was crisis. . . .
>
> After a few years it was as though the Pakistani army had come again. We were ruled by a junta. Pakistani culture was imposed. A big mistake was to release too many collaborators. We should not have done so. Most looked to continue their mischief. The defeat of collaboration on the soil of Bengal, that will be my life's achievement; the fundamentalists and the anti-liberation forces are more united than we. They are strong but not the majority. . . .[30]

For those given the title of freedom fighter there seems little to match 1971, nor any feeling of betrayal equal to observing those considered collaborators operating freely. Similarly, in the collection *Rising from the Ashes: Women's Narratives of 1971*[31] interviews with victims such as Rumana, who had survived a massacre when many of those sheltering in her father's house were killed (including her father and mother), make constant reference to the insult felt at seeing 'collaborators' operating freely in Bangladesh. Rumana expresses her distaste:

> In Bangladesh, collaborators . . . are walking about freely. They have been granted citizenship. When I see that I feel really bad. How can those who raped women, killed innocent people and freedom fighters walk about freely? . . . We want the collaborators in 1971 to be punished. If war criminals could be tried 50 years after the Second World War, why cannot our country try collaborators after 25 years?[32]

Television commentary on the WCT almost obsessively contains a Bangladeshi commentator who will refer to the atrocities as 'the worst genocide in history,' 'the worst genocide after Hitler,' and this is repeated in writings from the Liberation War Museum.[33] If the elite of Bangladesh are now cosmopolitan, the depth of the diaspora also means that references and texts are read in numerous locations including the US, Canada, the UK and Australia. It is no surprise that when the Second Tribunal of the WCT delivered its first judgment, on 21 January 2013, it attempted to place itself in a global meta-narrative.[34] In paragraph

30 Quoted in Jeremy Seabrook, *Freedom Unfinished: Fundamentalism and Popular Resistance in Bangladesh Today* (London: Zed Books, 2001), 109.

31 Shaheen Zaman, *et al.* (eds.), *Rising from the Ashes: Women's Narratives of 1971* (Dhaka: The University Press Limited, 2001 English ed. 2013).

32 Zaman, 49–50.

33 As put in the introduction to the 2001 publication simply called *Liberation War Museum* and on the current revamped webpages in the history section it is called 'the worst genocide after the second world war,' repeated in the 'About us' section; Liberation War Museum website, http://liberationwarmuseum.org/ [accessed 24 March 2017]. This is repeated in book after book. See for example Ahmed Salahuddin, *Bangladesh Past and Present* (New Delhi: APH Publishing Corporation, 2004).

34 See judgment at: http://bangladeshtrialobserver.org/category/tribunal-2/trial-of-abul-kalam-azad-bachu/ [accessed 24 March 2017].

47 it quoted Stan Cohen in *States of Denial*: 'After generations of denials, lies, cover-ups and evasions, there is a powerful, almost obsessive, desire to know exactly what happened.' The judgment continued: 'In Bangladesh, the efforts initiated under a lawful legislation to prosecute, try and punish the perpetrators of crimes committed in violation of customary international law is an indicia of valid and courageous endeavour to come out from the culture of impunity.'[35]

The structure of the judgment is repeated in all subsequent ones; it presents a particular, officially sanctioned, narrative as 'historical background.'

> Atrocious and horrendous crimes were committed during the nine-month-long war of liberation, which resulted in the birth of Bangladesh, an independent state. Some three million people were killed, nearly a quarter million women were raped and over 10 million people were forced to flee to India to escape brutal persecution at home during the nine-month battle and struggle of the Bengali nation. The perpetrators of the crimes could not be brought to book, and this left a deep wound on the country's political psyche and the whole nation. The impunity they enjoyed held back political stability, saw the ascent of militancy and destroyed the nation's Constitution.[36]

The judgment then immediately references two international scholars:

> A well-known researcher on genocide, R.J. Rummel, in his book, *Statistics of Democide: Genocide and Mass Murder Since 1900*, states:
>
> > In East Pakistan [General Agha Mohammed Yahya Khan and his top generals] also planned to murder its Bengali intellectual, cultural and political elite. They also planned to indiscriminately murder hundreds of thousands of its Hindus and drive the rest into India. And they planned to destroy its economic base to insure that it would be subordinate to West Pakistan for at least a generation to come.[37]

Women were tortured, raped and killed. With the help of its local collaborators, the Pakistan military kept numerous Bengali women as sex slaves inside their camps and cantonments. Susan Brownmiller, who conducted a detailed study, has estimated the number of raped women at over 400,000.[38]

Rummel has done valiant work attempting to establish the huge dark figure of state-sponsored crime worldwide, but his figures are always taken from media accounts and he then tries to get to a reasonable figure by taking a mean (his method is critiqued by Gerlach[39]). Brownmiller's famous 1975 text was rightly

35 Ibid.
36 Ibid, paragraph 5.
37 Ibid, paragraph 6.
38 http://bangladeshwatchdog1.wordpress.com/razakars/%5D, para 6 [accessed 24 March 2017].
39 Christian Gerlach, *Extremely Violent Societies: Mass Violence in the Twentieth-Century World* (Cambridge: Cambridge University Press, 2010), 257 and 468.

characterized as an 'overwhelming indictment' of the prevalence of rape and a critical take on male-dominated societies. However, like Rummel, she worked with secondary accounts, accepting sources now open to contestation.

The judgment rightly noted that Bangladesh is a signatory to various international conventions and states that the proceedings are in line with those commitments. It explains that 'the degree of fairness' embedded in the Act and the Rules of Procedure (ROP) formulated by the tribunals under the powers conferred in section 22 of the principal Act 'are to be assessed with reference to the national needs such as the long denial of justice to the victims of the atrocities committed during the 1971 independence war and the nation as a whole.' It explains that it will accept as given a history of 'common knowledge.' In paragraph 10 it sets the scene for the question: why try collaborators?

> In the war of liberation . . . all people of East Pakistan wholeheartedly supported and participated in the call to free Bangladesh but a small number of Bengalis, Biharis, other pro-Pakistanis, as well as members of a number of different religion-based political parties, particularly Jamaat-e-Islami and its student wing Islami Chatra Sangha (ICS), joined and/or collaborated with the Pakistan military to actively oppose the creation of independent Bangladesh and most of them committed and facilitated the commission of atrocities in violation of customary international law in the territory of Bangladesh. As a result, three million (30 lac) people were killed, near about a quarter million women were raped, about 10 million (one crore) people deported to India. . . .[40]

Again the figures of three million killed and of 250,000 raped are taken not as assertions but as common knowledge. It is undeniable that large-scale atrocities occurred in 1971 and that the vast majority of them were caused by the anti-liberation forces, whether the West Pakistan military or their paramilitary supporters, but the evidential basis for particular claims and particular events is weak. Yet the symbolic power of the court institutionalizes popular history; then uses its power to hold in contempt of court those who question it. As David Bergman, a journalist who runs a blog on the trials and who posted an intelligent and searching piece on the history of the numbers quoted, found out.[41] And when the defense team attempted to introduce as academic writing – to counter the piles of accepted texts, newspaper cuttings and 'memoirs' introduced by the prosecution – the revisionist history of Sarmila Bose, they were blocked.[42] This provides a deeply problematic account, but one can agree with her that the 'abundance of political rhetoric is matched by a paucity of

40 The thirty lac and one crore represent the numbers in Bangla.

41 See: David Bergman, personal blog at: http://bangladeshwarcrimes.blogspot.co.uk/ [accessed 24 March 2017].

42 Samila Bose, *Dead Reckoning: Memories of the 1971 Bangladesh War* (London: Hurst, 2011).

carefully documented data. If nobody knows, or different parties cannot agree on, what actually happened in 1971, it is impossible to embark upon any kind of analysis.'[43]

Does the court's narrative style construct any sense of historical accountability? Does it offer a feeling of historical justice? Reading the judgments, the events of 1971 become a formulaic presence, a recounting of the narrative of Bengali-Bangladeshi nationalism; there is no room for contingency, for accepting in good faith those who feared the loss of Pakistan. But for all of that they are still symbolic and compelling rituals, with accounts relayed on prime time TV. These are rituals that extend even to the executions of the condemned; although the executions are not filmed, the release of the bodies to families and their burial play out in video film reaching a wide audience via YouTube and other media. The rituals reply to and endorse a process which began with detailed criminal indictments. However, the language of law is intertwined with an historical accounting, problematic in its grasp for numerous reasons, aiming at society at large but in no way permitting reconciliation. The only victims narrated are the victims of the accused; in other words, the only victims of this great atrocity are those who supported succession ('liberation'). There are no accounts of pro-Pakistan supporters as victims. But can any true accountability be achieved without a broader historical inquiry?

Can Bangladesh be explained as a militant democracy?

For many of those I have spoken to in Dhaka the concerns noted above are of little consequence. Previous 'people's movements' to bring collaborators to justice have meant that 'these are not strangers, we have lived with the knowledge of what they have done most of our lives' (interview notes, a prosecution witness, 2014). This is reinforced by Mozammel Khan's 'performance review' of the tribunal in the *Daily Star* in January 2014: 'None of them [the accused] are strangers to us, rather [they] are nationally known as direct abettors of the [most] gruesome crimes ever committed against us as a people.'[44]

There is therefore little understanding of international criticism of the sort that Suzannah Linton gave in 2013: 'Heightened tensions always accompany such trials, but the politicization in Bangladesh has been extraordinary, raising passions, clouding reason and blinding otherwise seeing eyes to the obvious.' But whose eyes are these and exactly what is the obvious?

Consider again the memories of Prime Minister Sheikh Hasina recounted earlier; that the main opposition political party (the BNP) is feared as anti-democratic and subversive and its alliance with Jamaat-e-Islami is seen by supporters of the ruling Awami League (AL) generally as a direct renunciation of the narrative that

43 Ibid, 395.

44 Mozammel Khan, 'International War Crimes trials: a performance review,' *The Daily Star*, 1 January 2014.

stems from the 1952 language movement; the AL's six-point plan for autonomy; and the 'genocidal' crackdown of March 1971 and the successful 'war of liberation.' Even if, when it was announced, international observers gave the WCT a guarded welcome, the refusal by the Bangladeshi government of international assistance in setting up the trials indicated the State intended to have a large role in controlling the narrative of its operation.[45] By mid-2013 the trials were incorporated into what I elsewhere saw as 'authoritarian populism' responding, perhaps, to a crisis in hegemony and tending towards continual use of the image of the exceptional State. Such a way of making sense of the scene was borrowed from criminology and looks to the State as needing to refashion consent, to use a law-and-order moral panic to buttress power. However, I also wondered if Bangladesh had ever been a 'normal state' and whether the enemy was 'manufactured' or was 'actual, real and dangerous.'[46]

I now think that another, perhaps competing and overlapping, concept that may offer a way of interpreting the moves of the AL over time is that of Bangladesh – at least under, but not confined to, AL government – as a 'militant democracy'; that is, the attempt by democratic forces to guard from within the subversion of the democratic system, but in so doing resorting to anti-democratic methods. Militant democracy is, in a sense, the concept that solves the paradox that confronts one when a democracy acts as if to undercut itself but claims to do so to preserve democracy. It responds to what it considers the real risk – a form of tyranny that would lead to destruction. The concept originates with the immediate pre-war writings of Loewenstein, from 1935, analysing how democracies should counter the threat of fascism.[47] In the case of Bangladesh this was the dream of the liberation of a nationalist Muslim Bengali identity unravelling; first unable to find democratic expression in East Pakistan and then in Bangladesh itself. Then the maintenance of Bengali national identity results in the undercutting of some of the previous institutional structures of democracy, such as the decision by the AL government in 2013 to use its large majority in parliament to change the constitutional caretaker system to allow the government to stay in power while elections were held. Their offer to the BNP of a joint government ceased to be a requirement and became conditional only if the latter 'renounced violence.' The inevitable outcome was that the boycott by the opposition BNP alliance of the 2014 elections gave the AL constitutional domination. Continual opposition violence was used to justify the constitutional suppression of opposition political parties through new legislation. This included

45 Wayne Morrison, 'Bangladesh 1971, war crimes trials and control of the narrative: the state or collaborative enterprise?' *Critica Penal y Poder*, No 5 (2013) 338–357.

46 Wayne Morrison, 'Looking into the abyss: Bangladesh, critical criminology and globalisation,' in *Green Harms and Crimes*, edited by Ragnhild Sollund (Basingstoke: Palgrave Macmillan, 2015).

47 For an account of its history see: Giovanni Capoccia, 'Militant Democracy: The Institutional Bases of Democratic Self-Preservation,' *Annual Review of Law and Social Science*, Vol 9 (2013), 207–226.

the Foreign Donations (Voluntary Activities) Regulation Bill 2014, which restricts foreign funding to Bangladeshi NGOs, and the proposed Cyber Security Act 2015, which aimed to further tighten the control of the authorities over free expression, going beyond the existing Information and Communication Act which already criminalizes defamatory and 'anti-State' publications.

Consider again the narratives in the WCT's judgments: if this is a public ritual of accountability, there is no attempt at reconciliation; there is no apology for actions of the pro-liberation forces against Urdu-speaking minorities. When it refers to the need to renew the constitution it engages in a narrative where the failures of the succeeding period are blamed on the destruction of the war and the damage done by collaborators. The difficulties of the subsequent attempts to govern are placed in a narrative of attempted creation of a State and betrayal. It is not a story of the continuity of a State and the rule of law, but of a continual disruption of State responsibility by those who do not share the same narrative language. There is, of course, some sense to this, but it is an oversimplification.

After Mujibur's assassination the AL was cast aside under a chaotic set of military dictatorships that led to the strongman Zinur Rahman, himself a freedom fighter who had declared the independence of Bangladesh in the name of Mujibur. He formed the BNP on becoming president in 1978 and the assorted elements that made up the party – leftists to Islamists – shared a sense of victimization and disenfranchisement experienced under the AL, thus adding and institutionalizing a 'politics of grievance.' More political blocs than institutionalized parties, and often entering into electoral alliances with minor parties, the AL-BNP interaction has been contentious; with violent *hartals* called incessantly in street politics, rather than formal and sustained debate in parliament or the holding of government policies to account through committee oversight. Rahman was assassinated in 1983 and in the resulting military, then pseudo-democratic, regime of Hussain Muhammad Ershad the AL and BNP found some common ground in a struggle to achieve democratic governance.

While democratic elections have been held since, institutional patronage rapidly consolidated as a dominant form of political practice, severely hindering the development of any independent professional bureaucracy with the capacity to devise and implement policy. Patron-client networks insured that loyalty to the ruling party trumped any real investment in State activity, other than its use to further the interests of the party in power. The result, according to David Lewis, is that Bangladesh moved during the two decades since democracy was established in 1990 from being a 'minimalist democracy'[48] – with regular elections, peaceful transfers of government power, a guarantee of basic freedoms and civilian control over institutions and policy – to become an 'illiberal democracy.'[49] When accountability mechanisms are weak or fail to operate, confrontation rather than

48 David Lewis, *Bangladesh: Politics, Economy and Civil Society* (Cambridge: Cambridge University Press, 2011), 107.

49 Ibid.

negotiation becomes the tool of politics. Issues that may in 'normal' times be simply questions of the degree of good governance – such as law and order enforcement and the amount of loan defaults – when combined with a wide set of related issues, such as Bangladesh's politicization of the education system and pervasive corruption, become severe structural problems. They certainly proved beyond a three-year caretaker government (2006–09) which staked all on overcoming corruption when it decided to try to reform the political situation but ultimately oversaw a landslide victory for the AL. The AL presented a Charter for Change election manifesto in which addressing the desire for justice through a commitment to war crimes trials won electoral support. That the main defendants are from Jamaat is thus both contingent and politically determined.

Jamaat-e-Islami theoretically has no place in the AL narrative of what constitutes players in Bangladeshi democracy. Between 1991 and 2001, however, no party won an election by more than a four per cent margin – first the BNP then the AL then the BNP. The AL had banned religious parties but this restriction was lifted by Ziaur Rahman in 1979, and since the end of military rule in 1990 Jamaat has held a position of deal maker in election outcomes and has fronted the move towards public acceptance of Islam in Bangladeshi political life. This can be seen by the rise in political participation and the number of religious NGOs: in 1970 there were 11 Islamist parties, while in 2006 ten times that number represented a wide spectrum of Islamist thought. Of the 206,000 not-for-profit organizations documented by the World Bank, 189,000 were described as 'religious.'[50]

During the campaigns against the dictatorship of Hussain Ershad, both parties courted Jamaat; but the AL considered this a forced matter of *realpolitik* at odds with the principles on which they founded Bangladesh's initial constitution – 'nationalism, democracy, secularism and socialism.' After the AL's electoral landslide at the end of 2008 there would not be a better time to launch trials, with the defendants all ranked highly on a list of 1,597 persons suspected of atrocities according to a report that year from a war crimes fact-finding committee.

Jamaat-e-Islami is more than a political party; rather it has been described as a shadow government. It has extensive financial and organizational outreach (including the largest private bank in Bangladesh) and is linked to thousands of educational bodies varying from back-alley unregistered madrasas to large colleges. With a distinct financial base it does not need direct power to engage in patronage politics; moreover, its own brand of coercive politics can be seen as less corrupt, since its ideological goal is 'to establish an Islamic social order in society through the State' and to bring about an 'Islamic revolution.'[51] Its message is seductive in promising to end liberal voids, to provide answers where liberalism leaves it

50 Leon E. Irish and Karla W. Simon, 'NGOs in Bangladesh: Legal and Regulatory Environment,' International Consultants, International Centre for Civil Society Law (2005), at www.iccsl.org/pubs/bangladeshfinalreportmay15.pdf [accessed 24 March 2017].

51 Ibid.

to individual desire and to offer an enchanted land of Islamic purity in contrast to the real Bangladesh, a place I have elsewhere agreed is 'insufficiently imagined' and open to crushing shortfalls. Jamaat (and other Islamic groups) can offer a collective (and coercive) desire, an opposition to the cultural manifestations of liberalism, capitalism and the west in general. It has no need to debate the theoretical positions that call into question its key positions; its appeal ignores the arguments that there never can be an Islamic state as Islam is a religion and not a political project. It can accept technological advancement but cast aside any cultural baggage of western globalization. It offers an illusory Islamic homogeneity of peace and purity as it opposes difference, diversity and multiplicity; thus threatening to impose on the traditions of Bengali Islam a foreign power, one that destroys heterogeneity and from which there would be no return.

In my existential vertigo I have no knock-down arguments against those who criticize the WCT, other than it is a reflection of Bangladeshi democracy, albeit a flawed reflection. Whether this is a failed democracy, an illiberal democracy or a militant democracy may be a research question. The reality is that in between the ideal Bangladesh and the criticized Bangladesh there is the world of practice. This is a world of disappearances, of cross-fire deaths and of other memories that are not being allowed into the mainstream. For those who love Bangladesh, the task is always to tune the practice, always partially, crassly and faultingly, toward a better reality.

2 Modern Islamic memory and the ISIS 'caliphate'

John Strawson

The contemporary world is enthralled by its past. But the past is fractured through a kaleidoscope of memories. The proclamation of a 'caliphate' by ISIS represents a new twist in the cosmology of *modern* Islamic memory.[1] This chapter will seek to explain that the antecedents of the ISIS caliphate ideology lie not in classical Islamic history but in the first mass Islamist movement, the Indian Khilafat movement (1919–1924).[2] It was through this movement that the idea of a caliphate as an essential element of Islamic order was popularized among the international Muslim public. It was also a crucial moment in the evolution of Islamist ideology as it coarsened the humanistic discourse of Islam to justify or minimize the Ottoman atrocities against the Armenians.

ISIS today draws on this legacy as it attempts to legitimize genocide, crimes against humanity and war crimes as sacred acts of *jihad* sanctioned by the caliph. I will argue that this is a modernist version of Islamic memory that is at odds with history and jurisprudence. The emergence of a caliphate-centered Islamic discourse is a result of the confluence of the decline of the Mogul and Ottoman Empires and the results of the First World War. The ISIS claim to the caliphate, its understanding of the office and its view of its powers amount to a drastic rejection of Islam. This is an example of memory playing tricks on history.

Our story begins in July 2014 when, after sweeping military victories, the ISIS leader, Abu Bakr Al-Baghdadi, swaggered into the Grand Mosque in Mosul to publicly declare himself the caliph.[3] In the words of his spokesperson, Abu Mohammed Al-Adnani, 'the Khalifa [caliphate] has returned.'[4] For ISIS, Al-Baghdadi was the replacement for the last Ottoman caliph after a gap of 90 years. By the summer of

1 On ISIS generally see: Patrick Cockburn, *The Rise of Islamic State: ISIS and the New Sunni Revolution* (London: Verso, 2015). I have used ISIS throughout the chapter as the English acronym for the Arabic Daesh.

2 On the Khilafat movement, see: A.C. Niemeijer, *The Khilafat Movement in India 1919–1924* (The Hague: Martinus Nijhoff, 1972); Gail Minault, *The Khilafat Movement: Religious Symbolism and Political Mobilization in India* (New York: Columbia University Press, 1982); and M. Naeem Qureshi, *Pan-Islam in British Indian Politics: A Study of the Khilafat Movement* (Leiden, Boston, Koln: Brill, 1999).

3 See: Shiraz Maher, *Salafi-Jihadism: The History of an Idea* (London: Hurst, 2016), 3–4.

4 Ibid.

2014 ISIS had consolidated territorial control over large swathes of Syria and Iraq and had come to believe its own propaganda that it was indeed 'the Islamic State.' Its caliphate was projected as possessing a monopoly of Islamic authority through which it would enforce Islamic law within the areas under its control. It projected its caliphate as of worldwide significance and has been able to gain allegiance from groups in north Africa as well as from Nigeria, Somalia and parts of south and south-east Asia – and, of course, individuals in Europe and North America. Within the territories controlled by ISIS, religious and ethnic minorities have been selected for genocide. Yazidis, Shi'a and Christian communities suffered the brunt of this policy of destruction.[5] Women from such minorities were frequently captured as sex slaves and held in rape camps. Foreigners, including aid workers and journalists, were taken as hostages and their murders publicly broadcast. The group has also sought to destroy Islamic buildings, including mosques considered idolatrous and non-Islamic monuments and places of worship, including world heritage sites. In its military activities ISIS made no distinction between civilians and combatants and frequently committed mass murder of combatants taken prisoner.

Al-Baghdadi's appropriation of the title 'caliph' has sparked discussion among Muslims and non-Muslims alike as to the character of the office. Indeed, the *New York Review of Books* has even published pictures of Ottoman Sultan Mehmet Reshad alongside Al-Baghdadi with the caption 'two caliphs,' suggesting there is continuity between the two.[6] However, as our discussion will demonstrate, the concept of the worldwide caliphate was a diplomatic initiative of the Ottoman Empire, which was popularized by the Khilafat movement. This is not to suggest that the Khilafat movement espoused the same murderous criminality of ISIS, but rather that the latter has been able to draw on the ideological discourse which that movement so successfully circulated.

The Khilafat movement emerged in the wake of the Ottoman defeat in the First World War, which proved to be the final act in the history of the Ottoman Empire. In the first two years of the war the empire stood its ground and inflicted defeats on the British and Russians. In 1916 the tide was to turn. The Arab Revolt of that year initiated the rise of Arab national consciousness. By the next year the British had occupied Baghdad and Jerusalem. With British victories in Syria, the Ottoman Empire had in effect ceased to exist beyond Anatolia. The final denouement was the Allied occupation of Constantinople, the imperial capital where the sultan was in effect held under house arrest.

The Khilafat movement was a response to what many Indian Muslims saw to be anti-Turkish policies pursued by the British Empire at the 1919 Paris Peace Conference. For Indian Muslims the Ottoman surrender was particularly poignant

5 See for example, UN Office of the High Commissioner For Human Rights, UN Commission on Syria: 'ISIS is committing genocide against Yazidis' (June 2016), at: www.ohchr.org/en/NewsEvents/Pages/DisplayNews.aspx?NewsID=20113&LangID=E [accessed 22 July 2016].

6 Gerard Russell, 'Jihad: The Lesson of the Caliphate,' *New York Review of Books*, Vol LXII, No 8 (May 7–20 2015), 46.

as it removed from international politics the last great Muslim power. The Versailles Peace Conference would determine the status of the Middle Eastern part of the empire, which was then under the military control of the British and French. From 1916 the Allies had decided that the post-war world would be shaped by a new international order, with the League of Nations at its center. The League would create a mandate system to administer all the colonies of the defeated powers. The removal of the Ottomans from the Middle East meant that the Islamic holy places of Mecca, Medina, Jerusalem and Karbala would fall under the new dispensation. This struck at the heart of what the Khilafat movement understood as the role of the caliph. For the movement, these Arab cities were sacred territory over which the caliph and the caliph alone should exercise full political control. It saw the defense of Sultan Mehmet VI's territorial sovereignty as a religious duty, which surpassed any other consideration. As the key leader of the Khilafat movement, Mohammad Ali, wrote:

> It was our religious duty to prevent the further disintegration of the temporal power of the Khilafat, which was indispensable for the defense of our faith, to maintain the inviolability of the sacred regions of Islam and to see that [the] dying injunction of the Prophet with regard to the exclusive Muslim sovereignty over Jazirat-ul-Arab (or the Island of Arabia, including Syria, Palestine and Mesopotamia) was not disregarded.[7]

From the Indian nationalist perspective, the dismemberment of the Ottoman Empire was seen as the strengthening of Britain's imperial position. As a result there was an alignment between the avowedly religious content of the Khilafat movement's policies and the wider anti-colonial movement. However, this resulted in the paradox of placing the Ottoman emperor within the anti-colonial camp. In so doing, Arab self-determination was to be sacrificed in the interests of the sultan. At the same time the Khilafat movement, in becoming a defender of the Ottoman regime, sought to dismiss the Armenian genocide as an 'exaggeration.' Thus the crimes of the Ottomans were to be tolerated whereas those of the British were not. This binary division, not between good and evil but between the good camp and the bad camp, has come to haunt the twenty-first century.

Mohammad Ali and his brother Shaukat Ali[8] were interned by the British for pro-Turkish activities during the war. They both had a history of involvement in the Pan-Islamic movement,[9] which had attracted intellectuals who sought to project a united Muslim identity during the second half of the nineteenth century

7 Afzal Iqbal (ed.) *My Life A Fragment: An Autobiographical Sketch of Maulana Mohamed Ali* (Lahore: Shaikh Muhammad Ashraf, 1946), 183–184.

8 Mohammad Ali 1878–1931 and Shuakat Ali 1873–1938 were both journalists and graduates of Aligarh.

9 See: Umar Ryad, 'Anti-Imperialism and the Pan Islam Movement,' in *Islam and the European Empires*, edited by David Motadel (Oxford and New York: Oxford University Press, 2014), 131–149.

– with the Ottoman Porte at its center. While the Pan-Islamic movement had been confined to relatively small circles, the Khilafat movement rapidly became a populist force. Its leadership attracted a mixture of professionals, intellectuals, Islamic scholars and nationalist activists. Significantly it also drew support from the general nationalist milieu, including Hindus; among the nationalist leaders supporting the movement was Mahatma Gandhi.[10]

The Khilafat movement was formally founded in 1919. In its address delivered to the viceroy in 1920, its stated aims were:

> The preservation of the Khilafat, as temporal no less than a spiritual institution, is not so much part of their faith, as the very essence thereof; and no analogies from other creeds that tolerate the lacerating and devitalizing distinction between things spiritual and things temporal, between Church and State, can serve any purpose. . . . Temporal power is the very essence of the institution of the Khilafat, and Mussulmans can never agree to any change of its character, or to the dismemberment of its empire.[11]

The manifesto adopted by the All-India Khilafat Conference, held in Bombay between 15–17 February 1920, makes plain that this claim is framed in religious terms. The position of the caliphate and the control over the 'Jazirat-ul-Arab'[12] is said to derive from 'the Qur'an or from the traditions of the Prophet and . . . by other religious authority.'[13] Not to accede to this claim is said to be 'a violation of the deepest religious feelings of the Muslims.'[14] It is striking that these claims are made on behalf of all Muslims, not just Indian Muslims. The mobilization of religion to cultivate political claims is a feature of contemporary Islamists generally, and is a particular forte of ISIS and Al-Qa'ida.

When war broke out in 1914 the British authorities in India were understandably concerned by the implication of conflict with the Muslim Ottoman Empire. The British Empire contained the majority of the world's Muslim population, with some 69 million in India alone – which far exceeded the 15 million Muslims within the Ottoman Empire.[15] The British fretted that war with the Ottomans could easily become a source of instability from within, while Germany carefully

10 See: Minault, 67–72.

11 The address presented by the Indian Khilafat deputation to the Viceroy in Delhi on 19 January 1920, in The Turkish Settlement and the Muslim and Indian Attitude, (London: Indian Khilafat Delegation Publications, No 1, 1920), 6.

12 Literally the 'peninsular of the Arabs' but the manifesto is not just referring to this area which would include Mecca and Medina but also to Jerusalem, Najaf, Karbala, Samarra, Kaizmain and Baghdad. See: The Manifesto of the All-India Khilafat Movement passed at his Bombay Session held 15-17 February 1920, in The Turkish Settlement 10.

13 The Turkish Settlement, 11.

14 Ibid.

15 The Muslim population of the Ottoman Empire was 15.04 million. See: Stanford J. Shaw and Ezel Kural Shaw, *History of the Ottoman Empire and Modern Turkey*, Vol II (Cambridge: Cambridge University Press, 1977), 241.

cultivated such a policy.[16] Maintaining the loyalty of Indians was especially important as the Indian government and army would be relied on to deploy forces to the Ottoman theatre. On the outbreak of war, the British government issued a solemn declaration that the conflict with the Ottomans was entirely political and not religious. The war would be pursued for purely political objectives and would not include any attack on the holy places. The British pledged that there would be no threats to the sultan as caliph. The conflict was portrayed as one between the British Empire and Turkish nationalist politicians, not between the British and the sultan.[17]

British sensitivities on the subject of the Ottoman sultan derived from the victory of the Raj over the Indian Great Revolt of 1857. The British response to the rebellion was to end any pretense that rule was exercised through the *diwan* of the Mogul emperor. From the late eighteenth century the British East India Company had carefully set about inserting itself within the administrative structures of the existing empire. After 1857 there were drastic changes to the political order. The emperor, Bahadur Shah, was dispatched into exile, the East India Company ceased its governmental functions and the British state took control of government duties. This required the creation of the Indian Office as a department of state in London and the appointment of the viceroy and governor-general in India. At the same time the British authorities were well aware that a new compact was required if colonial governance was to be successfully restored. This was contained in a proclamation in the name of Queen Victoria (in legal terms, an order in council[18]). It enumerated the new administrative measures but also contained an express commitment to religious freedom. The proclamation noted 'with gratitude the solace of religion' and that it would 'disdain alike the right and desire to impose our convictions on any of our subjects' and continued that 'none be in any wise favored, none molested or disquieted by reason of their religious faith or observances; but that all shall enjoy equal and impartial protection of the law.'[19] It imposed a duty on those in authority not to interfere with religious belief or worship. The proclamation also contained a non-discrimination clause for those appointed to any office. This careful treatment of religion was to become a feature of British India after the rebellion. It is evident that the leaders of the Khilafat movement found this discourse useful as they formulated the policy that the political future of the Ottoman sultan and his empire was subject to Islamic belief. Thus, in this account, significant areas of British

16 See: David Motadel, *Islam and Nazi Germany's War* (Cambridge: The Belknap Press of Harvard University Press, 2014), 18–27, and: Eugene Rogan, *The Fall of the Ottomans: The Great War in the Middle East 1914–1920* (London: Allen Lane, 2015), 99–128.

17 Minault, 52.

18 Orders in Council refer to decree-making powers adopted by the monarch or a minister within the framework of the Privy Council.

19 *Proclamation, by Queen in Council, to the Princes, Chiefs and People of India* (Published by the governor-general at Allahabad, 1 November 1858) cmd. 1136.

foreign policy, and indeed aspirations of Arab nationalists, were to be subjected to a religious veto. It was this wrapping of politics in faith that was to prove decisive in mobilizing people on the ground and in gaining a hearing in the highest echelons in India and Europe.

With the removal of the Mogul emperor in 1857 a critical stage was reached in the formation of Indian Muslim identity. As has been noted, since the late eighteenth century the British ruled through the East India Company by inserting itself within the structures of the Mogul Empire. This form of governance had maintained a level of ambiguity that suited British interests. At the same time Indian Muslims felt a degree of protection with the titular emperor on the throne. However, once the emperor was gone the community had not only lost its sense of security but also its political and religious leader. It was in these circumstances that the Ottoman Empire became a factor in Indian Muslim discourse. If there was no emperor in Delhi, who was to replace him? As the second half of the nineteenth century progressed there was an increased interest in the religious role of the Ottoman sultan among intellectuals. An authoritative role for the Ottoman caliphate in India was to be a new development. The Mogul emperors had cast themselves as caliphs in their own right; indeed, from the reign of Akbar (1556–1605) Delhi had been known as *Dar ul Khilafat* (abode of the caliphate).[20] The Mogul rulers were certainly not subservient to the Ottomans. This was elegantly advanced in Mogul Emperor Humayum's letter to Suleiman the Magnificent in 1556 that reiterated his own status as caliph.[21] During the Mogul period, at the Friday *Khutbah* prayers it was the emperor in Delhi who was specifically named as the ruler of the Muslim community.[22] However, as British power asserted itself and Mogul power evaporated, so a section of Indian Muslims gave greater attention to the religious significance of the Ottoman Porte.

The interest in Ottoman authority was also accompanied by a new narrative about the history and character of the office of the caliphate. Despite the actual history of the Mogul caliphate, some Islamic scholars under the influence of the Pan-Islamic movement began to propagate the idea that, as there was one single worldwide Muslim community, there should be one single authority, the caliph. Indeed, despite the history of Islam in the sub-continent (and elsewhere), it was argued that, since the death of the Prophet, there had always been a central leader. The caliphate, it was said, had been handed down through the centuries until it was passed to the Ottomans. The Ottomans themselves had embellished this account by propagating a 'tradition' that at the beginning of the Ottoman occupation of Egypt in 1517 the last Abbasid caliph, Al-Mutawakki III,[23] had

20 Thomas W. Arnold, *The Caliphate* (Oxford: Clarendon Press, 1924), 159.

21 See: Naimur Rahman Farooqi, *Mughul-Ottoman Relations* (Delhi: Idarah-i Adabiyat-i Delli, 1989), 189.

22 Minault, 55.

23 The Abbasid Empire had in fact ended in the middle of the thirteenth century but the ruling family fled to Cairo, where they used the title caliph although exercising no power at all.

formally invested Salem I as caliph. However, the first accounts of such an event only began to circulate in the eighteenth century and are almost certainly mythical.[24] It is also the case that in the sixteenth century the Ottomans rarely used the title at all.[25] Nonetheless, the notion of an Islamic form of apostolic succession became increasingly popular in nineteenth-century India.[26] This was nourished by Indian Muslim involvement in the Pan-Islam movement, which was intimately connected with the Ottoman Porte's claims to international Muslim leadership. The weaker the empire grew politically and territorially, the shriller its claims to spiritual authority became.

As we have noted, after 1857 the British initiated an explicit commitment to religious freedom. This opened an important space for the colonized populations and this was especially the case with the Muslim population. Writing of the attitudes of Muslims in British India, Faisal Devji says:

> They were . . . assiduous in calling everything they did religious, cultural or traditional, thus increasing to a remarkable degree the role of these supposedly unexceptional categories played in social life. And this was simply another way in which colonial rule exaggerated the importance of religion and tradition within Indian society.[27]

This process neatly prepared the way for the discursive position that was adopted by the Pan-Islam movement and then by the Khilafat movement. The former spawned a series of groups and campaigns. For example, a group raised charitable funds and dispatched the Indian Red Crescent mission to Turkey in the Balkan wars.[28] Another group founded Anjuman-e-Khuddam-e-Ka'aba[29] in 1913 to commit the pious to defend the holy places. Through such activities the religious attachment to the Ottoman caliph was strengthened.

While the British were determined to portray the First World War war as entirely political, British imperial policy and the Pan-Islam movement had blurred the line between politics and faith. As Minault comments for Indian Muslims '[their] religious identity and their political identity were thus inextricably entwined.'[30]

24 See: Stanford J. Shaw, *The History of the Ottoman Empire and Modern Turkey, Vol I Empire of the Gazis: The Rise and Decline of the Ottoman Empire 1280–1808* (Cambridge: Cambridge University Press, 1976), 30–40.

25 Arnold, 164.

26 This was evident in the work of Ameer Ali who, although a Shi'a, increasingly saw the caliphate in this light. See: *The Spirit of Islam: The History and Evolution of the Ideas of Islam* (London: Christophers, 1922), 124–125.

27 Faisal Devji, *Muslim Zion: Pakistan as a Political Idea* (London: Hurst, 2013), 232.

28 See: Syed Tanvir Wasti, The Indian Red Crescent Mission to the Balkan Wars, *Middle Eastern Studies*, Vol 45, No 3 (2009), 393–406.

29 Society for the Servants of the Ka'aba – the central focus of Islamic ritual in Mecca.

30 Minault, 57.

Once the war was over the ideas of Pan-Islamism crystalized into the Khilafat movement. The defeat of the Ottomans and the perceived humiliation of the sultan fueled resentment against the British in India. As a result the Khilafat movement proved able to mobilize hundreds of thousands of people in support for its aims. Between 1919 and 1920 it organized branches in all major cities and towns and held well-attended public meetings. Vast demonstrations sometimes spilled over into violence. It was quite definitely a grassroots mass movement and for this reason Gandhi and the Indian Congress movement supported it and attempted to steer it towards non-cooperation politics.

While the movement was powerful in India, some of its leaders were dispatched as a special delegation to lobby support for its position in Europe – including at the peace conference. The delegation was led by Mohammad Ali and joined by a mixture of activists and scholars.[31] Meetings were arranged in Britain with Prime Minister Lloyd George and other ministers. Mohammad Ali also addressed the Labour Party conference. In other parts of Europe the group met French and Italian politicians and had an audience with Pope Benedict XV. Through carefully honing its program as the defense of religious belief, the delegation was able to gain a hearing among such powerful figures. The same program posed as political demands would no doubt have been rebuffed.

The issue of Arab self-determination was to prove particularly difficult to present as purely religious. This was compounded by the role that the Khilafat movement was playing in the demand for Indian freedom. Most of the more extreme contemporary Islamist movements, such as ISIS, have dispensed with national identity entirely, something which was difficult to do in the early nineteenth century when European colonial empires were well entrenched in the Muslim world. However, the Khilafat movement's argument for the maintenance of the caliph's temporal rule offers an interesting insight into the way faith is used in Islamist discourse more generally.

The 1916 Arab Revolt against Ottoman control of Arab lands was led by fellow Muslims and represented a major challenge to the Khilafat movement's beliefs. In its address to the viceroy, the Khilafat delegation lamented that 'we are most painfully aware that some sections of Mussulmans of Arabia have, in clear defiance of the laws of Islam, stood out from the solid mass of the rest of the Muslim world.'[32] This view was common among the Indian Muslim milieu, and indeed within three weeks on the revolt the All-India Muslim League Council denounced its leader Hussein for 'outrageous conduct.'[33] Abdul Bari, a scholar who was also a leader of the movement, called the supporters of the rebellion 'enemies of

31 See: M. Naeem Qureshi, *Mohamed Ali's Khilafat Delegation to Europe, February–October 1920* (Karachi: Pakistan Historical Society, 1980).

32 Address presented by the Indian Khilafat deputation to the viceroy in Delhi, on 19 January 1920 in *The Turkish Settlement*, 6.

33 Quoted in Qureshi, 83.

Islam.'[34] In 1920 he issued a *fatwa*, which defined the Jazirat-ul-Arab[35] as extending from Iraq through Jerusalem to the Arab peninsula. He argued that these lands had to be under the exclusive control of the caliph and thus prohibited any Arab self-determination. The Khilafat movement's manifesto was equally insistent on this position:

> The custody of the holy places has ever since the establishment of Islam been under the Khilafat, and unlike the boundary of the latter, which has fluctuated from the time to time, has never suffered any diminution whatsoever. This claim does not exclude genuine Arab self-government; but it does exclude the present arrangement because those who know the unreality behind it. The claim now said to be made by Sherif Husain and Amir Feisul is inconsistent, in fact, with their acceptance even of the spiritual sovereignty of the khalifa.[36]

Mohammad Ali in his meeting with Lloyd George reiterated such sentiments and is reported to have said he 'was not opposed to Arab self-government, although he could not agree that Arabs should be given full independence.'[37] The active campaign against Arab self-determination, argued at the highest level of the empire, indicates how central this policy was. Mohammad Ali assumed, however, that it would only be a matter of time before the Arabs would 'return' to the Islamic viewpoint. 'I hope that the Amir Faisal,' he wrote, 'when he looks at the matter from the point of view of a Muslim, as he is bound to do, will realize that his personal ambitions and even the ambitions of the Arabs can be entirely satisfied within the scheme of Turkish sovereignty.'[38] The failure of the Hashemites to 'repent' was seen in some circles as evidence they were complicit in imperialist intrigue. In a speech in Calcutta in 1921, Jalal-ud-Din Al Hussaini, an Islamic scholar, addressed the British, saying, 'you make the [Sharif] of Mecca the master of the holy places and bribe him into becoming your creature and into revolting against his sovereign.'[39]

The allegations of bribery and corruption against Arab nationalist leaders are a familiar part of the current Islamist discourse. ISIS and other Islamist groups use the image of corrupt governments in the Muslim world, which act as part of

34 Quoted in ibid.

35 The fatwa like the Khilafat Manifesto also included large areas of what are now Iraq and Syria beyond the geographical limits the Prophet would have recognized.

36 Manifesto of the All-India Khilafat Movement in *The Turkish Settlement*, 10. The assumption in this passage is that 'real' Muslims know that Arab independence is un-Islamic.

37 *Muhammad Ali, His Life, Service and Trial (Madras: Ganesh, 1922)*, 134.

38 Quoted in Minault, 88.

39 Muayyeed-Ul-Islam Jalal-ud-Din Hussaini, *Pan-Islam, Khilafat, Non-Cooperation, Swaraj and Hindu-Muslem Unity*, translated by Moulovi Syed Ibni Imam (Calcutta: The Hablul Matin, n/d).

a grand western conspiracy, as an effective recruiting tool. The gentler form of this narrative from the 1920s has entered Muslim memory with insidious results.

There were other accounts of the Arab Revolt within India, however. The jurist Siraj-ud-Din Ahmad argued in favor of what he called the 'revolution in Arabia.' 'Muslims should direct their united efforts, with a view to enable the Sharif of Mecca to consolidate his independence and to compel the Turks by all possible means to disconnect themselves from Arabia,' he wrote.[40] Interestingly he continued by referring to the attitude of other Arabs to the events:

> The Egyptian Muslims have given expression to their entire satisfaction at the declaration of independence by the Arabs and are anxious to see that independence assured. The Egyptian Mussulmans, who are the followers of the late Sheikh Muhammad Abdoo, the great Egyptian reformer, whose position in Egypt was similar to that which was held by the late Sir Syed Ahmed Khan in India.[41]

The reference to the two great Islamic reformers of the day is significant as he is attempting to establish a common intellectual link between Egypt and India. As with today's Muslim world there were major currents that sought to align Islam with progress. The rejection of conspiracy theories and western plots while trying to free Islam from the stultifying effects of the decaying Ottoman Empire was significant. Ahmad was not a lone voice. Faizul Karim argued in 1919 that:

> At this time there is a cry of self-government and self-determination all over the world, and what wonder then that Arabs, who taught the lesson of freedom to all the world thirteen hundred years ago, themselves shook off the Turkish yoke! It is indeed surprising that Dr. Ansari and his associates, who are so warm supporters of home rule for India, wish the Arabs to remain in everlasting bondage and servitude under the Turks![42]

Such views were significant but rather marginalized by the louder slogans of the Khilafat movement. This has similarities with the contemporary world, where Islamists have been able to dominate the discourse. Their ability to do so, as in the 1920s, is assisted by the prevalence of Orientalist images of Islam in the mass media. Whether the views of Ahmad and Karim went against the tide of opinion

40 'The Revolution in Arabia. The claims and conduct of the Turks,' originally published in the *Morning Post* of Delhi 28 July 1916 – a shorter version appeared in the *Bombay Times* of India 23 July, in Kazi Siraj-ud-Din Ahmad, *The Truth about the Khilafat* (Lahore: Khosla Bros, 1920), 81.

41 Ibid.

42 Moulana Faizul Karim, *Facts about the Khalifate* (Karachi: Daily Gazette Press, 1919), 9–10. Mukhtar Ahmed Ansari (1880-1936) had been a Pan Islamist activist and was a prominent member of the Khilafat Movement.

is uncertain. However, it was evident that Indian Muslim perceptions of Arab national consciousness could be problematic.[43]

Hussein, as the leader of the Arab Revolt, did cast his actions in an Islamic hue. He claimed that its 'principles are to defend the faith of Islam, to elevate the Moslem people, to found their conduct on holy law, to build up the code of justice on the same foundation in harmony with the principles of religion.'[44] These sentiments cut no ice with the Khilafat movement given its *a priori* position on the religious and temporal role assigned to the Ottoman caliph. The Khilafat leaders were convinced that there was a European Christian plot to undermine the Ottomans which included the revolt. In particular they speculated that British policy since the nineteenth century had been the creation of a rival Arab caliphate.[45] The revolt was portrayed as the hidden hand of the British in achieving this policy.[46] As with the Arab Revolt, the conspiracy theory often begins with a grain of truth. In April 1914 Hussein, through his second son Abdullah,[47] did approach the British in seeking assistance to mount a rebellion. The British refused on the grounds that they had no hostile intentions against the Ottomans. It was only after the war broke out in October 1914 that contact was resumed between the two sides.[48] However, the British found it quite difficult to deal with Hussein. Major Bray, the military intelligence officer who liaised with him, reported that the

> obstacles placed in our way in helping the Arabs were unbelievable. The Sheriff wished to decide every question which arose, whether [in] regard to policy or military action. He trusted no one, not even his own sons, whom he was as suspicious of and all with whom he had to deal. Every petty detail of supply, finance or administration was dealt with [by] him personally. . . . He daily became more and more imbued with the idea that he was the final arbiter of Islam and generalissimo of the forces in the field.[49]

This is hardly a description of a puppet. It is, of course, quite true that the British did aid the revolt through financial, intelligence and direct military support. However, that is rather different from directing it. Arab nationalism had developed

43 See: Qureshi, 83–85.
44 Hussein, quoted in Nurullah Ardic, *Islam and the Politics of Secularism: The Caliphate and Middle Eastern Modernization in the early 20th Century* (London and New York: Routledge 2012), 203.
45 See: Ibid.
46 A title he did in fact claim in 1924, although only after the new Turkish republic had abolished the caliphate. Hussein's claim was little recognized.
47 The future king of Transjordan.
48 See: Ronald Storrs, *Orientations* (London: Ivor Nicholson, 1937), 122–123, and Zeine E. Zeine, *Arab-Turkish Relations and the Emergence of Arab Nationalism* (Beirut: Kayat, 1958), 100.
49 Major N. N. E. Bray, *Shifting Sands* (London; Unicorn Press, 1934), 75–76.

quite independently by 1916 and the revolt became an iconic moment in the struggle for Arab freedom.[50] Arab nationalism and Britain's war against the Ottomans brought the two sides together with common interests. The idea that the west is so omnipotent that it dictates events is again common today. However, such views undermine the significance of autonomous agency of the non-western or colonial subject who is too easily re-inscribed as a one-dimensional artifact of empire.[51]

The aims of the Khilafat movement were to be defeated, not as it happens by European imperial policies but by the politics of modern Turkish nationalism. While the remnants of the Ottoman regime struggled to survive the allied victory, Greece attacked Turkey in May 1919 and scored lightning success in the early phase of the war. However, the war provoked Mustapha Kemal and other nationalists to create a rival provisional government in Ankara. From 1919 Kemal steered the national resistance to the Greek invasion. Within 18 months he had radically changed the military situation and in 1922 he decisively defeated the Greeks. In October 1923 the Turkish Republic was declared following the recognition of its borders in the Treaty of Lausanne. The sultanate was abolished but Abdilmecid II clung on to the title of caliph for a further year before being stripped of it and sent into exile. After 1924 the Khilafat movement declined rapidly but its ideas about the centrality of the caliphate took root in Islamic discourse and, indeed, in the popular western imagination.

In the immediate aftermath of the dissolution of the Ottoman caliphate major debates took place among Islamic scholars about its significance. There was a sharp exchange in Al Azhar University in Cairo, the center of Sunni thought. Ali Abdel Razek published his major work *Al Islam wa Usul al-Hukum* (Islam and the Roots of Government)[52] in 1925, which argued that Islam was a religion and not a state. In making his case he painstakingly analyzed the Prophetic period and argued that there was no particular system of governance but rather religious values, which can inform governance.[53]

In the political atmosphere in Cairo in the mid-1920s his fellow scholars considered these views unacceptable and he was removed from their number. However, his central argument was historically accurate. Indeed, the crisis that followed the Prophet's death was entirely connected to the fact that there was no blueprint for religious authority, let alone for governance. The creation of the early caliphate under Abu Bakr was the result of political struggles in the broadest sense. However, on Abu Bakr's death the succession was to prove fraught and

50 See: John Strawson, *Partitioning Palestine: Legal Fundamentalism in the Palestinian-Israeli Conflict* (London and New York: Pluto Press, 2010), 10–15.

51 For an incisive discussion of this issue see: Hamid Dabashi, *Can Non-Europeans Think?* (London: Zed Press, 2015).

52 See: Ali Abdel Razek, *Islam and the Foundations of Political Power*, edited by Abdou Filali-Ansary, translated by Maryam Lufti (Edinburgh: Edinburgh University Press, 2013).

53 Ibid, 81–96.

each of his three successors was murdered. In 661CE the creation of the Umayyad dynasty began a new departure; the sultanate in Damascus had aspects of Persian (Sasanian) and Byzantine features of governance. The use of the title caliph created a sense of continuity, but as Lapidus had observed:

> In practice . . . the caliphate did not transform the world; they were chiefs of conquering armies, heirs to imperial administration, the heads of privileged aristocracies. They patronized a court culture that gave the regime an Islamic identity, but a version of Islam that derived from Byzantine and Sasanian imperial concepts which emphasized the authority of the caliphs and the legitimacy of ruling elite.[54]

As we can see, the form of authority which the caliph claimed and the type of governance created was not Islamic in content. This borrowing of government practices from the Byzantine and Persian empires resulted in a government and administrative system that replicated those that had existed in the wider region. As a result, in many of the newly conquered lands the government system was unchanged. Lapidus viewed this result as meaning that, 'while the caliphate gave a distinctive Islamic identity to the Middle Eastern imperial institutions and court cultures, it also perpetuated a pre-Islamic imperial ethos.'[55] However, he regarded the subsequent arrival of the Turkish conquerors in the tenth century as effectively bringing even that distinctive characteristic to an end.[56] To a large extent the title of caliph was subsumed by the sultanate. What is also evident is that the idea of a single universal Muslim authority is mythical. Not only, as we have noted, were the Mogul and Ottoman caliphates contemporaneous but, as Arnold points out, in the eleventh century there were eight different claims to caliphate at the same time.[57] Thus the spread of Islam produced multiple centers of authority. Not only was authority diffuse, there was no model of Islamic governance and certainly no Islamic state. What Islamist authoritarians and Orientalists alike overlook was the development of a unique system of law.

Under the Umayyad Empire (661–750CE), and even more so in the early years of the Abbasids (from 750–1250CE), a new cast of jurist emerged. In the words of Messick, 'viewed in detail, the development of the shari'a across the Muslim lands was a phenomenon involving specific men and specific texts.'[58] Shari'a as a system of positive law is dependent on the work of the jurists in writing commentaries (*usul al fiqh*) and issuing *fatwas*. The jurists emerged not within

54 Ira Lapidus, 'The Institutionalization of Early Islamic Societies,' in *Max Weber and Islam*, edited by Toby F. Huff and Wolfgang Schuluchter (New Brunswick and London: Transaction, 1999), 141–156, 142.

55 Ibid.

56 Ibid, 143.

57 Arnold, 180–181.

58 Brinkley Messick, *The Calligraphic State: Textual Domination and History in a Muslim Society* (Berkeley, Los Angeles, Oxford: University of California Press, 1993), 15.

the court of the caliph but outside it. As Hallaq notes, 'the jurists and judges . . . emerged as civic leaders who found themselves by the nature of their "profession" involved in the day-to-day running of civic affairs.'[59] As he explains, the 'law of the Muslim court, as a judicial organ, is entirely under the authority of the private legal experts, the shari'a-anchored, shari'a-minded and socially embedded muftis and jurists.'[60] Islamic law thus emerges outside of the state and as a rival to political power. It is subversive in that the jurists serve their own conscience and not the contingencies of power.

This means the supremacy of law over all government functions, including the caliph. For ISIS the caliph is constructed as a center of power and law. On this point it follows in the tracks of the Khilafat movement for whom the caliph was the temporal ruler dressed in religious clothes. The part of Islamic law known as the *Siyar*,[61] which approximates to international law, is particularly relevant. It regulates the use of force and law of war and explicitly prohibits attacks on civilians, requires respect of prisoners of war and, in general, provides for humanitarian standards in warfare. The ISIS rejection of these legal principles shows how far from Islam the organization is. Its sponsorship of terrorism and suicide bombing, according to one Islamic legal scholar, places them and other such groups outside the Muslim community.[62]

ISIS has constructed Islam as an authoritarian dictatorship where Islamic law has been turned into its opposite. Far from restraining power it becomes a tool to perfect its unlimited violence. Its will to power has much in common with Pol Pot's Kampuchea. Like the Khmer Rouge, ISIS is determined to create a new year zero. The destruction of historical and religious sites, Muslim and non-Muslim, is part of a wider program to manipulate memory.[63] For ISIS the recall of Islamic history and jurisprudence is inimical to their aims.

On 21 September 2014 ISIS destroyed the Armenian Genocide Memorial Church at Der Zor in Syria. The church, which was completed in 1991, was built on land where upwards of 400,000 Armenians were murdered through death marches and camps in the last years of the First World War. The victims were part of the 1.5 million Armenians who died in the genocide. Successive Turkish governments have denied the genocide. At the time the Khilafat movement was keen to protect the Ottomans from what was described as 'a vigorous and most

59 Wael Hallaq, *The Impossible State: Islam, Politics and Modernity's Moral Predicament* (New York: Columbia University Press, 2013), 52.

60 Ibid, 54.

61 See for example, Majid Khadduri, *The Islamic Law of Nations: Shaybani's Siyar* (Baltimore: The Johns Hopkins Press, 1966), which contains an English translation of Shaybani's ninth-century work.

62 See: Shaykh-ul-Islam Muhammad Tahir-ul-Qadri, *Fatwa on Terrorism and Suicide Bombing* (London: Minhajj-ul-Quran International, 2010).

63 This is a mark of violent Islamist rule generally but the International Criminal Court has been successful in its first case on this issue, see: The Prosecutor v Ahmad Al Faqi Al Mahdi: www.icc-cpi.int/CourtRecords/CR2016_07244.PDF [accessed 29 September 2016].

effective and costly propaganda . . . being conducted on behalf of the Armenians. It was urged that the Turks were guilty of inhuman barbarities.'[64] The leader of the movement, Mohammad Ali, 'did all he could to condemn this propaganda.'[65] At the time the Khilafat movement saw those who sought to protest against this serious crime as attacking not just the Ottoman Empire but the whole Muslim community. It is a historic irony that while the Khilafat movement was denouncing the 'anti-Turk' propaganda, the remnant of the Ottoman regime was in fact holding trials of some of the officials responsible for the crime.[66] For ISIS and other violent groups, destroying the Der Zor memorial is part of cleansing the memory.[67]

The conjunction of ISIS action and the Khilafat movement's propaganda on the Armenian genocide is an unsettling moment in the formation of modern Islamic memory. Unrestrained violence in the name of Islam sanctioned by the 'caliph' becomes the motif of ISIS. Memory is deployed in this context to justify atrocities. The denial of the genocide of the Armenians opens the door to the contemporary crimes of genocide against Yazidis, Christians and Shi'a. The Khilafat movement was a brief episode, but through the mass popularizing of the caliphate as the all-powerful central force in Islam it bequeathed an inheritance that the people of the Middle East and beyond are forced to confront.

64 *Mohammad Ali: His Life, Service and Trial* (Madras: Ganesh, 1922), 131.

65 Ibid.

66 see: Vahakan N. Dadrian and Taner Akcam, *Judgment at Istanbul: The Armenian Genocide Trials* (New York and Oxford: Berghahn Books, 2011).

67 Indeed, academic genocide skeptics can also be found – see for example, M. Naeem Qureshi, *Ottoman Turkey, Ataturk and Muslim South Asia: Perspectives, Perceptions, Reponses* (Oxford: Oxford University Press, 2014), 82–94.

3 Peace and reconciliation in Northern Ireland

The case of Irish nationalism

Cillian McGrattan

Reconciliation has become a term of art in discourse on and about Northern Ireland's post-conflict transition. Within academic, elite and everyday political discourse, reconciliation is increasingly seen as synonymous with peace. A broad literature, for example, has emerged looking at how educational or residential divisions influence reconciliation between the two main communities in Northern Ireland – namely, Ulster Unionists (mainly Protestants who identify with British cultural traditions and wish to maintain the constitutional link with the rest of Great Britain) and Irish Nationalists (mainly Catholic, who identify culturally with the Irish Republic and who aspire to reunification of the island of Ireland).[1] The role of civil society, the churches, the education system, outside actors such as the European Union or philanthropic organizations, or inter-community mediation practices, often built around Jean-Paul Lederach's ideas, are seen as institutional ways of facilitating peace through reconciliation.[2] Often politicians and spokespersons for non-governmental organizations (NGOs) or community groups view reconciliation as intrinsic to peace. In this understanding, reconciliation is either the first step or the culmination of a peace process. Thus Dawn Purvis, the former leader of the Progressive Unionist Party (which is allied to one of the main loyalist terror organizations) and now chair of the NGO Healing Through Remembering, recently linked reconciliation to stability and good governance. Speaking to an audience at Duke University in February 2013, Purvis made a plea for continued investment in reconciliation work by international donors. 'Political parties in Northern Ireland,' she asserted, 'are recognizing that this [reconciliation] work is crucial in enabling them to do their jobs. They are beginning to appreciate the importance of dealing with the past to build the future

1 For an overview of the Northern Ireland conflict see: Aaron Edwards and Cillian McGrattan, *The Northern Ireland Conflict: A Beginner's Guide* (Oxford: Oneworld, 2012).

2 For recent overviews of this work see: Sandra Buchanan, *Transforming Conflict through Social and Economic Development: Practical Lessons from Northern Ireland and the Border Counties* (Manchester: Manchester University Press, 2014); Maria Power (ed.), *Building Peace in Northern Ireland* (Liverpool: Liverpool University Press, 2011).

and the type of society we want to live in. Having a cohesive, peaceful and stable society makes the government's [the Northern Ireland executive] job of attracting investment, growing the economy and creating employment much easier.'[3]

The merging of peace with reconciliation is having a profound and as yet under-appreciated and under explored impact on policy direction in Northern Ireland. I argue that the elision works to defer substantive issues of governance, democracy and justice. The findings of the recently published Peace Monitoring Report II – which suggest that, while Northern Ireland is becoming less segregated at an everyday level, its political leaders are becoming more and more deadlocked when it comes to agreeing policy (Nolan 2013)[4] – are merely indicative of this dynamic. In the process the Janus-faced dimensions of reconciliation (looking to the past as well as the future)[5] become drained and reformulated: reconciliation then takes on a meaning of transcending cultural and political division. In reality, this works to reaffirm ideological divides – a recent Ulster loyalist policy document, for example, argued that 'reconciliation' would 'not work if conceived as an extension of the political process,' meaning that nationalists need to 'acknowledge' Northern Ireland's place in the United Kingdom.[6] Meanwhile, the Irish Nationalists' linking of reconciliation to an 'agreed Ireland' seemingly requires Ulster Unionists to give up their constitutional allegiances to Britain: reconciliation then becomes synonymous with resignation to an inevitable constitutional break.

I suggest that if reconciliation is to actually mean something constructive in terms of policy, then it must be reimagined to include concerns with democracy and justice. I argue that this is quite distinct from the world-view represented by Purvis. In that view, reconciliation is logically prior to society; and the problem then becomes the people who won't move forward or who can't understand 'peace' and 'stability.' Unless a shared understanding of society is possible, then Purvis's ideas are either impractical or are easily put to the service of a range of political and socio-economic projects. As an alternative, I argue that reconciliation needs to be invested with the language of social responsibility and I turn to Iris Marion Young's final book for guidance on what that might look like.[7] I argue that this is an intermediary step, an initial and pragmatic one but one that is nevertheless vital. The situating of this analysis within Irish nationalism reveals that vitality because of the underlying objective of transcending the current constitutional framework that defines that ideology, a movement that the ephemerality of reconciliation facilitates.

3 Robin Kirk, 'Lessons from Northern Ireland: Dawn Purvis on Reconciliation,' 25 February 2013. Available at http://today.duke.edu/2013/02/dawnpurvis [accessed 4 May 2013].

4 Paul Nolan, *Northern Ireland Peace Monitoring Report: Number Two* (Belfast: Community Relations Council, 2013).

5 Andrew Schaap, *Political Reconciliation* (London: Routledge, 2005).

6 'Nationalists must accept UK status for reconciliation, say PUP,' *Newsletter*, 22 April 2013. Available at www.newsletter.co.uk/news/regional/nationalists-must-accept-uk-status-for-reconciliation-say-pup-1–5024090 [accessed 23 May 2013].

7 Iris Marion Young, *Responsibility for Justice* (Oxford: Oxford University Press, 2013).

Reconciliation and policy direction in Northern Ireland

Within Northern Ireland, reconciliation has been seen as a way of repairing the social fabric and is linked to ideas about having a 'shared society.' Yet even here ambiguity reigns. The idea of 'shared society' was supposed to be the foundation stone of the Northern Ireland Assembly's program for government. Yet disagreement over dealing with the past and residual sectarianism saw that program parked in 2005. Recently the Office of the First and Deputy First Minister issued a policy document to try to rectify this situation. The document states that 'good relations and reconciliation' should be a feature of departmental initiatives, yet the document itself is light when it comes to concrete proposals for dealing with the past – outlining the issue in little of two (well-spaced) pages and in effect passing it to a new all-party grouping.[8] In the absence of political leadership, the idea of shared society has taken on a peculiar meaning: rather than what might be expected – namely, integration and perhaps a weakening of ethnic identification – sharing has come to mean difference; governmental and societal provisions are shared between, rather than among, the two main ethno-nationalist blocs. The nature of the political divide is, thus, obscured: division is both maintained *and* painted out of existence through subtle changes in language. However, that fluidity only goes so far in masking basic political dynamics such as constitutional implications or socio-economic inequities.[9]

In policy terms the actual debate over dealing with the past in Northern Ireland seems to have stalled. There is no political consensus on establishing a truth and reconciliation commission. While the British government's favored position seems to be a commission of historical clarification, this has not proceeded; although a dedicated commission and a Forum for Victims and Survivors have been established, recent legislative changes have seen a medicalization of victimhood and trauma care, the establishment of a new victims' service and, arguably, an attempt to remove it as a live issue in the public realm. In reality a drip-drip effect has been created by the concatenation of a series of high-profile juridical and coroner cases together with a chain of stories about collusion and the investigation of murders by the police's historical enquiries team. Whether these trends are seen as piecemeal or as an intrinsic part of contemporary politics, the result is more of the same. This stasis may be either guillotined by sweeping legislative changes by the British government, which would undercut the victims' industry (the assorted NGOs and the legal processes) or it may be ameliorated by the fostering of a new political culture in Northern Ireland. The implications and counterfactuals of the former lie beyond the scope of this chapter (although it may be assumed that a quick fix may in the end exacerbate matters rather than

8 OFMDFM [Office of the First and Deputy First Minister], '*Together: building a united community*.' Available at; www.ofmdfmni.gov.uk/together_building_a_united_community.pdf [accessed 8 June 2013].

9 Cillian McGrattan, 'Moving On: The Creation of a Peaceful Community in Northern Ireland,' *Studies in Ethnicity and Nationalism*, Vol 12, No 1 (2012), 172–189.

help – and that that calculation may militate against it being chosen by policy-makers). One thing that can be said, however, is that the idea of reconciliation is a foundational policy objective of the peace process. The Belfast/Good Friday Agreement of 1998 includes it as a key aim; according to the second paragraph of the text:

> The tragedies of the past have left a deep and profoundly regrettable legacy of suffering. We must never forget those who have died or been injured, and their families. But we can best honour them through a fresh start, in which we firmly dedicate ourselves to the achievement of reconciliation, tolerance and mutual trust, and to the protection and vindication of the human rights of all.[10]

Reconciliation has therefore been an integral part of the debate over dealing with the past in Northern Ireland. Yet the Agreement's representation of reconciliation is problematic: the past is utilized – or, more accurately, commodified – and put at the service of building peace in the present and for the future. Inevitably, within this educative understanding, justice becomes limited to the extent to which it can contribute to peace. The possibility that victims of violence and injustice may have to forgo their desire for truth, punishment or reparation in order to maintain peace and stability is, therefore, ever present. Yet it is this very circumscription that creates the conditions for continuous repackaging of peace. The linking of peace with limited justice can thus be seen as having instituted a path-dependent process as the dynamic reproduces itself until the political culture itself becomes saturated with the type of expediency that valorizes sharing and separation above hopes for integration and inclusion. This process conforms to the ideal of tolerance, mentioned in the same paragraph of the Agreement, which ensures plurality by building fences rather than cooperation. As the political theorist Andrew Schaap reminds us, 'toleration unduly limits reconciliation by grounding social harmony on the exclusion of substantive conceptions of the good from the legitimate ends of politics. In doing so, it precludes the possibility of discovering good reasons for political antagonists to live together in the first place.'[11] Writing within a similar logic, the historian Theodor Zeldin argues that toleration, by itself, only ends in indifference and so it must be seen as a 'stepping stone' towards greater understanding of the other.[12] For Zeldin that understanding comes by gaining new understandings of ourselves: '[t]o have a new vision of the future, it has always first been necessary to have a new vision of the past.'[13]

10 'The Agreement: Agreement Reached in the Multi-Party Negotiations,' April 1998. Available at http://cain.ulst.ac.uk/events/peace/docs/agreement.htm [accessed 4 May 2013].

11 Schaap, 5.

12 Theodor Zeldin, *An Intimate History of Humanity* (London: Minerva, 1994), 272.

13 Ibid, vii.

Reconciliation, the legacy debate and Northern Irish nationalism

Due to the vagueness over the nature of the Northern Irish state and its constitutional future and the concreteness of ethnic bloc divisions, views on peace and reconciliation are deeply contested and constantly renegotiated. The case of Northern Irish nationalism is instructive, particularly because Northern nationalists hold that the state is illegitimate because of a constrained democratic vision – the island of Ireland is ultimately the unit in which questions of self-determination and societal progress should be decided.[14] Northern Irish nationalism is represented by two political parties. Sinn Féin, the largest grouping, has in the past supported armed resistance to end Irish partition and promote a strong defense of Irish cultural values north and south of the border; the late Martin McGuinness was the Deputy First Minister of Northern Ireland and was in the early 1970s the leader of the Provisional Irish Republican Army (PIRA) – a terror group responsible for almost 60 per cent of the 3,700 deaths in the conflict – in Derry, the province's second largest city. The Social Democratic and Labour Party (SDLP) is a more moderate grouping, traditionally linked closely to the Catholic middle class; the SDLP was seen as a key architect of the peace process but has lost ground electorally to Sinn Féin following the ceasefires of the 1990s.

Because nationalists hold that the current constitutional settlement is untenable and favor reunification with the Republic of Ireland, questions concerning the revisiting of historic crimes or unpicking old wounds are not just simply mechanical or narrowly political (What can we know about the past? How can we know it? And might the effort endanger the current peace?), juridical (Can evidence be found to prosecute?) and moral (What truth will we find? How best might it be publicized? What responsibility do we have to forgive and forget?). They are also structural in so far as the answers will say something about the nature of the Northern Irish state. Charles Tilly's thesis that '[s]truggles over collective memory pivot on credit and blame'[15] holds true for the intra-bloc competition within Northern nationalism – ideas and narratives about value, competence and commitment are marshaled by way of accruing credit, while ideas about damage and guilt are evoked to suggest blame for political outcomes. At heart the debate centers on whether the conflict was unjustifiable or inevitable and then (and thus) how the key defenders of nationalist interests during the conflict are the same today.

Sinn Féin's mobilization of the past is a necessary part of its political project. Linked to the main paramilitary organization in the conflict, the PIRA, its role in the peace process is difficult to square with the intractability of its attitude towards the necessity of violence, which it espoused for almost four decades. This

14 Jonathan Tonge, *The New Northern Irish Politics* (Basingstoke: Palgrave Macmillan, 2004).

15 Charles Tilly, *Credit and Blame* (London: Princeton University Press, 2008), 125.

is compounded by the fact that, despite the loss of life and sacrifice of its own volunteers, Sinn Féin singularly failed to achieve any of its policy goals (or the PIRA's war aims) and now finds itself administering British rule in a devolved power-sharing assembly. As such its policy agenda has taken on characteristics of path-dependency: accrue gains through political leverage (typically the appeal that they are necessary for sustaining peace) and move forward from the concessions that are 'banked' or pocketed. The 'path' then established is one of ethnic particularism, for not to win concessions would mean facing up to historical responsibilities, and facing up to those responsibilities would mean conceding ground to the inter-bloc 'others' (namely Ulster unionism). The zero-sum dynamic is self-reinforcing and might only be escaped by a broadening of the question regarding what ethnic parties represent to those they are (or ought to be) responsible.

The interesting element of Sinn Féin's attempt to answer that question is that the language of inclusivity and pluralism, of democracy and accountability and of acknowledgement and responsibility is placed at the service of a particularistic, ethnic agenda. Thus the rhetoric of Declan Kearney, party spokesperson on reconciliation and the past, is based around catch-allisms that are superficially plausible and politically difficult to argue against (for example: 'There is a shared obligation to ensure that future generations grow up in a better place than we did. Discussion is needed now on how to do that. There is no alternative to dialogue.'). As with the best self-help manuals, Kearney's rhetoric is apparently neutral, yet also replete with feelgood terms that lend it a transformative dimension: 'acknowledgement,' 'set aside recrimination,' 'focus on the future and new possibilities,' 'generosity.'[16]

Of course, the political effect is to tilt the playing field decisively towards the Sinn Féin position. This occurs through subtle rhetorical tricks. Although easily discernible once recognized, their nebulousness means they retain an intellectual slipperiness that makes them difficult to pin down. These tricks depend on the false logic that 'there were many victims on all sides . . . All sides were party to the context in which this arose and continued.' The political, the social and the ethical in this type of rhetoric congeal into an aspic of equivalency; in other words, where everyone is to blame so no one is culpable. Second, subversion is placed on the same level as the state, meaning that murder becomes confused with the law. This type of equivalency slides effortlessly into an almost willful blindness of the reality of killing and continued trauma. That reality is often displaced by invoking the South African or Latin American examples – in the process distorting the nature of the violence by the allusion to instances where the state was responsible for the majority of killings – or by an unironic summoning of Orwell's ghost: 'Our future will remain contested for as long as we continue to contest the past.'

16 Declan Kearney, 'Reconciliation and Legacy,' address to the *Ard Fheis* [Sinn Féin Annual Convention], 2013. Author copy.

How do the SDLP's proposals for dealing with the past relate to notions of reconciliation? The party's 2012 policy document explicitly rejects the equivalency involved in 'acknowledgement' processes and calls instead for 'robust mechanisms of truth.'[17] Yet beyond allusions to party self-interest we are not really told what the problem is with acknowledgement. One reading might conclude that, in fact, acknowledgement and understanding are red herrings: we already know that it was the PIRA that was primarily responsible for the vast majority of the killings; we understand that only a small minority of the North's population participated in violence and that to be rendered a victim did not mean that individuals lost all sense of autonomy and automatically joined terror organizations; and the British government has already acknowledged that its forces indulged repeatedly in amoral, anti-democratic, extra-judicial killings such as Bloody Sunday (1972).

The SDLP's document places the onus of responsibility on the London and Dublin governments for instituting what it refers to as a 'comprehensive truth process.' Two questions again emerge: what will it mean for the SDLP if that does not happen and what will it mean for the peace process if it does not happen? As regards the first, the SDLP, if it is not going to happen (and the document alludes to 'state vested interests' being 'central to the resistance' for truth), then why mention it? A moral victory of sorts may be claimed for trying to put the issue on the political agenda, but moral victories on losing issues do not translate into easy electoral success.

The document goes on to claim that there 'is a singular test for Sinn Féin and the IRA – will they endorse a comprehensive truth process, support robust mechanisms of accountability and agree that those who were in command and control of the IRA have a higher and a particular responsibility to account for IRA actions?' Again the point should be made as to whether this is realizable. Sinn Féin have undoubtedly opened doors ('things we wish had been done differently or not at all' . . . 'foundations for the society we all claim to want and have formally committed to build') that the SDLP could capitalize on, but the party's approach remains enveloped in such ill-defined terms as a 'comprehensive truth process,' an 'ethical approach to the past,' and 'national reconciliation.' Although ambiguity can be constructive (see, for instance, Sinn Féin's deliberate but hazy language referred to above), it can also be counterproductive; and the type associated with the central SDLP terms seemingly fails to resonate at any intellectual or emotional level.

The SDLP's idea of an ethical approach raises more questions than it provides answers to. Does it, for instance, consist in recognizing the (SDLP's) 'truth' about the past? Does it mean foregrounding victims' testimonies and experiences? It most likely means both but, even so, while the term itself is intellectually and morally defensible it may not resonate to the same degree as 'generosity' or 'acknowledgement.' To return to the point about pedagogy: while a lesson can

17 SDLP, 'Addressing the Past: A Comprehensive Truth Process and the Ethical Way Forward, 2012.' Author copy.

be imparted in a number of different ways, the 'ethical approach' rhetoric seems somewhat monochrome. Furthermore, the very idea of 'national reconciliation' raises a question regarding whether it represents the SDLP trying to strategically outflank unionism and foist an 'agreed Ireland' on them. The idea of ethics is then rendered problematic by reconciliation when unionist roles are taken into account; for the SDLP's vision seems to consist in unionists agreeing to the terms of debate and that, really, the only question is not why, but when, a united Ireland of some description will come about. The SDLP's reluctance to critique the Irish government's role in establishing or lending tacit support to the IRA (and later the Provisionals) is similarly problematic. The connection is no longer really a matter of conjecture: political historians have for the past ten years been granted access to state papers and their findings are coalescing around a positive relationship between the two. There are, of course, ideological points to be scored in this debate, but if the SDLP is genuine about robust, hard approaches to the past then state collusion in the South needs to be 'acknowledged.'

The SDLP's emphasis on legal theory seems to have recently led it on to a similar terrain as Sinn Féin. It refused, for example, to support a Bill that would ban terrorists convicted of serious offenses (defined as resulting in gaol terms of five years or more) from taking up posts of special ministerial advisers.[18] Obviously reticent about being attacked by Sinn Féin as anti the peace process and advocates of discrimination, the party ignored the political patronage emphasis of the Bill in favor of a framing that encapsulated wider employment dimensions (particularly as regards people who had laid aside violence and served their sentences). Regardless of the question over whether the Bill was in the 'spirit' of the 1998 Agreement as regards prisoners and victims, in terms of straightforward party politics in trying to protect its flank from Sinn Féin, the SDLP's approach works to reaffirm the old nationalist tendency towards what is known as 'sneaking regard' – that is, the willingness to turn a blind eye to unsettling moral issues about reasons for violence and the idea that, along with victims, there may also be perpetrators. The threat by the SDLP to invoke a Petition of Concern – essentially an ethnic veto mechanism that requires cross-community support (rather than a simple majority) for legislation and that has worked exclusively to end Bills – in effect handed power over to other parties to set the agenda in this area. Certainly the SDLP's position places it firmly within Sinn Féin's broad approach to dealing with the past. Whereas the proposed legislation was ethically and politically exclusive in that it positively discriminated, the SDLP's position in effect removed victims from being the prime concern and replaced them with perpetrators. Whereas the original legislation arguably sent the symbolic message that politicians were taking concrete steps towards recognizing their responsibility for caring for

18 SDLP, 'Bradley: SDLP guided by what is right law and right by victims,' 21 May 2013. Available at www.sdlp.ie/index.php/newsroom_media/newsarticle/bradley_sdlp_guided_by_what_is_right_law_and_right_by_victims/ [accessed 23 May 2013].

their citizens, the SDLP's stance repudiated that idea. Instead of a robust attitude to the past, the decision moved the SDLP towards what it characterized as the 'soft' approach of Sinn Féin – an approach that has recently extolled the benefits of decoupling truth from reconciliation.[19]

Between reconciliation and responsibility

In a much-cited report for a Northern Ireland think-tank, Brandon Hamber and Gráinne Kelly set out a typology of reconciliation.[20] Their 'working definition' involves five elements. First, reconciliation, the authors argue, requires the 'development of a vision of a shared future' involving 'the whole society.' More specifically, this does not mean individuals or groups giving up their opinions or beliefs; rather it entails 'the articulation of a common vision of an interdependent, just, equitable, open and diverse society.' Second, reconciliation involves 'acknowledging and dealing with the past.' This includes an institutional focus in the form of establishing mechanisms for dealing with 'justice, healing, restitution or reparation, and restoration.' Third, relationship-building is seen as essential. This includes the fostering of trust and acceptance of difference as well as the breaking down of prejudice and intolerance. Fourth, 'significant cultural and attitudinal change' is required. This consists in the opening up of space 'in which people can hear and be heard' and seems to imply a commitment to empathy along with popular participation in society. Finally, reconciliation entails steps towards a (Lederachian) conception of positive peace that involves 'substantial social, economic and political change.'

The authors suggest that these are 'interwoven strands,' implying that while each is essential none is necessarily *more* important than the others. It also implies there is no causal chain and, because of this, I believe, the model can potentially be more harmful than is intended. In short, unless the first point is satisfied, it (and arguably points three, four and five) can be undermined by the second. In other words, it may – as the Sinn Féin case demonstrates – be easily possible to espouse beliefs in pluralism, equity, openness and diversity while still holding particularistic views on the past. The logic is as follows: violence occurred because we were denied equity, openness, fairness; now that we've proved our point, we will continue to ensure that such denials never happen again; and we will ally ourselves with other human rights activists across the world because a threat to liberty anywhere is a threat to liberty everywhere. Quite what this means to other citizens – who believe that, while society was or is not ideal, the resort to violence

19 Stephen McCaffrey, 'Should truth be separated from reconciliation?' *The Detail*, 20 May. Available at www.thedetail.tv/issues/209/reconciliation/should-truth-be-separated-from-reconciliation [accessed 23 May 2013].

20 Brandon Hamber and Gráinne Kelly, *Reconciliation: A Working Definition* (Belfast: Democratic Dialogue, 2004). Available at http://cain.ulst.ac.uk/dd/papers/dd04 recondef.pdf [accessed 5 May 2013].

needs to meet strong criteria before it can be justified – is a critical question that is not resolved by a simple evocation of pluralism. Pluralism in this case might be seen to work against social cohesion and operate to marginalize voices that might also favor a fair and shared society. The Hamber/Kelly definition falls short of the Schaap/Zeldin ideal mentioned above; for, as Schaap explains, reconciliation depends on shared understandings of what actually occurred or, rather, where the grievance happened. It is the agreement on facts that allows a meeting of minds over explanations. As such, Schaap may be seen as adopting a straightforward but lucid empirical standpoint on which to base his theory; namely, that 'reconciliatory politics requires respect for factual truth, of that which is simply because it was not otherwise.'[21] In other words, Hamber and Kelly's second item is normatively and practically prior to the others: an agreed version of reality is necessary in order to have a point around which reconciliation occurs; and that reality is not simply a matter of perception – it consists in absences and the reasons for absences or the persons responsible.

Iris Marion Young attempted to tackle this question by distinguishing between responsibility and guilt at a conceptual level. There are things for which we are, by dint of our participation in society, responsible. We have a duty, for example, to try to tackle injustice where we can identify it occurring; however, there are other events for which individuals, by either act or omission, are culpable – for these we may not be liable, directly or indirectly, unless we contribute in some way to their perpetuation by our negligence or lack of interest. Guilt is, in this framework, linked to blameworthiness and the principle of 'but for' – that is, but for what I did (or omitted to do) the resulting harm would not have taken place, or would not have occurred to the extent it did.[22] As Young explains:

> To the extent that we participate in the ongoing operations of a society in which injustice occurs, we ought to be held responsible. This does not, however, make us guilty or blameworthy or directly liable for paying compensation to victims of harm. Responsibility does not, however, make us guilty or blameworthy or directly liable for paying compensation to victims of harm.[23]

Collective responsibility therefore does not exist and, in fact, ends by draining the idea of responsibility of all meaning, as alluded to above. It becomes meaningless to talk of victims' experiences or trauma because if everyone is complicit no one is truly guilty, and if everyone is a victim of conflict then no one is really a perpetrator: we are, in short, all victims of a system. Intent becomes important in differentiating between degrees of culpability, and understanding is essential

21 Schaap, 8.
22 Young, 101.
23 Ibid, 104.

to ascribing responsibility, which of course is attenuated in instances of limited knowledge. Young outlines what she calls a 'social connection model of responsibility' in which she argues responsibility can be ascribed to individuals for 'social injustice because they contribute by their actions to the processes that produce unjust outcomes.'[24] She goes on to define responsibility as deriving 'from belonging together with others in a system of interdependent processes of cooperation and competition through which we seek benefits and aim to realize projects . . . All who dwell within the structures must take responsibility for remedying injustices they cause, though none is specifically liable for the harm in a legal sense.' Thus, in Young's understanding, responsibility derives not simply from living in a society; rather it comes from 'participating in the diverse institutional processes that produce structural injustice.' As such, responsibility is not collective; it is 'shared' and, as such, it can be 'discharged only through collective action.'[25]

Young contrasts her social responsibility model with liability and describes five features that distinguish the kind of structural bonds that concern her from concerns about legal culpability. The first condition she identifies is the need to avoid isolating individuals from their broader societal contexts, which can work, she argues, to absolve others 'whose actions contribute to the outcomes from bearing responsibility in a different way.'[26] Second, she argues that to ascribe responsibility means paying attention to the background conditions in which injustice occurs; in so doing it will be possible to evaluate harm over and above 'normal and acceptable' hurts. Third, she argues, responsibility is forward-looking. Unlike guilt, which is focused on the past, social responsibility is centered on the imperative of ending injustice and establishing a better society. Fourth, responsibility is shared within society; every person 'is personally responsible for the outcome in a partial way, since he or she alone does not produce the outcomes.'[27] Since culpability cannot be isolated (as distinct from a more legal understanding of liability), responsibility is to an extent shared. Finally, the promotion of social justice must be predicated on collective action – it is not simply the duty of the state or particular organizations or agencies to remedy injustices. Instead, these bodies should be viewed as 'mediated instruments for the coordinated action of those who share responsibility for structures, rather than as actors independent of us.'[28]

Young's ideas about social justice arguably help to clarify the terms of debate in an ethnically divided, post-conflict society such as Northern Ireland's. Extrapolating from her distinction between guilt and responsibility, for example, helps to demarcate exactly who was culpable for violence and gives lie to the notion that conflict was somehow inevitable and that, as the Northern Irish novelist Glenn

24 Ibid, 105.
25 Ibid.
26 Ibid, 106.
27 Ibid, 110.
28 Ibid, 111.

Patterson has argued, continued outrages are 'wrong not just regrettable.'[29] The focus on the shared nature of responsibility, meanwhile, contains an imperative to not let victims be remarginalized for political and/or societal expediencies. Her commitment to asserting culpability and blameworthiness, and her conceptual distinction of guilt from responsibility, opens up space for some kind of shared understanding about what actually occurred. As such, Young's ideas prepare the ground for the kind of reconciliatory politics theorized by Schaap and desired by Hamber and Kelly.

Although Young's future-oriented emphasis serves to delimit guilt and separate it from responsibility, it may, when placed with the context of a deeply divided and post-conflict society, actually work to delegitimize her central interest in sharing obligations. By placing the onus on the future, the risk arises that the past will be forgotten. The point is subtle but important – of course, societal interests should be on building better societies for future generations and at one point drawing a line under the past.[30] The question arises, however, as to at what point that line can be drawn. If it is drawn too soon then we obviously risk revictimizing those who have suffered the most from conflict. If the balance of concern is placed too squarely towards the future then we risk forgetting what went on in the past; history is again relegated to a subservient role and questions concerning culpability and responsibility are excised and deferred as an unintended consequence. If social responsibility is about sharing and, in the process, opening up debate or even consciousness-raising, then the tilt towards the future and away from the past might be seen as a shutting-down and an analgesic amnesia. This certainly seems to be an unresolved anomaly within Young's considerations.

Conclusion

The fact that both shame and scrutiny can work to defer admission of culpability does not exhaust the possibilities for engendering reconciliation through responsibility. One further option lies in the social nature of responsibility itself; for the admission of responsibility for actions (or omissions) on the part of one person or group creates an onus on others to respond. This can be done through a negative or pragmatic ethic or through a more selfless impulse – what is known in German as *Fremdscham*, that is vicarious embarrassment or shame for the other. The result is arguably emblematic of the dynamics involved in social responsibility: difference and distinction is created and the self and the other are (re)affirmed – I accept responsibility for these actions, events and omissions,

29 Glenn Patterson, 'The IRA is a tradition, not an army. It hasn't gone away,' *The Guardian*, 26 April 2011. Available at www.guardian.co.uk/commentisfree/2011/apr/26/ira-tradition-army-martin-mcguinness [accessed 5 May 2013].

30 Max Weber, 'Politics as a Vocation' [1919]. Available at www.sscnet.ucla.edu/polisci/ethos/Weber-vocation.pdf [accessed 5 May 2013].

the others must be shared between us or are your responsibility. 'Reality' or 'historical accuracy' does not, of course, have much bearing on this beyond what is credible and logically sustainable. Instead, the ethic (whether positive or negative) of responsibility becomes self-reinforcing and the only escape is to adopt an ethic of indifference or complete cynicism. I would suggest with an admitted degree of cynicism that such a dynamic might come easily to the political discourse in Northern Ireland, where the term 'whataboutery' is part of everyday parlance. But whereas 'whataboutery' indicates a vicious circle of blame and counter-blame that is always aimed at the other ('You talk of X atrocity/ broken promise/example of bad faith, what about Y. . .?'), the admission/ acceptance/attribution of responsibility is something that reaches the other by first going through the self. I am not suggesting that initial step is in reality any less cynical or calculating than the 'whataboutery' cycle (certainly not in the negative or pragmatic impulse). Rather, I am suggesting that instead of a confrontational, circular and ultimately self-interested debate about history, the admission of responsibility may inculcate discussion about why actions were taken and what could have been done differently. The peace process would then, perhaps, become less about historical justifications and more about agreed and concrete ideas concerning what Northern Ireland went through and where it is going.

Such a debate would require a certain amount of soul-searching among Northern Ireland's political elites. The SDLP might, for example, have to face up to historic 'mistakes' made by their totemic leader John Hume – mistakes such as his rejection of dialogue with Ulster Unionists in favor of talks with Sinn Féin in the late-1980s.[31] Whether the SDLP would regard this as a 'mistake' or not is in some ways irrelevant. The critical point is that admitting responsibility would entail raising the question of whether its actions delayed peace. Why such a step is critical is simply because it would entail the party loosening its grip on an aspect of its foundational mythology – namely, that it has always been the party of peace; that it was the architect of the peace process.

However, it is a smaller step than what it would mean for Sinn Féin to loosen its grip on its history, for its policy direction seems to be solely predicated on a particular (and particularized) attitude to the past. This entails it 'banking' concessions in the debate over dealing with the past (such as the recent decision to construct a Conflict Transformation Center at the site of the former Maze gaol) and moving forward, drawing on their capital and returns to continually hollow-out or simply transcend the Northern state. The problem, of course, is that Sinn Féin needs to repaint the past to avoid facing up to the compromises it has made. To do so would be to admit that the IRA's decision to take a war to the 'Brits' was profoundly misguided; to admit the political and strategic vacancy of the decision to continue that war after the fall of Stormont and during

31 Cillian McGrattan, *Northern Ireland, 1968–2008: The Politics of Entrenchment* (Basingstoke: Palgrave Macmillan, 2010).

the Sunningdale Assembly; to admit the moral degeneracy of prolonging its campaign despite the rising death counts during the 1970s and 1980s. In short, such a change in policy direction would be to admit the Republicans' key and unjustifiable role in the perpetuation of murder and mayhem and the selling out by Sinn Féin of their undemocratic and imperializing project. However, this can only go on for so long. Indulging the party may stave off the inevitable collapse, but unless Sinn Féin begins to articulate a vision of politics based on social responsibility, rather than craven self-interest, a vision of society based on pluralism, inclusion and accountability, rather than universal blame and exculpation, then it will continue to run into delusional dead-ends.

This chapter has suggested that conceptionalizations of reconciliation and peace that sidestep questions of political analysis end in facing similar limitations. Rather than serving the purposes and stated goals of integration and stability, by removing the political from the equation, they can potentially end up reinforcing ethnic boundaries and established power relations. I have suggested that this is the inevitable result of moving too quickly to a Lederachian vision of socio-economic justice allied with clarity about the past. The chapter has instead argued for an initial step of recognizing and adopting an attitude of social responsibility. I have suggested that, although this is ultimately forward-looking, it needs to entail a decisive element of historical recognition. Such a recognition may help to move beyond sterile debates over truth recovery – especially when everyone knows the basic, fundamental facts of who committed historic crimes. Instead, the focus switches to linking those crimes to society. I have not theorized the political philosophical implications of such a vision, but instead focused on its pragmatic benefits. However, by way of conclusion it may be worthwhile pointing out that such a vision entails a radical politics that must be distinguished from neo-conservative discourses on responsibility, for the idea of taking responsibility and attributing responsibility for past actions is predicated on the social and the democratic, suggesting that the past must be approached not simply from an individualistic, historicist or narrowly empirical point of view. The past is not a foreign country. Like the present and the future it must be envisioned, constructed and approached with the normative and the ethical in mind; such an approach logically entails consideration of the social.

4 Selecting the memory, controlling the myth

The propaganda of legal foundations in early modern drama

Eric Heinze

It is an ancient view that we obey law solely in pursuit of self-interest, shunning the disadvantages of non-compliance.[1] At times we surely do. But it by no means contradicts another, equally ancient, view: people follow law because they sense it is right to do so.

That feeling of 'right' rarely flows from seminar-style deliberation. More often it arises from long-inculcated and shared attitudes,[2] sometimes propelled through stories.[3] Few American or French citizens today, for example, possess a detailed knowledge of their eighteenth-century revolutions. Most have inherited socio-political values layered atop those historical events – not as meticulous chronologies, but as legends animating values such as liberty, democracy or nationhood.[4]

But let's travel a bit further back in time. In medieval Europe, rival jurisdictions had often maintained nebulous and shifting balances of power. The English monarch, for example, reigned only as 'first among equals,' alongside a still-powerful aristocracy and church. By the late sixteenth century, however, a progressively absolutizing monarchy absorbs those rival powers, holding itself out

1 See for example, *Republic* 2.359d-61d (suggesting that many people would violate law if they knew they could avoid penalties), in *Plato: Complete Works*, edited by John. M. Cooper (Indianapolis: Hackett, 1997), 1000–1002.
2 See for example, *Nicomachean Ethics* 2.1103a15–18 (relating ethics [as *ēthos*] to habituation [as *ethos*]), in *The Complete Works of Aristotle* (Vol 2), edited by Jonathan Barnes (Princeton: Princeton University Press, 1984), 1742.
3 See for example, *Republic* 2.379c–92c, in *Plato: Complete Works*, 1997, 1018–1030.
4 See for example, Martial Poirson (ed.), *La Révolution française et le monde d'aujourd'hui: Mythologies contemporaines* (Paris: Garnier, 2014); Ray Raphael, *Founding Myths: Stories That Hide Our Patriotic Past* (New York: The New Press, 2014).

as the ultimate source of law.[5] The doctrine of absolute sovereignty comes to define the emerging nation-state as a hallmark of political modernity, nowhere more memorably advocated than in Thomas Hobbes's *Leviathan*. Strong justification is required for a single human authority to be asserted over law.[6] It is no accident that the making and dissemination of new political mythologies reaches a pinnacle through dramatists – Shakespeare, Corneille, Racine – whom time would soon elevate to national bards.

Performing legitimacy: a Shakespearean transition

Shakespeare's middle-period 'tetralogy' comprises *Richard II, Henry IV: Part One, Henry IV: Part Two* and *Henry V*. Those plays seem at first glance to stage events of a medieval past already distant for late Elizabethans. Yet it has never been a secret that Shakespeare is commenting more on his Tudor present than on England's Plantagenet past. The tetralogy mythologizes an ascendant political modernity. It offers a 'How To' guide for fabricating memory, for disseminating myths of political legitimacy, and for mobilizing a populace to abide by an increasingly centralized regime founded on a myth of divine right.[7]

Political propaganda is, of course, ancient. Accounts of kings and emperors from China to Egypt to Rome confirm the role of iconography in public art, be it through temples, pyramids or coinage, to promote the legitimacy of an existing regime. Shakespeare's English histories mirror the dramatic amplifications of such imagery under Henry VIII and Elizabeth I as essential tools for entrenching the authority of a central monarchical power within the bourgeoning nation-state.[8]

The second tetralogy stages the following sequence. The Lancastrian Henry Bolingbroke overthrows Richard II to become Henry IV. Bolingbroke is then succeeded by his eldest son as Henry V, also commonly called Harry or Hal. Shakespeare depicts this father and son intent on manufacturing political and legal legitimacy as doubts about Richard's overthrow haunt their reigns. Striving to

5 See for example, Peter C. Herman, 'Macbeth: Absolutism, the Ancient Constitution, and the Aporia of Politics,' in *The Law in Shakespeare,* edited by Constance Jordan and Karen Cunningham (Basingstoke: Palgrave Macmillan, 2007), 208–232; Ernst Kantorowicz, *The King's Two Bodies* (Princeton: Princeton University Press, 1997); Paul Raffield, *Shakespeare's Imaginary Constitution* (Oxford: Hart, 2010), 82–116; Ian Ward, *Shakespeare and the Legal Imagination* (London: Butterworths, 1999), 20–44.

6 See: Eric Heinze, 'Sovereign Legitimacy in Shakespeare's English History Plays,' in *Shakespeare: Authority and Authorities,* edited by Katie Halsey and Angus Vine (Basingstoke, UK: Palgrave Macmillan, 2017); Eric Heinze, 'The Literary Model in Comparative Law: Shakespeare, Corneille, Racine,' *Journal of Comparative Law*, Vol 9, No 2 (2014), 17–27.

7 See for example, Graham Holderness, *Shakespeare: The Histories* (New York: St. Martins Press, 2000); Phyllis Rackin, *Stages of History: Shakespeare's English Chronicles* (Ithaca: Cornell University Press, 1990).

8 See for example, Leonard Tennenhouse, *Power on Display: The Politics of Shakespeare's Genres* (New York: Methuen, 1986).

legitimate Lancastrian rule in the face of rebellion, Bolingbroke despairs about his heir keeping company with the debauched Sir John Falstaff and their alehouse companions.

Creating a myth of divine grace

Far from undermining Lancastrian legitimacy, however, Hal pursues his secret plot to entrench it. Hal will become Shakespeare's exemplary self-propagandist. (And it works. After four centuries, countless viewers still hail Henry V as Shakespeare's model ruler.[9]) He shall turn himself into a legend, subtly directing the population's opinion about him. He will spawn a story, a memory, of his quasi-miraculous transformation, in the sense of conversion or redemption, such as to be deemed divinely favored even despite his father's breach of lineal succession.

After all, at the core of divine right lies God's choice of the monarch. Hal's task is daunting, since that choice ordinarily depends on orderly succession and shuns overthrow. Hal will fabricate myth and memory by manufacturing his own mythology of divine grace. His plan consists of two steps. He will first lower others' expectations of him, deliberately shrouding himself in 'base contagious clouds'[10] (1H4, 1.2.186), seeming to confirm their fears about the illegality and indeed sin of his father's rebellion and of God's manifest disfavor. When those onlookers least expect it, however, Hal will then suddenly 'break[] through the foul and ugly mists' (190). Like 'the sun' (185), this 'son' will become all the more 'wanted' (189), all the 'more wondered at' (189), all the more 'wished-for' (194), when the people behold him suddenly shining 'like bright metal on a sullen ground' (200).

Public memory, public opinion

The prince savors the time he has to forge his long-term interest. His father, enjoying no such leisure, must myth-make more shrewdly. Unaware of his son's plan, the king perceives only its unseemly surface. Henry IV sees only his son's stage-managed 'fault' (201), lacking the lustre which the prince later intends to add to it. Bolingbroke would never have found his way to the throne without, from the outset, currying public opinion to his advantage and to Richard's detriment. Bolingbroke recognizes his own self-iconography, his own fashioning

9 See for example, Sara Munson Deats, 'Henry V at War: Christian King or Model Machiavel,' in Sara Munson Deats, Lagretta Tallent Lenker and Merry G. Perry, *War and Words: Horror and Heroism in the Literature of Warfare* (Lanham, MD: Lexington Books, 2004), 83–102, 83–84.

10 Unless otherwise indicated, Shakespeare citations are to Stanley Wells, Gary Taylor, John Jowett, and William Montgomery (eds.), *The Oxford Shakespeare*, 2nd ed. (Oxford: Oxford University Press, 2015). Alternative references are to Richard Proudfoot Ann Thompson, David Scott Kastan (eds.), *Arden Shakespeare, Third Series* (London: Bloomsbury, 1998).

Figure 1 Henry VII: undistinguished dignity[11]

11 Henry VII, ca. 1505, artist unknown, National Portrait Gallery, London.

Figure 2 Henry VIII: dispensing with humility[12]

of popular memory, as crucial to his legal legitimacy as monarch. Without cultivating their favor, the aristocracy would have 'kept loyal' to Richard's 'possession' of the throne (3.2.39–45). In telling Hal as much, the king directs the prince's memory, all the while teaching him how to create political mythology.

12 Henry VIII, 1535–1540, circle of Hans Holbein, Galleria Nazionale di Arte Antica, Rome.

Figure 3 Elizabeth I: dazzling attire[13]

What Henry IV and the future Henry V share is the early modern strategy of presenting themselves as near-miracles of nature, each being 'wondered at' in the style of the Tudors' political self-modelling. Hal's ploy may well be to show himself redeemed from seeming incompetence, but his father's more pragmatic self-mythologizing can take no such risks. Bolingbroke keeps his public appearances few and, by carefully controlling their timing, 'wondered at' as a sheer rarity,

> By being seldom seen, I could not stir
> But like a comet I was wondered at,
> That men would tell their children, 'This is he!'
> Others would say, 'Where, which is Bolingbroke?' (46–49)

13 Elizabeth I ('Armada portrait'), ca. 1588, artist unknown (formerly attributed to George Gower), National Portrait Gallery, London.

The myth that had conferred legitimacy on Richard was, again, divine right, precisely what Bolingbroke had violated by breaking the sacred bond of lineal succession. Now, as Henry IV, he must restore it, but on a new foundation. Bolingbroke presents here a version of Richard's downfall rather different from the one we see on stage. In *Richard II* (R2, 1.4.23–36) the forces joining the rebellion speak more effusively against Richard than for Bolingbroke. We certainly learn about this upstart currying popular favor, but witness him far more like a cunning operator than 'like a comet,' a miracle of nature. Still, he certainly scripts the legitimating myth he wishes his son to embrace. *Vox populi, vox dei:* the first step towards restoring lineal succession 'from heaven' lies in securing popular 'courtesy':

> And then I stole all courtesy from heaven,
> And dressed myself in such humility
> That I did pluck allegiance from men's hearts,
> Loud shouts and salutations from their mouths,
> Even in the presence of the crownèd King. (1H4, 3.2.50–54)

Richard, too, comes to an 'Elizabethan' understanding about the new necessity of performed legitimacy, but only too late, after a coup from which he learns that 'heaven's' choice of ruler lies to no small extent in being able to 'pluck allegiance from men's hearts.' Legitimacy flows from the show of legitimacy, from its trappings, which not only the 'deputy elected by the Lord' (R2, 3.2.57) but anyone at all can don. Bolingbroke wins few votes among more perceptive audiences for his 'humility.' What he does know is the importance of having 'dressed' himself in it (1H4, 3.2.55–49. Cf. H5, 4.1.248–56). The dazzling royal attire of Tudor monarchs, far surpassing that of their medieval forebears, is crucial to the iconography, to the mythology, of legal legitimacy.[14] Compare the transitional Henry VII (Figure 1), certainly dignified yet scarcely more so than a distinguished mayor or magistrate, to his quasi-palatially presented progeny Henry VIII (Figure 2) or Elizabeth I (Figure 3).

'He needs will be Absolute'

The Tempest offers a further study of bourgeoning state centralism. For ages the play had been read as a universalist fable, unfolding in a fairy-tale nowhere because its supposed humanist themes of self-realization and reconciliation could presumably be discovered everywhere. A deeply wronged yet instinctively paternal Prospero, so it was thought, seeks only to nurture his untainted daughter Miranda. He fruitlessly strives to civilize the ungrateful 'native' Caliban. And he aims only to redress injustices wrought on his lost Milanese domain, preparing it for

14 See: Tennenhouse.

enlightened rule under a scrupulously initiated Ferdinand, son of the Neapolitan King Alonso.[15]

That humanist-universalist perspective has, since the mid-twentieth century, faced dogged attacks. Feminism, new historicism, cultural materialism and post-colonial studies have dissected that 'universal,' seeing in it not the self-actualizing lives of humans on all continents but rather a rhetorical strategy for naturalizing privilege within repressive hierarchies, strategically justifying existing power structures under the mantel of a self-evident moral code.[16] With the tide of 1960s decolonization movements, new understandings of Prospero's isle were afoot. The Martiniquais Aimé Césaire rewrote the play, calling it *Une Tempête* (1969), bearing the hallmarks of anti-colonialist critique associated with Frantz Fanon's *Peau noire, masques blancs* (1952) or *Les Damnés de la Terre* (1961). Césaire gives voice to a Caliban politically and psychologically colonized, yet having gained critical consciousness of the mental processes of colonization, as he rebels against European domination. But are those altogether recent insights? Did Shakespeare's Caliban ever really differ from Césaire's? Or is Césaire quarrelling with a naively humanist *Tempest* that was never Shakespeare's to begin with? No one today can easily read *The Tempest* other than as the story of a politically absolutist patriarch practicing pervasive surveillance and control on a commodified daughter and a degraded, brutalized Caliban, all in preparation to transform his Milan – England – from a factious medieval backwater into the engine of a modern, global empire.

By the late twentieth century, readings and performances of *The Tempest* were passing from classical humanism to socio-critical approaches. Its regime of power was increasingly deemed violent and oppressive. That approach contrasts with humanist readings, which viewed Prospero's realm as generally benign and saw actual or threatened violence, if at all, only in the supposed savagery of the colonized.[17] Domination within Prospero's 'brave new world' (Tmp 5.1.183) runs in one direction only. It emanates from the privileged European male, exercised on his underlings. Of course, Prospero's Milan has itself become subordinated within the Neapolitan king's imperial structure. Should Prospero's plot succeed, however, Milan will become ostensibly subsumed by Naples, like Elizabeth's England under Scottish James, only to emerge as dominant after all.

15 See: critically, e.g. Meredith Anne Skura, 'Discourse and the Individual: The Case of Colonialism in The Tempest,' in *Shakespeare: An Anthology of Criticism and Theory 1945–2000*, edited by R. McDonald (Malden, MA: Blackwell, 2004), 817–844, 817.

16 Cf., e.g. Skura, 818–819.

17 See for example, Paul Brown, 'This thing of darkness I acknowledge mine: The Tempest and the discourse of colonialism,' in *Political Shakespeare: Essays on Cultural Materialism*, edited by Jonathan Dollimore and Alan Sinfield (Manchester: Manchester University Press, 1994), 80–81; Francis Barker and Peter Hulme, 'Nymphs and Reapers Heavily Vanish: The discursive contexts of The Tempest,' in *Alternative Shakespeares*, edited by John Drakakis (London and New York: Routledge, 2002), 195–209, 205.

The edgier a political barb, the more an early modern writer must encode it. The techniques of political hegemony that Prospero is perfecting, controlling bodies by engineering minds, become packaged as the play's famous 'magic.' Meanwhile, in a tell-tale sign of the late Shakespeare's newly Jacobean world, that sovereign absolutism which Prospero is confecting, he also dissimulates through an accusation against his usurping brother Sebastian: 'he needs will be / Absolute Milan'[18] (1.2.108–09).

Plays like *Hamlet* and *Measure for Measure* have, since Foucault, been read with an eye towards diffusion of power as a technique of control in modernity,[19] notably through institutions such as schools or prisons, presented providentially as pathways to individual liberation and enlightenment. *The Tempest* altogether fits that mold, with Prospero's island indeed increasingly imagined as a prison.[20] Power is imposed by this seventeenth-century autocrat on Miranda, always in the guise of her own self-interest. Miranda remains vigilantly preserved as endogenous to a culture of European supremacy,[21] anticipating the ethnically delineated enclaves that white overlords would later create within their colonial outposts.[22] That same power overwhelms Caliban, indigenous yet enslaved, and rendered culturally exogenous within his own land (332–44, 363–64). It descends on Ariel, Prospero's culturally appropriated agent (270–71, 294–96). Most importantly, at least for Prospero's designs, he wields power on that Milanese-Neapolitan socio-political microcosm, that 'ship of state,' which he lures into his dominion, a vessel carrying Europe's highest and lowest social orders, all bursting into open conflict with each other (1.1.16–48).

Miranda's 'good dullness'

Miranda grows up on her father's island, his psychological guinea pig. Despairing at her incapacity to aid the shipwreck victims, Miranda cries out to him,

18 That mode of ironic self-revelation is familiar in the corpus. Recall the disguised and spying Henry V's jibe at a common foot soldier 'you speak this to feel other men's minds.' *H5,* 4.1.120–21. Recall also Antonio's slur in *The Merchant of Venice:* 'The devil can cite Scripture for his purpose.' *MV* 1.3.95.

19 See for example, John Dollimore, 'Transgression and Surveillance in Measure for Measure,' *Political Shakespeare: Essays on Cultural Materialism,* edited by Jonathan Dollimore and Alan Sinfield (Manchester: Manchester University Press, 1994) 72–87.

20 See for example, Margaret Atwood, 'A perfect storm: Margaret Atwood on rewriting Shakespeare's Tempest,' *The Guardian* (24 September 2016), at www.theguardian.com/books/2016/sep/24/margaret-atwood-rewriting-shakespeare-tempest-hagseed [accessed 24 March 2017]; Nick Curtis reviewing Harriet Walter's setting of *The Tempest* in an all-women's prison, *The Evening Standard* (14 September 2016), at www.standard.co.uk/goingout/theatre/harriet-walter-on-the-donmars-allfemale-shakespeare-trilogy-we-didnt-want-to-be-coy-about-addressing-a3344456.html [accessed 24 March 2017].

21 See below text accompanying notes 31–32, 38–37.

22 See for example, Gijsbert van Es Multatuli, *Max Havelaar, of de koffie-veilingen der Nederlandsche handelsmaatschappij* (Amsterdam: de Ruyter, 1860); Louis Couperus, *De stille kracht* (Amsterdam: L.J. Veen, 1900).

underscoring her condition of engineered disempowerment *vis-à-vis* her father by reminding us that she is anything *but* 'any god of power':

> Had I been any god of power, I would
> Have sunk the sea within the earth or ere
> It should the good ship so have swallowed, and
> The fraughting souls within her. (1.2.10–13)

One might perhaps stress the word 'power,' as if to question the existence or character of God or of the gods. Above all, however, the weight falls on the word 'I,' contrasting herself, being no such supernatural entity, with her father, set up as the island's god.[23] If that power is one that not she but only a god can have, then such is, as far as she knows, her father. Yet Prospero immediately directs our attention away from whatever it is Miranda does know, towards that which she does not know, which also turns out to be a good deal: 'my daughter, who / Art ignorant of what thou art; nought knowing / Of whence I am' (17–19).

The purely surface meaning of 'what thou art,' in light of 'whence I am,' can be limited to sheer matters of geography and heredity. Its existential dimension, by contrast, has not gone missing on scholars, particularly from feminist perspectives. By sheer homonymy, the repetition of 'art' evokes the early modern noun, closer to the Latin *ars* than to today's narrower notions of 'fine' or 'decorative art,' leaving a sense of Miranda as the product of Prospero's workmanship, created by careful molding of her mind (cf. 25). Prospero's attention to what his daughter 'is' links to what she knows, which in turn will emerge from a studious engineering of her memory.

Prospero's philosophy of what traditional readings have deemed a loving father, justifying all he has taught and not taught, proves paternalist indeed. Prospero assures his daughter, 'I have done nothing but in care of thee' (16). That maxim recalls the stock political rationales of national interest, the *raison d'état*. Miranda's education has proved perfect, not merely because Prospero has determined what she does and does not know, but because, as a matter of her individual will and disciplined obedience, she does not *want* to know beyond what Prospero, whom we might almost call Kim Jong-Prospero, deems she ought to know: 'More to know / Did never meddle with my thoughts' (21–22). With just 999 more chirpy Mirandas we could witness an impressive flag dance.

This is not to say that Miranda fails to raise objections (445–84), as do the other islanders under her father's control. Like Henry V, Prospero nonetheless remains attuned to any deviance. Not merely content, but timing becomes decisive. What Miranda may know becomes a function of when she may know it. It is imparted not for its sake, nor for her sake, but for the sake of generating a mythology of legitimacy. The content is not an end in itself, but a means to some other end, a political project. Having posited her constitutive ignorance,

23 Cf. below, text accompanying note 35.

Prospero proceeds not through instruction but through interrogation to extract all relevant memories from Miranda's mind. She is not free to make what she will of the narrative she is about to hear. Instead, before recounting that story, Prospero must first prepare the way in which she will hear it, because the knowledge is imparted with the aim of control more than instruction:

> Canst thou *remember*
> A time before we came unto this cell?
>
> ---
>
> Of any thing the image tell me that
> Hath kept with thy *remembrance.*
>
> ---
>
> But how is it
> That this lives in thy mind? What seest thou else
> In the dark backward and abysm of time?
> If thou *rememb'rest* aught ere thou cam'st here,
> How thou cam'st here thou mayst. (38–52 (emphasis added))

We encounter three times in that excerpt cognates of 'remember' and 'remembrance' (the play as a whole counts 19, with several more in this scene alone). When Shakespeare methodically reiterates a word or idea (as with *The Merchant of Venice*'s variations on the concept of surface appearances or *King Lear*'s references to animals) it is not that we may take the notion at face value. Remembrance is presented as anything but the indifferent, dispassionate re-'collecting' of 'facts.' Memory in *The Tempest* becomes actively dictated and constructed. Having first solicited from Miranda the extent of her recollection, Prospero then judiciously grafts on to it the remaining 'remembrance' which he charges her to nurture.

That invention of memory remains an age-old method of political propaganda. When citizens are asked to 'remember' the fallen of a national liberation struggle, which may date back several generations, that recollection consists mostly in renewing their faith in what subsequent ages have taught. This does not mean that such stories are lies. To the contrary, events in *The Tempest* confirm much of Prospero's story. Political knowledge, germane to political justice, is not always a locus of sheer lies. It is often more a matter of strategically managed memory through craftily selected and contextualized facts.

One detail has long attracted interest. As victim of what is otherwise a straightforward political coup, Prospero explains his delegation of and withdrawal from political authority. He cites his interest in 'the liberal arts' (73), his library famously being 'dukedom large enough' (100). The 'liberal arts' traditionally encompassed the *trivium* of grammar, logic and rhetoric, and *quadrivium* of arithmetic, geometry, music and astronomy.[24] Recall, however, that such studies

24 Orgel, 1987 (Oxf[4]), 105; Vaughan and Vaughan, 2011 (ARD[3], rev'd), 176.

are not, in early modernity, divided from religion or the supernatural as strongly as post-Enlightenment thought would do. Prospero refers to his 'magic garment' (24), and his supernatural powers are taken for granted. Scholars have observed how Prospero's *magus* figure had become a familiar type in the Renaissance. Prospero compares, for example, to Marlowe's Dr Faustus,[25] for whom boundaries between astronomy and astrology, chemistry and alchemy, in short the natural and the supernatural, remain more fluid than we generally see them today. The 'scientist' may well be depicted as a magician type, like the more comical Dr Pinch in *The Comedy of Errors* (comparable figures include Friar Laurence in *Romeo and Juliet,* Helena in *All's Well That Ends Well*, or Lord Cerimon in *Pericles*).

In *The Tempest* that association of knowledge with magic, pre-modern in our eyes, serves as a cornerstone of political modernity, as Prospero perfects his propagandizing techniques. King James had famously inveighed against witchcraft,[26] against autonomous pretenses to power exercised particularly among lower classes, while pursuing through political propaganda an absolutism as godlike, as akin to magic, as the terrestrial world had ever known. Prospero tutors Miranda in each detail of his political history that she, groomed as his posthumous political agent, will need to know, with the roles of good and evil, of perpetrator and victim, clearly demarcated. He does not simply recount that story but, at each juncture, quizzes his pupil's memory:

> **Prospero** [. . .]
>
> Dost thou attend me?
>
> **Miranda**
>
> Sir, most heedfully. (78)
>
> **Prospero** [. . .]
>
> Thou attend'st not!
>
> **Miranda**
>
> O, good sir, I do.
>
> **Prospero**
>
> I pray thee, mark me. (87–89) (Ard[3] (rev'd)) [. . .]
> Dost thou hear? (106)

Miranda's 'tutorial' certainly conveys facts aimed at persuading her, whereby Prospero eloquently recites the memory of his political overthrow. More

25 Vaughan and Vaughan, 2011 (ARD [3], rev'd), 64–66.
26 See for example, Orgel, 1987 (Oxf[4]), 21; Vaughan and Vaughan, 2011 (ARD [3], rev'd), 64–66.

important is his interpolation of linguistic 'performatives' or 'illocutions.'[27] Prospero's words serve not merely a denotative function. They actively perform the task of molding Miranda's mind. They discipline and rectify her thought processes. That strategy draws on grammatical imperatives ('Obey and be attentive,' 'mark me') and interrogatives ('Canst thou remember?' 'Dost thou attend me?' 'Dost thou hear?'), and not merely on the conventional grammatical indicative of 'factual' history. Those grammatical constructs may be either formal or functional. Strictly construed, the emphatic 'Thou attend'st not!' forms only a grammatical indicative. Functionally or rhetorically, however, it serves not merely to convey information but as equivalent to a grammatical imperative: 'Pay attention!'

Prospero's concentrated focus indifferently blends the command 'hear' with the adverb 'here,' as if grasping any subliminal occasion to reissue the command. Like his 'art'-'art' or his 'remember'-'remember,' this 'hear'-'here' forms part of the hypnotic drip-drip by which Prospero's *logos* enters his listener's mind as much through form as through content, be it through hypnosis or through osmosis:

> Sit still, and *hear* the last of our sea-sorrow:
> *Here* in this island we arrived; and *here*. . . . (170–71 (emphasis added))

Prospero manages the story as a means to achieve a specifically desired political aim: '*Hear* a little further, / And then I'll bring thee to the present business' (135–136 (emphasis added)). Prospero's method consists, then, not merely in imparting information but in meticulously parcelling out those data which Miranda is, and those which she is not, to know. Prospero precisely times all intervals and dosages, again admonishing Miranda that she exercises no individual autonomy: 'Know thus far forth' (177); '*Here* cease more questions' (184, (emphasis added)).

Caliban – the 'devil himself'

Miranda complies through steady psychological pressure, as does Ariel through threatened torture. By contrast, Prospero's third subject, Caliban, viewed not just metaphorically, but literally in animal terms, feels Prospero's full physical force. Unlike Ariel, whose promised freedom offers an incentive, Caliban nurtures no such hope. Much has been written on Caliban. Older readings often acquiesce in the face-value presentation of Caliban as expressing the 'material,' in contrast to Ariel's 'spiritual.' Post-colonial analyses have reversed those readings, seeing in Caliban a symbol of European atrocities.[28]

27 See generally, Rae Langton, 'Speech Acts and Unspeakable Acts,' *Philosophy and Public Affairs*, Vol 22 (1993), 305–330.
28 See for example, Barker and Hulme; Brown; Skura.

Prospero calls Caliban sluggish, contrasting with Ariel's instant obedience. From the outset, before meeting the island native, Prospero and Miranda prepare the audience's minds with the standard stereotypes of the recalcitrant servant as 'slave' and 'villain.'[29] The complex semiotics of the word 'kind' in Shakespeare[30] remind us that, in introducing Caliban as un-kind (307–309), Prospero constructs Caliban from the start as not 'kin,' as alien, foreign, Other and not human. Miranda's tutoring on that point, too, is consummate: 'tis a villain, sir' (309). While Caliban's earlier sexual advance towards Miranda[31] explains her revulsion, she expresses her abhorrence in terms similar to those of Prospero (recalling more general fears often expressed in the corpus towards miscegenation, and attributions of sexual impurity in ethnic terms[32]). It is Prospero, not Miranda, who 'remembers' Caliban in the discourse of offspring begat through polluted sexual mixing and degeneracy (319–320). The epithets 'poisonous' and 'slave' are also illocutionary, speaking not so much information as *confirmation* of the construction of Caliban as sub-human.

The privileges of socio-legal hierarchy and bondage accrue to Prospero and Miranda in their newly colonized land, as part of the obvious and natural order of things. To compare, we have no reason to believe that Prospero's threats to Ariel ever progress, or need to progress, any further than words. Caliban's meaner fate is unequivocal. For spiting his master, Prospero assures Caliban of violence which appears as Caliban's constant routine (albeit ambiguously; the text leaves reason to think that Caliban finally heeds Prospero's call only through 'cramps' and 'pinches' inflicted through a command to Ariel (318)).

Prospero's tortures are far from crude. They entail 'cramps' and 'pinches,' finely tuned to his drip-drip methods of moderate and steady, but nonetheless 'zero-tolerance,' coercion. Caliban's account indeed differs little from Prospero's (2.2.4–14). Given the quasi-eroticism of Prospero's cruelty, we might wonder at the earlier relationship between them. That earlier time is evoked only obliquely: 'When thou cam'st first, / Thou strok'st me and made much of me' (1.2.332–33). What emerges are two sexual dimensions of colonialism, reflecting imperial power relations.[33]

Caliban's reply has been of particular importance for post-colonial readings. Caliban recites a lineal claim to the island: 'This island's mine by Sycorax my mother, / Which thou tak'st from me' (331–332). But Prospero has trumped it through brute force. Caliban does not use 'indigenous' reasoning. He instead

29 Cf. Eric Heinze. 'Were it not against our laws: Oppression and Resistance in Shakespeare's Comedy of Errors,' *Legal Studies*, Vol 29 (2009), 230–263, 250.

30 See for example, *Ham.* 1.2.65. Cf. Eric Heinze, *The Concept of Injustice.* (Abingdon and New York: Routledge, 2013), 130–138.

31 See below text accompanying notes 37–38.

32 See for example, *MV* 1.2.127; *Tit* 4.2.64–70.

33 Cf. Eric Heinze, Imperialism and Nationalism in Early Modernity: The 'Cosmopolitan' and the 'Provincial' in Shakespeare's Cymbeline, *Journal of Social and Legal Studies*, Vol 18, No 3, (2009) 373–396, 383–387.

turns the hypocrisy of European reasoning, ownership of land and exclusive property rights through lineal conveyance, against Prospero.[34] Locke would later, as Prospero anticipates, deny the possibility of 'title' in property to 'savages' who had 'not yet learned' to acquire title by 'mixing their labour' into the earth with adequate yield.[35] Prospero again turns up in the role of God, having originally taught Caliban, like Adam in Eden, 'how / To name the bigger light and how the less' (334–335). We are reminded also of today's 'local knowledge' claims, challenging global corporations which have sought exclusive copyrights with little or no compensation to peoples from whom marketable goods or technologies have been appropriated: 'and then I loved thee, / And showed thee all the qualities o' th' isle, / The fresh springs, brine pits, barren place and fertile' (336–338).

From our standpoint, Miranda and Ariel had seemed equally under the spell of Prospero. Things look different to Caliban. Like Miranda he has been kept in ignorance about Ariel, while Miranda in his eyes only shares Prospero's privilege. The result, Caliban naively exhorts Prospero, is: 'I am all the subjects that you have' (341), an image of isolation Prospero would have every reason to foster. Prospero formulates justice on his own terms with respect to what counts as to truth or lie. We again find him obsessed with rectifying and entrenching a single, legitimating historical memory about power on the island (recalling again the lexicon of 'kindness'): 'Thou most lying slave, / Whom stripes may move, not ***kindness***, I have used thee – Filth as thou art – with human care' (344–346 (emphasis added)).[36]

In his memory-making, Prospero cites not just any old example of his 'human care' for Caliban: '[I] lodged thee / In mine own cell, till thou didst seek to violate / The honour of my child' (346–348). Generations of audiences under Prospero's spell have taken that accusation on face value, assuming a rape attempt, which would in some measure justify Caliban's harsh treatment. Yet fears of miscegenation, of ethno-sexual impurity, had arisen earlier in Shakespeare.[37] There, as here, questions arise as to what is meant by 'violate' and 'honour.' Are those two concepts defined identically for Europeans and others? Does any erotic inclination towards a European woman – even one that, for a white, aristocratic European, would amount to routine courtship – translate as a 'violation' of 'honour' when stirring Caliban? Did Caliban act with intent to rape, or can Prospero and his daughter imagine this non-European's bestial sexuality in no other terms? The more worldly-wise Portia had scarcely needed any

34 Cf. Heinze, above n. 33, pp. 375–376. Cf. also Eric Heinze, 'Legal Hybridity in Shakespeare: Revisiting the Post-Colonial in The Tempest and Cymbeline,' in *Hybridity: Exploring power, social structures, and institutions beyond the liberal west*, edited by Rosa Freedman and Nicolas Lemay-Hébert (London and New York: Routledge, 2017), 122–140.

35 John Locke, Second Treatise of Civil Government. In *Two Treatises of Government*. (Cambridge: Cambridge University Press, [1689] 1988), ch. 5, para 41.

36 Cf. Ard[3] (glossing 'stripes' as 'strokes of the whip').

37 See: above text accompanying n. 32.

physical threat to feel repulsed by none less than a Moroccan prince because he bore the 'complexion of a devil.'[38] The rape allegation proceeds, moreover, not from Miranda but from the *man*, her father (she might, for example, have been sleeping at the time – has she simply been drilled on this point, too?), whose 'honour' is deemed 'violated' by the rape of any woman of his class and in his charge.

We have long been asked to guard against dismissing rape allegations, or viewing rape in solely sexual terms. Caliban by no means denies his desire, yet does not express it in sexual terms. Albeit in blunter language, his motives are no different from countless heroic European men in the corpus. Caliban recalls the time when he was 'mine own king,' and expresses the same yearning to secure progeny that we find stated in high-minded language when sought by Shakespeare's Europeans. Caliban makes the altogether rational calculation that strength in numbers, via the only means available to attain it, might win his island back through the self-same coercion by which it was seized from him (348–350). The rape allegation nevertheless suffices for all and sundry invective against Caliban to seem partly credible, warranting Prospero to construct a memory of the 'goodness' of his rule, in contrast to this native's congenital evil (350–352). Both Prospero's and Miranda's illocutionary naturalizing of Caliban's bestiality succeed, as Caliban is repeatedly confirmed as not human. Miranda translates the colonists' 'goodness' into a standard civilizing narrative. Arguably like many a missionary, she had at first 'pitied' Caliban (352–361). Throughout the play, however, Caliban expresses only satisfaction with his life before the Europeans had arrived.

New shores encountered: Racine's seventeenth century

'Yes, now I've found you here, my loyal friend, / my fate begins again, my sorrows end' (1.1.1–3).[39] Rarely have a few brief verses so pithily captured an entire era.[40] Racine begins his third play, like his preceding two, with a return to ancient Greece. In *Andromaque* we find ourselves confronted with heroes more familiar to a classically educated early modern audience than they are to us. But the characters and action are not as hard to master as they seem. The Trojan War has just ended. The Greek side had been led by the joint forces of Agamemnon, Menelaus and such warriors as Ulysses and the slain Achilles. Achilles' son, Pyrrhus, reigns now as king over their own north-western Greek homeland of Epirus. Pyrrhus has taken into custody the Trojan princess Andromache, widow of Hector, as well as their infant son, Astyanax. And he has fallen in love with her.

The Greeks had forged unity against Troy. But tensions now surface between, on the one hand, those allied powers and, on the other hand, a renegade

38 *MV* 1.2.127. Cf. *MV* 2.7.79. Cf. Heinze, 2013, 126–130.

39 References to Racine citations are to G. Forestier (ed.) *Oeuvres complètes* (Vol 1) (Paris: Gallimard (Pléiade), 1999).

40 Evocations of fate (*la fortune, le sort*) and destiny (*le destin*) recur almost as mantras throughout the opening scene, cf., e.g. 1.1.22, 25, 27, 34, 65, and elsewhere in the drama.

Pyrrhus. In order to consolidate the pan-Hellenic alliance, Pyrrhus had earlier pledged to marry Menelaus's daughter Hermione. Having now fallen in love with Andromache, however, Pyrrhus openly slights Hermione. The allied Greeks wish Pyrrhus to honor that earlier pledge of marriage. He resists their demands to hand over Andromache's son, sole male heir to the Trojan crown and thereby the greatest spark of hope for a Trojan rebirth. By refusing, even pursuing marriage to the royal Trojan Andromache, Pyrrhus asserts Epirus's sovereign autonomy.

To deliver that message the Greeks have sent Agamemnon's son, Orestes, who opens the play speaking those words of hope and renewal. Orestes is scarcely ideal as the allied Greeks' choice of emissary. Unlike Pyrrhus, Orestes loves Hermione. He arrives in Epirus invested more in the failure of his mission than in its success. His sanguine opening turns out to conceal more political conflict than he at first leads us to believe. The purely dramatic elements are certainly in place, perhaps more elegantly than in any other early modern tragedy: Orestes loves Hermione; but Hermione loves Pyrrhus; but Pyrrhus loves Andromache (Jean-Paul Sartre's existentialist *Huis-Clos* ('No Exit') seems like little more than a redrafting of *Andromaque*).

A political template is, however, equally evident. The standoff between Epirus and the allied Greeks mirrors that between the emerging consolidation and centralization of the early modern European state and resistance by local overlords. The latter often have little to gain from their provinces' absorption into the new state machinery, and much to lose by it. Although rejoicing at the sight of his friend Pylades in personal terms, Orestes evokes his recent arrival on the shores of Epirus in the language of a newly – colonially – seafaring Europe, recalling that period's admixture of fear of the unknown combined with revelatory discovery (1.1.5–6 (variant b)).

Erstwhile forbidding shores seem suddenly to offer a renewed hope for this ambassador, who will nevertheless confront, to the end, the ambiguity of his mission. Either he fulfills the Greeks' imperial task, but at the greater personal risk of sacrificing Hermione to Pyrrhus, or he pursues her, but at the greater diplomatic risk of betraying that political office. Europe's bold maritime ventures were indeed rewriting 'fate' itself, albeit with often highly divergent interests on the parts of, as well as unexpected consequences for, government officials, individual fortune-seekers and, of course, indigenous populations. If the standard European discourse of state formation appropriated the language of civilization over the supposed barbarity of the provincial warlord, Pyrrhus asserts his regional autonomy by turning that myth on its head:

> Who would think a mission like this one
> Demands none less than Agamemnon's son?
> That Greeks who soundly thrashed their foe in Troy
> Would still be plotting murder on a boy?
>
> ---
>
> Must my own pity cause me endless pains,
> To watch them soak blood from this child's veins? (1.2.177–80, 213–217)

Only by both preserving her son's life and maintaining his independence can Andromache nurture Troy's last hope of a future revival. Pyrrhus certainly offers Astyanax survival, refusing to turn the boy over to the allied Greeks. If Andromache marries him, however, she and her son nevertheless risk absorption into his realm – final destruction of Troy, not by death but by marriage. Andromache refuses Pyrrhus's overtures by recalling her lost nation. Her later plans for reviving Troy will draw their force precisely from a story of its hideous destruction, sidestepping questions of right and wrong as between the warring sides. Crucial to the foundation myth she will create is a story of catastrophe, as a survival myth – not in the sense of falsehood, but of *mythos* as symbolic tale – such that any Trojan survival at all becomes the mission of a phoenix rising from its ashes:

> Sir, see what I'm reduced to, see me lame,
> I saw my father dead, Troy's walls aflame,
> I saw my family slain, such was our luck,
> My husband drenched in blood, dragged through the muck,
> His son and I saved – to be bound in chains. (3.6.931–35)

Andromache pursues the memory with her confidante Céphise, invoking the impossibility, or inhumanity, of forgetting, through the anaphoric 'Must I forget':

> Must I forget, because he [Pyrrhus] cannot remember?
> Must I forget my spouse, denied a grave
> Dragged all around Troy's walls, worse than a slave?
> Must I forget his father drenched in red
> Clutching at the altar where he bled? (3.8.996–1000)

Andromache then immediately follows with the quasi-hypnotic repetition (*epizeuxis*) 'Think, think,' which in French carries a stronger sense of imagining or even dreaming ('*Songe, songe*'). The events thus far recited, albeit eloquently, as straightforward facts now steadily become retold as myth. Andromache draws Céphise into memory as reconstruction, with wartime brutality retold as calculated sadism:

> Think, think, Céphise, of that night's degradation,
> One long eternity for our whole nation,
> Recall in Pyrrhus' eye that sparkling glow
>   Darting from our palaces burned low,
> Marching on the corpses of my brothers,
> Their blood on him a spur for killing others.
> Think of those killers' shouts; think of the victims. . . . (1001–03)

Almost every speech made by Andromache in the play invokes painful yet necessary memory, becoming more overt as she persists:

> Céphise, you bring grim memory back to me.
> Must I relive foul deeds done to those fair,

The death of Hector and his son, his heir,
This child, this hope, this gift of love he gave,
I remember. . . .

[quoting Hector's last words:]
'If the *memory* of our bond you cherish,
Then show our son your love. Let it not perish.' (1019–22. 29–30)

By Act IV, Andromache's plan, although it will turn out rather differently, is to marry Pyrrhus then to kill herself, binding Pyrrhus to preserve Astyanax without dishonoring Hector or Troy. It will be Céphise's task to oversee the young prince's education, which Andromache formulates as a quasi-ritual re-enactment of preserved memory:

Teach my son about his nation's heroes,
Retrace their steps, and then make sure he knows
The deeds that crown them with immortal fame. (1117–22)

Racine observes the processes of selection and omission that transform factual accounts into political myths. Andromache steers Céphise away from what the Trojans 'did' (*'ce qu'ils ont fait'*) and towards what they had 'been' (*'ce qu'ils ont été'*):

Yet just those deeds most worthy of their name.
Tell him of the virtues of his father,
And mention sometimes too those of his mother. (1117–22)

What effect are these stories supposed to have? As the modern European state is emerging from feudalism, scarcely a political drama by Shakespeare, Corneille or Racine will lack a 'death of chivalry' motif. As the centralizing state is eliminating any independent jurisdiction locally held by the old aristocracy, the 'nobility of the sword' (*la noblesse d'épée)*, must lay down its arms, renouncing all regional autonomy. It must either perish entirely or become wholly subsumed within the increasingly absolutist state, reborn as subordinate officers and magistrates, *la noblesse de robe*. Any rebirth of Troy will rely not on the old 'blood is their argument' models of cyclically feudal revenge, but rather on cleverly managing those in control of the dominant political power:

Ban every thought of vengeance from his heart,
We've left him with a master to outsmart. (4.1.1119–20)

Under the great power of the bourgeoning modern state, the old aristocracy must temper all-too eager nostalgia for past glories:

On memories of his forebears place some reins,
He's Hector's blood, but he's all that remains. (1121–22)

5 Sin carries the penance

The Spanish Civil War's conflicts of guilt and justice

Ignacio Fernández de Mata

In total impotence, the sole remaining possibility is a spiritual appeal to the ideal right.

Karl Jaspers[1]

The value of memory

We live, in Spain at least, in a post-memorial time. This does not mean that memory has been superceded, gone out of style or become irrelevant. On the contrary, it refers to the fact that memory – qualified or not by the adjective 'historical' – has become part of our permanent social and political landscape. 'Post-memorial' signals that memory's relative novelty as a category of analysis and social demand has given way to its integration in the social fabric; it has been normalized, in a way. Spain's explosion of memory experienced at the turn of the twenty-first century has passed, and we can now observe its decanting, so to speak, as a solidary remembrance, embodied in associations that contribute to resolve memory-related personal and cultural conflicts. These groups have successfully occupied public spaces ripe with symbolic capital, and have developed their own political agenda, with significant international repercussions. They are indeed consolidated and, as far as the government is concerned, uncomfortable public actors.[2]

We have also witnessed debates that have placed historical memory and history as opposing, or separate, concepts. From the trenches of a militant activism and idealism inspired by post-modern discourses, some citizens and intellectuals propound the dethronement of history as the source of knowledge of the past, proposing memory in its stead.[3] History, they say, leaves out people's real stories.

1 Karl Jaspers, *The Question of German Guilt* (New York: Fordham University Press, 2001), 39.

2 Ignacio Fernández de Mata, *Lloros vueltos puños: El Conflicto de los 'Desaparecidos' y Vencidos de la Guerra Civil Española.* (Granada: Comares, 2016), 195–198.

3 Colectivo Contratiempo, *Menos templos y más ágoras.* http://www.contratiempohistoria.org/?page_id=288 [accessed 27 April 2015]; Colectivo Contratiempo, *Por una gobernanza acerca del pasado.* http://www.contratiempohistoria.org/?page_id=472 [accessed 27 April 2015].

On the other side, serious academics such as Santos Juliá point to the changing nature of memory and its inaccuracy to underline its inappropriateness as a historical source. Memory, they say, has feet of clay.[4] The latter argument abets the entrenchment of a social sector that is not uncomfortable with Spain's Francoist past by providing it with munition to attack those who wish to alter the way the dictatorship, repression and the civil war are remembered. Thus, instead of contributing to clarify or construct broader understandings, such maximalist debates have simply added noise to the conflicts.[5] Both radical positions sidestep two issues that should be taken into account to make the relationship between history and historical memory more productive.

First, there is no doubt that the concept and practice of *historical memory* are invaluable for a significant sector of Spanish society; people who suffered in their own flesh, or that of their loved ones, not only Francoist repression but the subsequent manipulation of history that erased, silenced or justified its abuse. The historical narrative constructed by the dictatorship to grant itself political and social legitimacy in post-war Spain defined the nation from a patrimonial and ideological vantage point, and tied it to an exalted Catholic religiosity that legitimated the violence against so-called Reds. It thus excluded the ample segments of the population that had been defeated in the civil war from their nation, silencing their experience and proscribing their politics. In the last two decades or so the circulation of written and recorded testimonies of the defeated, the opportunity to bear witness (a.k.a. historical memory), has paralleled the legitimation of leftist and democratic politics more broadly. This has brought a respite for their long-lived subalternity and silent suffering by providing collective narrative frameworks in which to fit their personal and familial experiences, allowing them to make sense of past traumatic experiences and condemn the violence perpetrated against them as illegitimate. Professional historians such as Julio Aróstegui and Javier Rodrigo rightly complain that many of these post-dictatorial narrative frameworks lack rigor, respond to idealizations of the Republican past, or contain deficient historiographic and historical analyses.[6] However, instead of lambasting the deficiencies of popular narrative frameworks produced by amateurs and survivors whose education in historical methodology is lacking, academics should participate

4 See: Juliá Díaz, 'Echar al olvido: Memoria y amnistía en la transición.' *Claves de razón práctica*, 129 (2003), 14–25; and *Elogio de historia en tiempo de memoria* (Madrid: Marcial Pons, 2011).

5 See: Pedro Ruiz Torres, 'Los discursos de la memoria histórica en España.' *Hispania Nova, Vol* 7 (2007), http://hispanianova.rediris.es/7/dossier/07d001.pdf [accessed 30 April 2015). See also Ricardo García Cárcel, *La herencia del pasado. Las memorias históricas de España* (Barcelona: Galaxia Gutenberg, 2011).

6 Julio Aróstegui, 'Traumas colectivos y memorias generacionales: el caso de la Guerra Civil,' in *Guerra Civil. Mito y memoria*, edited by Julio Aróstegui and François Godicheau (Madrid: Marcial Pons, 2006); Javier Rodrigo, 'Los mitos de la derecha historiográfica. Sobre la memoria de la Guerra Civil y el revisionismo a la española.' *Historia del Presente*, No 3, (2004) 185–195.

in their production. We all need a better grasp of the methodological and theoretical issues that surround the practice of oral history, and we need to encourage its inclusion in academic curricula if we are to engage in more productive critiques and rigorous historiographic revisions.

Second, memory has value beyond its usefulness as a historical source. Reducing people's testimonies and narratives to data (that can or cannot be checked) is a near-sighted exercise that privileges form over content, scorns individuals' and communities' historical experiences, and disregards the problematic translation of past sorrow and horrors into a coherent and well-structured discourse spoken in the present. Francoist victims' narratives of remembrance are constituted by multiple elements, mirroring in many ways the multiplicity of victims or survivors themselves. In the case of those whose loved ones were 'disappeared' (extra-judicially executed and buried in unmarked, mass graves), a traumatic core was generated around 'frozen' memories. They remember the events from the perception of who they were at the time – children.[7] This traumatic core is surrounded by layers of other painful experiences accrued in their life histories – both personal and collective – throughout the long dictatorship and forgetful democracy that followed. Despite, and sometimes precisely because of, their incoherencies and mistakes, these kinds of testimonies provide us with much more than data. Indeed, because of their very origin and constitution, narratives of repression and persecution are often inaccurate or lacking in data. This is even more severe in the Spanish case, given that decades of imposed silence and discursive manipulation have passed between the events and their telling. Such testimonies are like windows into the negotiation of personal, familial and communal dramas and frustrations related to experiences of political violence. In their imprecision, confusion, self-interested retelling or incoherence, survivors' testimonies can powerfully reflect sufferers' states of mind and emotional effects *vis-à-vis* exploitation, marginalization, and subjugation, discourses that are usually inaccessible to historical research. What survivors say, how they say it and when they say it constitute in and of themselves sources of data that help us understand the historical experience of a significant part of the Spanish population – surely all historians would agree that this is an exercise that enriches historical knowledge.

One of the main reasons behind the Spanish memory explosion was the lack of direct attention to the cultural dramas of the disappeared and the complete absence of transitional justice – or justice of any kind – for the victims of the dictatorship.[8] In his study on German guilt, Karl Jaspers points out that 'victorious

7 My work focuses on the victims of the early wave of political violence unleashed right after the coup in the province of Burgos.

8 Ignacio Fernández de Mata, 'Mass Graves and the Emergence of Spanish Historical Memory,' in *Recorriendo la memoria – Touring Memory*, edited by Jaime Almansa (Oxford: Archaeopress, 2010), 49–55; Ignacio Fernández de Mata, 'Rude awakening. Franco's Mass Graves and the Decomposition of the Spanish Transition Dream,' in *Legacies of Violence in Contemporary Spain. Exhuming the Past, Understanding the Present*, edited by Ofelia Ferrán and Lisa Hilbink (New York: Routledge, 2017), 121–147.

might does not make right,'[9] but he also argues that while the victors hold power they operate as if it did:

> Success apparently justifies. The man on top believes that he has the truth of a good cause on his side. This implies the profound injustice of blindness for the failures, for the powerless, for those who are crushed by events.[10]

In Spain, this perception survived the dictatorship, and permeated the transition from Francoism to democracy, important segments of Spanish society rejected the possibility of any sort of justice or reparations for the dictatorship's victims. This, along with the Left's discursive weakness and the prioritization of democratization over other political needs (such as redress for past injustice), necessarily marginalized the victims' needs and demands, becoming a case-in-point of Jasperian injustice.

Guilt and justice

In his text on the analysis of 'German guilt' in the aftermath of the Second World War, Jaspers seemed to be speaking directly to and about the survivors and victims of the Spanish Civil War – its defeated. Proposing that justice for the vanquished of any war is necessarily 'illusive,' Jaspers argues that

> every war is blamed on the loser. He is forced to admit his guilt. His subsequent economic exploitation is disguised as restitution. Pillage is forged into a rightful act. If the right is not free, let us have naked force – it would be honest, and it would be easier to bear. In fact, there is nothing beside the victor's power. Recrimination as such can always be made mutual, but only the victor can make his charges stick, and he does so ruthlessly and solely in his own interest. Everything else merely serves to disguise the actual arbitrary force of the powerful.[11]

Indeed, surviving victims in Spain knew the crimes that had been committed; they often knew the identities of the culprits. But they also knew that they could denounce nothing, for the brutal power of the regime suspended all procedural safeguards. Rubbing salt in their wounds, the new State forbade them from mourning their dead – who, as Reds, had betrayed the Spanish nation reproducing the tale of Antigone – while the Church denied them solace by legitimating the crimes against them, and their communities showed little or no solidarity. The local power holders (civil and military officers, members of the Falange, the Guardia Civil, the parish priest, etc.) were permanent reminders of the impunity

9 Jaspers, 50.
10 Ibid, 8.
11 Ibid, 50.

of those who committed crimes; as perpetrators, accomplices, instigators and concealers, but also as representatives of the new system, in which relatives of Reds who did not wholeheartedly embrace the regime were permanently vulnerable to new injustices. Unable to grieve – and, for relatives of the disappeared, with no remains to grieve over – surviving victims were incapable of using the channels available in their cultures to gain solace and closure in the face of bereavement.

Their narratives of war, repression and dictatorship reveal that despite their social degradation – as individuals and as a community – most of them did not renounce the expectations associated with the cultural milieu they shared with the broader society. They did not give up their demands for justice, nor did they renounce recovering the remains of their loved ones: they simply bided their time. The latter was evinced in the exhumations carried out immediately at the end of the dictatorship by hundreds of families across the country. These exhumations were typically conducted without archaeological and forensic rigor, but they did allow the bereaved to inter their loved ones in cemeteries.[12] The former was illustrated by the emergence of associations for historical memory in the first decade of the millennium. Those who shared this memory still held perpetrators (most of them individually identified) accountable for their crimes; the surviving victims hoped that if the perpetrators could not be tried in a court of law, at the very least they could be made to acknowledge their guilt. The victims also hoped the State and the broader society would understand their desire for accountability as an element that Spanish democracy could not do without.

The surviving victims' need for perpetrators to carry their guilt is inherent to their need for justice, because guilt and justice are consubstantial. It is not that Francoism's victims are particularly vengeful: in every modern society the legal process is meant to determine the guilt of the accused so that the guilty can pay for their crimes and thus be allowed to partake in communal life once more.

Deprived of the legal process to achieve reparation, many victims could not ignore their need to feel that perpetrators had to pay for their crimes. The scale of the victims' sorrow made perpetrators' impunity unfathomable. This is why many of the survivors and victims that I have spoken to, or whose testimonies I have read, are convinced that the perpetrators suffered (or still suffer) a gnawing, even unbearable, remorse. However, since there could be no public manifestations of remorse and no apologies (therefore, no forgiveness) for abuses that were considered rightful, the perpetrators' guilt was a covert and festering burden known only to the victims, who became silent witnesses in a sort of secret trial carried out in their name. Only they knew the tell-tale codes and signals that indicated expiation and, above all, penance; only they witnessed the workings of divine justice in the souls and bodies of the perpetrators.

12 See: Marije Hristova-Dijkstra, *Memoria, olvido y la apertura de las fosas comunes de la guerra civil en 1978–1981 y 2000–2006* (unpublished undergraduate thesis. University of Groningen, 2007), 31–45.

Procedural justice

Legal anthropologists have analyzed the diverse ways in which societies across the world resolve situations in which an aggrieved party perceives that they have been treated unfairly: these go from abstention, community action, negotiation and mediation, rituals of reconciliation-apology, oaths and ordeals, trials and tribunals, to blood feuds, violent incursions and even war.[13] In modern societies justice is a notarized and institutionalized value, subject to certain controls and procedures, as laws and codes determine the action of the courts and tribunals charged with meting it out.

The steps of the judicial process – accusation, identification of the accused and the victim, hearings, interrogations, presentation of evidence, declarations, deliberations – serve to channel the anguish and unease produced by a crime. The sense of attention and reparation that stems from the process seems to be confirmed by the sentencing of the guilty party. Moreover, the public character of these activities suggests that society is implicated in the process; that is, that the community of the aggrieved is accompanying them.

For the victims of Francoist repression there was no such rerouting of grief or feeling of accompaniment. The dictatorship disarticulated a rights-based legal system and replaced it with a repressive model that relied heavily on military trials and a civil system purged of all those who were not committed (*desafectos*) to the regime. Since crimes committed against Reds during the civil war were not considered crimes, perpetrators reaped with impunity and apparent legitimacy, the profit and rewards secured through illegitimate means in the heat of repression. The defeated were to live in the permanent confirmation that they were social pariahs.

Marginalized by the system, the victims only had each other for comfort. Their social isolation led them to configure a veritable 'community of sorrow,' which articulated means for solidarity and support, as well as marriages and social relations.[14] However, this community could not counteract the effects of the broad spectrum of repression that they suffered: blocked access to certain social services; loss of lands, all kinds of property, businesses and jobs; public humiliations; physical punishments; sexual abuse; and more.[15] Moreover, without the victims' remains,

13 See: Ignasi Terradas Saborit, *Justicia vindicatoria. De la ofensa e indefensión a la imprecación y el oráculo, la vindicta y el talión, la ordalía y el juramento, la composición y la reconciliación* (Madrid: CSIC, 2008); Carol Ember and Melvin Ember, Antropología cultural (Madrid: Prentice Hall, 2003), 309–319.

14 Ignacio Fernández de Mata, 'The Rupture of the World and the Conflict of Memories,' in *Unearthing Franco's Legacy. Mass Graves and the Recovery of Historical Memory in Spain*, edited by Carlos Jerez-Farrán and Samuel Amago (Notre Dame: University of Notre Dame Press, 2010), 279–303, 285–286.

15 Paul Preston, *The Spanish Holocaust: Inquisition and Extermination in Twentieth Century Spain* (London: Harper Press, 2012); Gutmaro Gómez Bravo and Jorge Marco Carretero, *La obra del miedo. Violencia y sociedad en la España franquista (1936–1950)* (Barcelona: Península, 2011).

the regime's authorities did not consider the disappeared dead, which meant that heirs could not properly use or dispose of their spouses' properties; claim widow or orphan status, remarry etc. The disappeared were like ghosts; simultaneously present and absent.

So how did these vanquished families deal with their frustration and despair, their thirst for justice and reparation? How did they articulate solace and support?

Divine justice

In the 1940s, many victims tried to configure alternative historical narratives to locate, and somehow resolve, their intimate cultural conflicts. They did so using the information and propaganda circulated by the Republican side during the civil war (pamphlets, biographies, literature etc.) as well as whatever reached them from the outside world through underground radio stations and other means. Treasuring the political traditions at stake during the Second Republic, they wove these strands along with those of their own personal experiences into a narrative tapestry of resistance that circled through secondary circuits, rooting their identity to their memories and representations of the past.

The defeated of humbler origins, many of whom had minimal or no formal education, had to deploy other cultural resources. Instead of relying on the 'moral superiority' of the politics of the deceased, they intermingled faith, rumor and legend in narratives of divine justice. In these brief tales – which shared elements of old stories, urban legends, ballads and popular curses – God, or the Heavens, punished the perpetrators and thus granted victims redress.[16] The notion of divine justice developed, as a matter of fact, after countless persons (whom I interviewed in the context of my investigations related to Francoist mass graves) answered with tales of this sort when I asked: 'Do you think that those who committed crimes have somehow paid for what they did?' Divine justice can be defined as unsolicited interventions of (a/the) divinity to assist those without access to formal justice. It is thus configured as a source of cultural solace in societies where the presence of religion in everyday life is very strong, and especially where the exercise of political power is cloaked in divine legitimacy or sanction.

In the stories told by civil war victims, God-as-Judge assumes the responsibility that the community and the State refuse. He does not accuse, interrogate or threaten; his presence is implicit and absolute; and his participation is silent and covert. In the face of unquestionable evidence and the heinousness of the crimes, there is no need for a trial to determine guilt. God's intervention restores a lost order, one ruptured by the Church and the regime when they murdered or sanctioned the murder of thousands of citizens and pretended to get away with it.

16 Luis Díaz Viana, 'Homero o el Folklore: del origen, transformación y fijación de las leyendas,' in *La cultura tradicional en la sociedad del siglo XXI. IV Jornadas nacionales Folklore y Sociedad*, edited by Ignacio Fernández de Mata (Burgos: Instituto Municipal de Cultura, 2009), 169–178.

This type of justice is outside the human orbit, extraneous to human capacity for action; moreover it does not act only on the soul, but on the perpetrators' bodies. Indeed, it is in its retribution that its restorative and consolatory character lies, for it is a type of last – or highest – judicial instance that metes out punishments, usually illnesses, chosen by divine will as befitting the crimes.

These condensed narratives share a common structure and various elements. First, they address the crime's immediate context and reasons, never reaching beyond their short radius to the higher, inaccessible authorities of the Francoist regime. Second, they generally begin by presenting the villain – whose name or moniker is widely known by the audience, which is always local – and recalling his participation in countless repressive actions. It is also common to highlight a particular circumstance that placed the perpetrator beyond the boundaries of recognizable violence – his viciousness, his infliction of physical or mental torture etc. – epitomizing his evil character and dictating the punishment that divine justice will later deliver. This particular part of the tale is often very dramatic. Since the incidents described generally took place during extra-judicial executions carried out secretly, in isolated spots and in the dead of night, the source of its description is unclear. Either narrators do not mention it; they give the impression that they know it, but must conceal it; or they claim the source is a third party, as happens with many urban legends (this third person can be a neighbor's cousin or someone of this sort). It is not the victims' demands, then, that bring down the wrath of God but the guilty party's actions.

Third, the narrations have clear biblical models. On the one hand, the plight of the disappeared parallels those of Saint Job and/or Jesus Christ himself, in the sense that God allowed for the maximum chastisement and sorrow of those he loved best, because in the end He would repair all the wrongs inflicted on them and punish the wrongdoers. This conception of the victim as *chosen*, as the Just submitted to the worst evils, stems from their superior morality and 'absolute innocence' and provides a semblance of solace to Catholic relatives who have been abandoned by the State, society, their church and their communities.[17] Being able to count on cultural models that underline the unfairness of pain and suffering reaffirms victims' condition of innocence. The story of Job is especially useful, not only in relation to the dead and the disappeared, as we have seen, but for survivors as well. It foreshadows the surviving victims' unexpected and unfair undoing, their sudden loss of shelter and support, and explains why God allowed the unleashing of absolute evil; in Spain's case embodied in Falangists and other right-wing militias, the Guardia Civil, soldiers, vindictive priests etc. Such innocent victims demand sympathy from the listener.[18] They were good people, valuable, responsible, hardworking; they discharged their family duties and were admired by others. In the narratives told by relatives there is sometimes a trace of so-called survivors' guilt, but the greater guilt is born from their failure to give their loved

17 Javier Moscoso, *Historia cultural del dolor* (Madrid: Taurus, 2011).
18 Ibid.

ones a proper burial that would allow them to rest in peace. Those with disappeared relatives – who lay 'like dogs in ditches' – cannot even mourn their dead and experience ritual/cultural closure. This ritual incompletion fills them with impotence and frustration, as well as debts towards older family members who die with the promise that their missing relative will be found and buried properly. Guilt and frustration become terrible legacies that weigh heavily on family life. Until the exhumations came, only the tenuous solace provided by tales of divine justice had alleviated it.

The exercise of justice that is present in these stories is based on the juridical principle of the *lex talionis*, 'an eye for an eye and a tooth for a tooth.' One of my informants best expresses popular Catholicism's approximation to this retributive justice: 'the sin carries the penance.' The conflicts related to the absence of formal juridical processes are resolved in the direct relationship established in the tales of divine justice between the crime committed and the punishment received. In what constitutes an interesting, Catholic-style transfer of acts/effects, akin to Hinduism's karma, the perpetrator suffers rigors and agonies similar to those he caused others.

In this form of simplified justice the criminal gets what he deserves because he deserves it. The possibility of coincidence does not enter anybody's mind. The meanings read onto the evils that befall perpetrators acquire the character of evidence and proof, and the relatives of the disappeared (as well as surviving victims) are called on to contemplate the sentencing and punishing of wrongdoers. After all, it is they who understand the sense and reason behind the illnesses, tragedies and sorrows that ail the perpetrator. It is necessary to know the intricacies of the assassinations – with rumors and legends as main sources – to understand and recognize the exercise of divine justice. They bear witness to justice in a trial that only they know to be so.

One of the first such narratives that I came on, that of Juan Giménez, related that:

> Many people were assassinated here, including Eladia Pérez, la Jaboneta. They went to get her son Guillermo, who was later *paseado* [taken out of prison to be killed], and she refused to open the door, so *Cagalubias*, Anastasio González, shot her and killed her [*Cagalubias* is a nickname that means 'bean-shitter']; then they took her to the cemetery, but her body did not fit in the grave, and *Cagalubias* cut her head off with a shovel . . . ¿*Cagalubias*? Oh, he died, that bastard, **but before he died he was delirious, screaming for someone to take Eladia off him** . . . The killers were people from the town and also foreigners. . . . Falangists? Yes, Falangists, priests, friars and the Holy Ghost. Don Pablo Martín Dorado, the priest, was one of the worst; he gave his blessing to the '*paseos*'. . . . They also shaved the hair off a hundred women and, in the rain and all, they paraded them, with music playing and the Falangists yelling hails to Spain and Franco . . . and bloody hell! (*¡me cago en la madre que los parió!*)]. . . . And they raped a lot of women . . . this one [pointing to his wife], they raped! [Emphasis added].

In this narrative the supposed decapitation of Eladia by *Cagalubias* constitutes the act that qualitatively exceeds the limits of decency. All crimes against 'the weaker sex' appear as acts of cowardice, compromising the honor and masculinity of perpetrators, and thus *Cagalubias* is revealed as an antihero. But Eladia represents the ultimate victim, and the circumstances of her death (assassinated for attempting to protect her son) more than just the killing (or rape) of a woman. This is why the symbolic weight of the story rests on Eladia: she procures the listeners' sympathy, just as she procured the criminal's punishment. The figure of the victim, as in a curse, returns to haunt her killer in his deathbed as an instrument of (divine) justice.

Among my informants I have encountered diverse narratives of divine justice. One of them (BSG) related that her brother's killers 'had paid dearly' for their crimes. Her husband corroborated this: 'Of course they have paid.' One of the killers had tortured BSG's brother and his companions, before shooting them, by hitting them on the legs with his rifle butt. According to BSG this man, who was nicknamed *El lechugo* (The lettuce), had his feet, and then his legs, amputated when he was older. He came and went often to Burgos because of his disease. 'I have seen him going to the doctor's office, alone, without his wife or anybody, holding on to the walls, half-falling [here BSG arose and demonstrated how *El lechugo* had walked]. He was bedridden for a long time. His own son did not talk to him.' As for the other two men who participated in her brother's assassination, they died 'before their time' when they were still young: Alejandro 'broke his neck making tinder' and 'Quintiliano drowned when he went to turn some baskets.'[19]

In a conversation with another informant, BR related how a man who was about to be finished off said to one of the perpetrators: 'Take pity on me, I have six mouths to feed.' On his deathbed this man's killer raved that he had a 'basket on his chest' with the heads of the six children saying they were hungry.[20]

Speaking of her father's killer, TCM said: 'I don't think that that man ever slept in peace, because he not only killed my father, he killed many more . . . he died screaming . . . from a terrible disease, with lots of pain.'[21]

In an interview with FG I asked her if she believed that the killers had paid for their crime. When another person who was present shook their head, FG retorted by rhetorically asking: 'What do you mean, they did not pay?. . . . *El Samal* died from a haemorrhage in his groin right when he was going through Costaján [a site strewn with mass graves].' *El Samal*, by the way, was the same man who according to other popular stories would urinate on his victims when they asked for water. FG added that another perpetrator ranted that he was chased by the children of one of his victims. 'Trying to escape from this hallucination, he would fall in the gutter. The one who hit the condemned [*El lechugo*] got his leg cut

19 Interview, BSG. Ribera del Duero, June 2004.
20 Interview, BR. Ribera del Duero, June 2004.
21 Interview, TCM. Ribera del Duero, May 2004.

off. . . .'[22] *El Samal's* story embodies the above-mentioned elements: the audience knows him and there is a specific, humiliating and callous thing that he does (urinating on the thirsty, dying men), which explains the importance of his fatal haemorrhage happening in his groin (and near the site of the mass graves).

SMB recalled how in 1936, when she was still a child, a girl at school told her that 'in the house where they had killed three [SMB's home] they shouldn't have left even the smallest one alive. . . [SMB herself].' She had never forgotten that girl's cold and cruel comment, and she added that:

> Two years ago [2002] I was in a funeral, and I saw the one who had told me that. She had a child . . . all wrong . . . one of those children who are defective, and I said to myself, 'God chastises without shouting.' And I also said, 'in the sin they carry the penance. . . .' Well, if there is a God, because I don't know if there is.[23]

SMB's last remark is worth highlighting, for it reveals divine justice as a total retributive principle (like karma) that is above the existence of a divinity itself. Thus, although she interprets that woman's misfortune as a retribution for past wrong-doing, this gives her no redress (she does not participate in the *divine* experience).

In Ribera del Arlanza I was told that:

> *El Tocino*, the shepherd of Ruyales del Agua, next to Lerma, who knew how to read, was killed first. He is buried in the *cruz alta*, on the road to Ruyales. *El Chino* killed him, but he later had a bad death and they told him, 'that's *El Tocino*, who gives you repugnance.'[24]

My informant meant to say 'reflux,' not 'repugnance,' as if the assassinated man, whose nickname means pork fat (a common dietary staple of the lower classes), caused his killer a deadly indigestion. Here is another interesting game of symbolic transference, in this case between the nickname as a representation of the person and the object through which chastisement/revenge is performed: the food that the murdered shepherd is named after. There is another, paradoxical symbol here: *chino*, as an abbreviation of *cochino*, is another popular name for pig. That *Chino* and *Tocino* repel each other is a symbolic representation of the social body's repudiation of a part of itself, a symbol of its fragmentation and polarization.

Ending these examples, we have the conversation between BBT and his wife, in which they differentiated between basic Catholic terms that explained why Francoist perpetrators were not, and could never be, forgiven by God. According to BBT, 'assassins felt remorse, but they did not feel repentance.' Well, he added,

22 Interview, FG. Ribera de Duero, July 2005.
23 Interview, SMB. Ribera de Duero, July 2005.
24 Interview, CF. Burgos, March 2011.

'they repented in the end, in any case.' But his wife interrupted him, saying: 'No, they did not repent. They died burdened by remorse. They did not have clear consciences.'[25] Had they truly repented, felt contrition and sought forgiveness, they would not have been punished as they were, wracked by remorse, for eternity.

Divine justice was not reserved for direct perpetrators only: it also reached those who should and could have avoided the killings or, at the very least, consoled the bereft: Catholic priests. According to FG, a priest who had supported the insurgents actually delayed a mass so that a group of Falangists could finish their misdeeds and arrive on time. However, 15 days later, 'because of remorse. . . the priest poisoned himself.' He was buried in the chapel 'but his grave exploded, perhaps because there was too much lime in it, and his body was exposed.'[26] If he had taken his own life the priest's soul would be banned from heaven and his remains could not be buried in hallowed ground, which is symbolically expressed by the expulsion of the body from the grave. The unbelievable nature of this narrative reveals just how deeply the 'divine judge' rejected the priest's behavior.

Some narratives reproduce medieval juridical forms, in which the injured party is himself charged with dispensing justice. Carlos Gil Andrés analyses several tales of this sort, including the case of Carmen Campo, whose brothers were killed in Haro in January 1937.[27] After the socialist victory of 1982, Carmen walked up to one of her youngest brother's executioners and warned him: 'I will tell you this in the street, loudly, so that everybody can hear me. . . . Criminal! Murderer! Criminal!' According to Carmen, 'everybody came to their windows' as she continued yelling:

> You did not have the balls to kill him unrestrained. You killed him with his hands tied. . . . Why didn't you untie him? Because he would have eaten you up. Criminal! Murderer! All I ask is that, if there is a God, those whom you have killed surround your bed each day you have left to live. Because it was not only my brother. You carry a lot of crimes on your shoulders. Criminal! Murderer! . . . Anyway, he walked on and when he got to his doorway he broke down and they had to help him up. . . . I did this three times, and after the third time he died.[28]

In this case divine justice acts through the victim herself, whose verbal assaults cause the perpetrator's death.

Paul Preston grants credibility to some of these narratives, arguing, '[t]here is some second-hand evidence of the perpetrators of atrocities suffering some sort

25 Interview, BBT. Ribera de Duero, May 2004.
26 Interview, FG. Ribera de Duero, July 2005.
27 Carlos Gil Andrés, *Lejos del frente: la Guerra Civil en la Rioja Alta* (Barcelona: Crítica, 2006).
28 Ibid, 429–430.

of psychosomatic illness or other distress as a result of repressed guilt.'[29] However, he also considers that they may simply respond to 'popular fantasy.' The tales, which seem to be cloaked in Catholic imagery and discourses, have much older roots, evincing an ancient, reiterative and traditional substrate traceable all the way back to Mesopotamian trials by ordeal and Greek myths in which divine intervention resolved human conflicts.[30] This is the literary-cultural motif of the choleric tyrant who is chastised in the end for his unfair treatment of the innocent, or his flaunting of God's merciful mandates.[31] Moreover, Spanish medieval legal codes, such as the Castilian *Siete partidas*, mandated a retributive death, which contemplates sentencing murderers to suffer deaths similar to those they had caused.[32] The *partidas* also executed after a given period of time nobles who ordered the illicit death of a subject. In keeping with this legal tradition, stories of 'summons,' in which a king or noble who ordered an unfair execution was given a brief period to live by his victim or a third party, also circulated widely across Spain. An example is a tale told of King Ferdinand IV of Castile (1285–1312). According to legend, King Ferdinand ordered the execution of the Carvajal brothers for murder. The brothers were to be thrown from the heights of the Peña Martos in a cage filled with sharp spikes. Before their execution took place, however, the brothers summoned the king to appear before God within 30 days to respond for their unjust death. Thirty days later the king died.[33]

This kind of tale is common in popular literature, as the various ballads and stories in which divine interventions re-establish equilibrium in the face of the inaction of human justice show. In these narratives we find the formula adapted to the popular context, with violent evildoers and hapless victims standing in for the choleric tyrant and the archetypical innocent. A legion of ballads (*romances*) with this theme were sung and published across Spain, constituting a widely accepted morality tale: God re-establishes balance in the world by doing justice to the innocent.

It is impossible to know if there were indeed cases of 'psychosomatic illnesses' among the perpetrators of atrocities during and after the Spanish Civil War. However, given the cultural framework in which the narratives of divine justice are inserted, what matters most is not their veracity but their function. Such tales are meant to readjust a world of unreserved and utter injustice. The surviving relatives of the disappeared, after all, suffered a rupture of their world, in which the loss of their loved ones was compounded by the impossibility of paying their

29 Preston, 673.

30 Terradas Saborit, 299–303.

31 See: Abbé Barbier, *Les trésors de Cornelius a Lapide: extraits de ses commentaires de l'écriture sainte à l'usage des prédicateurs, des communautés et des familles chrétiennes* (Paris: Poussielgue-Rusand, 1859).

32 Alfonso X (1252–1284) ordered the compilation of the *Siete Partidas* in an attempt to establish a uniform body of normative rules of common law for his kingdom.

33 Antonio Benavides, *Memorias de Don Fernando IV de Castilla*, Tomo I (Madrid: Imprenta de Don José Rodríguez, 1860), 242–243.

respects to the dead. On the other hand, they also suffered the permanent opprobrium attached to their condition of vanquished, Reds, second-class citizens. Narratives of divine justice provided a semblance of solace to these victims, giving them a sense of reparation and accompaniment.

Conclusion

Forty years after Franco's death the absence of memory-related public policies, symbolic reparations, apologies or the re-interment of the thousands buried in mass graves in sites known and chosen by relatives, has left surviving victims feeling politically bereft. The narratives analysed in this text show that the immense emotional burden generated by political violence is carried and passed down through generations, unless the State and the other responsible institutions initiate (or partake in) a process of reparation and closure.

A significant part of the Spanish population has accepted the Right's dememorialization strategy as a positive way of negotiating the past. With its Benjaminian conscience of 'possessing' history and the use of catchy metaphors – such as 'we must turn the page' – it has promoted the disarticulation of the most personal memories in favor of the social frameworks constructed by the dictatorship. Exclusivist and sectarian, the dictatorship's beneficiaries and apologists hope to protect the past, sealing it safely from critical interpretations. Today's discursive turbulence is perceived as an assault on their possession and dominion of the past, an attempt by the vanquished to overturn their defeat and claim a moral victory. The vigor with which the so-called Movement for the Recovery of Historical Memory (RHM) erupted in Spanish society had nothing to do with a 'war of versions' or an ideological revenge, as some have claimed. Its strength lies in the intensity of the cultural and personal dramas linked to the disappeared, those who suffered bad deaths, who had not said their farewells and cannot rest in peace.

Narratives of divine justice provide victims with some relief, but not with a resolution to their anguish. With the arrival of democracy the anguish of victims' families was transformed into permanently frustrated hope. It is as if the RHM movement's frustration with the limits of Spanish democracy anticipated the crisis of Spain's political institutions, provoked by the government's handling of the 2008 financial collapse and revelations of widespread political corruption. Popular discontent exploded in 2011 when the *indignado* movement occupied central Madrid, openly questioning the democratic character of modern Spain. RHM activists had been among the first to criticize the transition from Francoism, questioning its representation as a model process, pointing out the deep injustice entailed by its lack of attention to Francoism's victims. Faced with the Spanish State's impassiveness, the RMH association has internationalized the conflict, seeking the involvement of the United Nations Committee on Enforced Disappearances and other countries' judicial systems (such as that of Argentina).

The State's general indifference toward the depth of the conflict of memories foreshadows the permanence and, indeed, the strengthening of the confrontation between irreconcilable historical narratives in Spain. The timidity of the official measures, such as the Law of Historical Memory[34] and the condemnation of Francoism by a parliamentary commission (and not the whole of parliament), has made it impossible to overcome the dictatorship's narrative. The State's unwillingness to pursue reconciliation has fostered an environment of cultural and historical rivalry between bereaved relatives of opposing ideological camps. Thus, Francoism's heirs confront the demands of the relatives of the disappeared with their own dead and their own mourning.[35]

In the end, blame is still placed on others and nobody assumes their own guilt. In the meantime, surviving relatives carry the heavy burden of their victimization.

34 Ley 52/2007, de 26 de diciembre, por la que se reconocen y amplían derechos y se establecen medidas en favor de quienes padecieron persecución o violencia durante la guerra civil y la dictadura. BOE 310, 27 December 2007.

35 See Ignacio Fernández de Mata, 'So That We May Rest in Peace: Death Notices and Ongoing Bereavement,' *Journal of Spanish Cultural Studies*, Vol 12, No 4 (2011), 439–462.

Part II

Addressing injustice

6 Beginning anew

Exceptional institutions and the politics of ritual

Paul Muldoon

The novel political institutions that states now commonly use in order to 'come to terms with the past' – criminal tribunals, truth commissions, administrative purges, reparative gestures and political apologies – invariably perform a double function. Though explicitly set up as vehicles of justice, whether in its retributive or reparative form, such institutions are also charged with constituting (as well as serving as signs of) a new order. Beyond simply punishing perpetrators and healing victims, in other words, these 'exceptional institutions' carry symbolic weight as moments of re-foundation for the political community as a whole. To the extent that they operate (or are perceived to operate) as terminal points for the history of wrong-doing, they introduce a break into the flow of time, a rupture between the past and the present, characteristically expressed in terms of the motif of the 'new beginning.' Though clearly an important part of what makes them exceptional, this investment of symbolic power in what are otherwise simply alternative tools for the work of justice, lends exceptional institutions a special kind of aura – an aura, which in modern politics, has historically been reserved for the phenomenon of revolution. This auratic quality is attested in many ways, but most dramatically and most suggestively through the appropriation of terms denoting some kind of special or otherworldly power: 'miracle,' 'mystery,' 'magic' and 'enigma.'

Looked at from a political perspective, this appropriation of the revolutionary notion of the 'new beginning' for transitional settings (that is, for scenes of transitional justice) has an inherently ambiguous quality. On the one hand, the assertion of a radical break would seem to be pivotal to the efficacy and stability of the newly instituted political order. Were it not to completely disassociate itself from the injustice of the past, the State would forever lack legitimacy in the eyes of those it had persecuted. Continuity with the previous (criminal) regime would spark fears of a repetition and undermine the promise of 'never again' that serves as both the rationale for, and the objective of, exceptional institutions. On the other hand, the figure of the 'new beginning' would appear to work against the need for ongoing reflection on the causes of the injustice and the allocation of responsibility. To the extent that it implies that the State is *already* other, already non-identical with its former self, it renders further critical interrogation unnecessary. Irrespective of the kind of changes it makes either to its constitutional structure or its political culture, the work of prosecuting, confessing, purging, apologizing and repaying, gives it the right to claim a renewed innocence. Not unlike the purification rituals known to us from the ancient Greek and medieval Christian worlds, such institutions provide opportunities for erasing the past as a burden or a stain.

My aim in what follows is to problematize this appropriation of the revolutionary motif of the 'new beginning' for transitional justice where the risk of taking on religious connotations of rebirth are especially great. The difficulty, as I see it, is how one might pass judgment on the previous regime, consigning it to a time that is now over, without simultaneously giving in to the presumption that the political community has thereby been purified. How does one insure that the rupture in time that the exceptional institution marks through its ritualized act of judgment on the past does not bring a premature halt to the work of self-interrogation that such institutions set in motion? As I will go on to show, this is not just a logical problem – a problem of how to mark a break in time that is not one – but a political problem. If it is only by slowly and patiently working through the past that the flaws in the underlying grammar of political communities can be identified and redressed, the revolutionary motif of the 'new beginning' may be not only historically misleading but politically dangerous. I argue that the injustices of the past live on after the 'transformative event' and require political communities to sustain a 'work of memory' – a work, that is, of continually sifting through the past and digesting its significance with respect to keeping faith with the promise of 'never again.'

The argument is developed in two stages. In the first section of the paper I make a case for treating exceptional institutions as *sui generis*. Eschewing the common tendency to criticize them on the basis of their procedural flaws, I suggest they ought to be approached as political, as opposed to simply legal, institutions that make use of ritual forms in order to facilitate the transformation of the political community. I suggest that such institutions are 'exceptional,' not simply because they lack the formal integrity that we customarily expect from politico-legal institutions but because they serve as symbols of rupture in the life of the political community – that is, as moments when the polity attempts to mark its own transformation *as a polity* by dividing itself from its violent past. In the second section I take a critical look at exceptional institutions as 'transformative rituals' and reflect on how far the analogy between transition and revolution can (and ought) to be pressed. To what extent, I ask, can these transformative rituals deliver on the, expressed or implied, promise that they allow the political community to 'break free' of the past and 'begin anew?' I conclude by suggesting that rituals of purification are dangerous, to the extent that they blur the distinction between the finality of judgment and the finality of the injustice.

Exceptional institutions as transformative rituals

The pressure applied in the post-war period to respond to (and, as best as possible, make amends for) state-sponsored violence has given rise to a collection of novel institutional forms. While the most celebrated of these, particularly in the wake of the South African iteration, has been the truth commission, its relative prominence on the global stage should not blind us to the fact that it is simply one institutionalized expression of politico-legal innovation, other instances of which include administrative purges, reparative gestures and political apologies. Nor should it be forgotten that the criminal tribunal, against which the truth commission is so regularly compared (and in relation to which it assumes its status as an 'innovation'), was itself a novel invention of the post-war period. Though the criminal tribunals at Nuremberg and Tokyo clearly drew on the established precedent of domestic criminal trials, the fact that they were carried out under the auspices of the 'international community' (not to mention the uniqueness of the crimes on which they were called to pass judgment) made a certain kind of institutional torsion inevitable. More alike than unlike the truth commission in this respect, the international criminal tribunal was an attempt to secure justice under exceptional circumstances – under circumstances, that is, in which the State had become an agent of violence rather than an instrument of protection, or rather an agent of violence against certain (usually racially differentiated) groups under the *pretext* of providing protection for everybody else.[1]

Conventional critiques of these exceptional institutions have tended to focus on the manifold ways in which they fail as instruments of justice. Within the terms of this legalistic approach, such institutions tend to be found wanting for two primary reasons: first, because their legitimacy *qua institutions* remains dubious (by what right does this court stand in judgment or this apology become offered on behalf of the political community?) and, second, because they fail to meet basic standards of procedural fairness (how can legal and moral norms be applied retrospectively or why is this person being removed from office and not that one?). Exactly how these criticisms are couched, and how damaging they are deemed to be, depends in large measure on the specific institution being addressed and how rigorously it adheres to established principles of procedural justice. In the final analysis, however, all of them tend to boil down to one essential concern: exceptional institutions are unacceptably arbitrary. Either they lack the authority to which they lay claim (that is, they have no right to stand in judgment at all) or they breach the procedural rules that lend legitimacy to specific decisions (that is, the judgments they make in individual cases are wholly capricious). By failing in these ways, such exceptional institutions are deemed to undermine the very distinction between the past and the present that they are, at once, seeking to embody and to enact. They mirror the old regime in it arbitrariness at the very moment they seek to differentiate themselves from it.

1 Martha Minow, *Between Vengeance and Forgiveness: Facing History after Genocide and Mass Violence* (Boston: Beacon Press, 1998); Elazar Barkan, *The Guilt of Nations: Restitution and Negotiating Historical Injustices* (Baltimore: Johns Hopkins University Press, 2000); Mark Gibney, Rhoda E. Howard-Hassman, Jean-Marc Coicaud and Niklaus Steiner (eds.) *The Age of Apologies: Facing Up to the Past* (Philadelphia: University of Pennsylvania Press, 2009).

In part because it was the first experiment in 'transitional justice' – the first, that is, to which the term might be applied without risking serious anachronism – and in part because the crimes it addressed were so staggering in their originality, the Nuremberg War Crimes Tribunal has historically served as the principal testing ground for this kind of critique. Although, as Minow points out, Nuremberg had, by the end of the twentieth century, been rehabilitated to the point where human rights activists could cite it as a landmark in the struggle for a just world order, it was commonly condemned in its own time as a travesty of justice.[2] The ambiguous status it enjoyed as the 'court of the victors,' the retrospective manner in which it applied 'international norms,' the arbitrariness of the criteria it used to select individuals for prosecution, its readiness to punish individuals for acts of State, and the symbolic role it played as a trial of Nazism more generally, all worked to blur the line between retribution and revenge that the 'rule of law' is designed to inscribe.[3] While few followed Chief Justice Stone of the US Supreme Court in his suggestion that Nuremberg was simply a 'high-class lynching party,' the perception that it failed to live up to its own criteria of formal justice was widespread. The issue was not just that Nuremberg was 'victor's justice,' but that it was 'sloppy justice,' procedurally compromised to the point where its judgments became unconscionably arbitrary.

That Nuremberg, perhaps one of the greatest tributes that has ever been paid to law, should have done so much to expose its frailties remains one of the great ironies of history. Though the codification of the Nuremberg principles into international law has done a great deal to legitimate it retrospectively, the mist of arbitrariness surrounding the international criminal tribunal as an institution has never quite lifted and continues to plague subsequent iterations in Yugoslavia and Rwanda.[4] This is not to say, of course, that other exceptional institutions have fared any better. If anything, the abrogation of the 'duty to prosecute,' which Nuremberg established as a precedent, has made them even more vulnerable to the claim that they fail as vehicles of justice. Hence truth commissions have been denounced on the grounds that they 'sacrifice justice' for the sake of truth or, worse still, for the elusive goal of reconciliation[5]; administrative purges on the grounds that they are unconstitutional and their criteria of selection open to party-political manipulation[6]; material reparations on the grounds that they make arbitrary decisions about who qualifies as a victim and how much they ought to

2 Minow, 27.

3 See for example, Martha Minow, *Between Vengeance and Forgiveness* and Mark Osiel, 'Why Prosecute? Critics of Punishment for Mass Atrocity,' *Human Rights Quarterly*, Vol 22, No 1 (2000), 118–147.

4 Martii Koskenniemi, 'Between Impunity and Show Trials,' *Max Planck Yearbook of United Nations Law*, Vol 6 (2002) 1–35.

5 Robert Rotberg and Dennis Thompson (eds.), *Truth v Justice: The Morality of Truth Commissions* (Princeton: Princeton University Press, 2000).

6 Cynthia M. Horne, 'The Impact of Lustration on Democratization in Post-Communist Countries,' *The International Journal of Transitional Justice*, Vol 8 (2014), 496–521.

receive in damages[7]; and political apologies on the grounds that it is illogical for political leaders to offer apologies for things they did not do and about which they can feel no remorse.[8]

Such critiques are inarguable insofar as we hold firm to the view that conventional conceptions of justice provide the right yardstick against which to measure exceptional institutions. However, they lose a great deal of their bite once we begin to attend to the unusual circumstances that make these kinds of institutions necessary. As Bronwyn Leebaw has argued, transitional justice institutions such as criminal tribunals and truth commissions respond to a 'unique set of dilemmas.'[9] Unlike 'ordinary' institutions, which are only required to uphold the principles of justice that secure the integrity of the existing order, 'exceptional' institutions must create the possibility of justice at the same time as they enact it. Instead of simply passing judgment on individual cases, they have to establish the conditions under which such judgments can become recognizable *as expressions of justice* by instituting a new *grundnorm* for the political community. Exceptional institutions are, to this extent, instruments of foundation as much as they are instruments of justice – they institute the (new) normative order at the same time as they uphold it. It is this double function of instituting and upholding that makes exceptional institutions appear arbitrary in the eyes of their critics. Yet it is entirely possible that their nature and significance will continue to elude us until we recognize them as *sui generis*, defined by their own functions and subject to their own criteria of evaluation.

Looking at exceptional institutions in this way does not overcome the procedural problems customarily associated with them. Such institutions, precisely because they make judgments about the past based on the new norms they institute, will always be vulnerable to charges of arbitrariness. What it does do, however, is allow us to shift the grounds of critique. Rather than simply condemn exceptional institutions as imperfect versions of more conventional, procedurally correct, legal and moral forms, it focuses attention on the broader role they play as vehicles of political re-foundation. Looked at from this perspective, the critical issue is not so much what these institutions achieve (or, perhaps more to the point, fail to achieve) by way of justice for individuals, but how they function as 'transformative rituals' – that is, as rituals that stage moments of rupture in the life of the political community. What, we need to ask, do these rituals entail and how efficacious are they? What kind of benefits do they provide for the political community and what kinds of risks are associated with them? Responding to these questions requires us to pay more attention to the ontological dimension of time in transitional situations than has hitherto been the case. In particular, careful attention needs

7 Barkan, 308–350.

8 Michael Cunningham, 'Saying Sorry: The Politics of Apology,' *Political Quarterly*, Vol 70, No 3 (1999), 285–293.

9 Bronwyn Leebaw, 'The Irreconcilable Goals of Transitional Justice,' *Human Rights Quarterly*, Vol 30 (2008) 95–118.

to be given to the frequently repeated claim that transformative rituals 'interrupt the flow of time' and allow political communities to 'break free' of the past.

Political rituals, self-interrogation and purification

Perhaps the best way to get our bearings in this inquiry is to take note of the fact that claims of this kind have, since the eighteenth century, generally been couched in the name of revolution. From that point onwards the old, naturalistic, notion of revolution as a cyclical movement, returning always to the same point, was first supplemented and then, to a large extent, displaced by a sense of revolution as a dramatic upheaval that altered the course of time. For obvious, and entirely understandable, reasons, political scientists have tended to be more interested in the systems of government that appear before and after such revolutionary moments than in what this new conceptualization of revolution implied about our understanding of temporality. However, there is no question that this new-found belief, that it was possible not simply to accelerate the flow of time but to interrupt it, was of momentous political significance. To the extent that it allowed human beings to imagine themselves as the masters of something that had always mastered them – namely, time itself – it invested worldly action with an unprecedented status. The power to 'start afresh,' hitherto the prerogative of the gods, now lay firmly in human hands. This human potential to 'make revolution' in the form of a temporal displacement rather than a temporal return was already anticipated by the Glorious Revolution of 1688 in England. However, it found its historical referent *par excellence* in the world-historical revolution of 1789 that marked the beginning of the end of the European monarchies.[10]

The French Revolution now enjoys a certain mythological status as the archetypal instance of political rupture. However, as Connerton points out, this revolution of revolutions is notable not simply for the historical beginning (or beginnings) it made but for the manifold problems of beginning it brought to the fore. In politics, as in life, new starts tend to be marked by, if they are not in fact *performed through*, some kind of ritualized act of judgment on the past. 'To pass judgment on the practices of the old regime is,' according to Connerton, 'the constitutive act of the new order.'[11] Such judgments are, however, radically different from those that take place under the authority of an established regime. To begin with they are wholly without precedent – they must invent, rather than simply apply, the normative criteria on which right and wrong will henceforth (and retrospectively) be distinguished. Second, they are beyond appeal – the normative criteria they bring into effect cannot be open to contestation or subject to challenge because they are the foundations on which the new order is built.

10 Reinhart Koselleck, *Futures Past: On the Semantics of Historical Time* (New York: Columbia University Press, 2004), 43–49; Paul Connerton, *How Societies Remember* (Cambridge: Cambridge University Press, 2006), 6.

11 Connerton, 7.

Connerton is thus quite right to suggest that '[t]here is a measure of complete arbitrariness in the very nature of any such attempted beginning.'[12] Every new start, if it really is a new start, is self-legitimating. The appeals that revolutionaries often make to the transcendent figures of God or Nature ought, to this extent, be seen as an attempt to dispel the feeling of groundlessness that beginning induces. In moments of upheaval, even an allegiance to old idols can, it seems, be preferable to having nothing solid under one's feet.

There is, of course, one obvious way in which the situation of transitional societies today is not analogous to that of revolutionary France. The emergence of human rights as an internationally recognized standard of legitimacy provides them with a ready-made, pre-authorized, normative order – an order that stands outside the jurisdiction of any one state and which is not, therefore, tainted by any particular national history. At least since Nuremberg, states transitioning from authoritarianism to democracy (or, for that matter, from colonialism to post-colonialism) have been able to allude to a 'new dawn' of human rights without becoming mired in the bog of arbitrariness that plagued the Declaration of the Rights of Man and Citizen in 1789. And yet the distance between them may not, in other respects, be all that great. As Connerton's work helps us to see, both seek to establish the total and complete substitution of a new social order (an order built on a new *grundnorm*) and both lean heavily on ritual in order to insert a rupture between the present and the past. In 'transitional' as much as in 'revolutionary' situations, in other words, the problem of beginning tends to center on the issue of judgment and its ritual performance. In both cases an exemplary act of judgment, enacted on the stage of the exceptional institution, is used to separate the present from the past and to erect a barrier against future transgression.[13]

That the exceptional institutions deployed in transitional situations incorporate powerful ritualistic elements has long been acknowledged; if only because such elements are, in the eyes of the critics, part of what compromises their legitimacy. Whether it is the allusion to the 'last judgment' that recurs in criminal tribunals, the 'emotional catharsis' associated with truth commissions, the explicit invocation of 'ritual purification' in administrative purges, the 'devotional sacrifices' that lie at the origin of acts of reparation or the 'penitential rites' that shadow political apologies is, to this extent, of little consequence. The important point is that all of these exceptional institutions exceed the legal realm in one way or another – all of them operate simultaneously at the level of legal mechanism and symbolic performance. To say this is not to deny that the ritualistic dimension may be more clearly marked or, as Danielle Celermajer puts it, more 'purely' manifested in some transitional justice institutions than others. On her reading, it is strongest in political apologies, where virtually all the work of justice is done at the symbolic

12 Ibid, 6.
13 Ibid, 7.

level of recognition, and weakest in criminal tribunals, where the juridical dimension of prosecution and punishment acts as a powerful, independent source of moral correction.[14] However, there is no instance in which the pseudo-religious element of ritual is wholly absent, no instance in which it is not entangled in the juridical apparatus in some way.

Scholars and practitioners who treat human rights as sacrosanct are apt to find this entanglement of the ritual and the juridical within the exceptional institution deeply problematic. Seen from their perspective, these ritualistic elements are not simply an unnecessary, but potentially also a dangerous, intrusion into the legal process. The best one might say about them is that they are wholly extraneous to the work of justice, forms of 'symbolic excess' that have no consequence in the world and therefore no real efficacy. Hence the frequently repeated claim that political apologies are 'merely symbols,' ritual charades that make it possible for perpetrator states to regain legitimacy in the eyes of the 'international community' but which do little or nothing to help the victims.[15] The worst that one might say about them is that they actually seep into the work of justice, 'coloring' (which is to say, distorting) the way in which it ought to function. Hence the recurrent concern that criminal tribunals become perverted, turned into 'show trials,' as soon as the performative element of ritual intrudes. The worry in this case is that the defendants will be tried less as individuals who have committed specific crimes than as symbols of the previous (now despised) regime. One condemns them in order to condemn or, better still, symbolically 'kill off' the old order.[16]

The role played by ritual in transitional processes may, however, be more complex and more efficacious than this juridical critique allows. To begin with, ritual would seem to be indispensable to the attempt, re-enacted in all transitional settings, to divide the present from the violence of the past. Unlike the juridical element in exceptional institutions, which always addresses itself to individuals and to the crimes they have perpetrated or suffered, the ritual element addresses itself to the collective. Ritual speaks of and to 'the nation' and its 'sins.' It summons a 'we' up out of the fragments of the social, allowing the political community to appear before itself as a subject on whom judgment can be passed and against whom a new order can be constituted. That the, now completely ritualized, incantation 'never again' should take center-stage in the transitional scene is, from this perspective, scarcely surprising. By saying 'never again' the polity 'finalizes' the injustice in question, simultaneously terminating any further contest over its status as a wrong and extinguishing any potential for its rehabilitation. 'Never again' is, to this extent, the last judgment on the *ancien regime*, the judgment from which there is no right of appeal. In line with the modern understanding of revolution,

14 Danielle Celermajer, 'Merely Ritual? Displacing the Myth of Sincerity in Transitional Rituals,' *The International Journal of Transitional Justice* Vol 7 (2013) 286–305, 288.

15 Michel-Rolph Trouillot, 'Abortive Rituals: Historical Apologies in the Global Era,' *Interventions*, Vol 2, No 2 (2000), 171–186.

16 See: Koskenniemi.

this judgment breaks the flow of time by erecting a wall between the past and the present. Once it is uttered, a return to the old order and the old ways becomes, morally speaking at least, out of the question.[17]

Eradicating ritual entirely would, then, seem to be an unachievable and undesirable goal. So long as some kind of symbolic act differentiating the present from the past remains a moral requirement, no transitional society will be able to do without it. However, to assume that ritual does nothing more than 'symbolize' transformation may be to undersell it. In her seminal work on political apologies, Celermajer has, for instance, insisted that ritual is not simply ineradicable in transitional settings but something that does important work, *in its own right*, at the level of the public culture. On her reading, the ritual performances endlessly repeated in transitional contexts do not simply address themselves to the nation in an artificially contrived 'other world' where new beginnings are possible. They actively reshape its political culture by habituating citizens to the new *grundnorm* of universal respect. By publicly condemning practices and acts that had previously worn the mantle of political legitimacy, transformative rituals can, according to Celermajer, shift the 'normative compass of the nation' and reorient individual behavior around a new set of values. Ritual, on this reading, does not simply reflect normative orientations but actively shapes them. Just as children can learn to respect others as independent centers of value by performing the ritual of apology (if initially in an inauthentic way), so too can citizens acquire the ethical disposition needed to sustain the new order of universal dignity by participating in its transformative rituals.[18]

If, following Celermajer, ritual performance is granted the capacity not simply to reflect but to actively reshape normative predispositions, it assumes a special importance in situations where gross violations of human rights have been committed. In cases of this kind, cases where the injustice is systemic rather than episodic, prosecuting or purging a select group of perpetrators is never going to be sufficient to bring about the required transformation. While specific acts of wrong-doing can hardly be ignored, the possibility of real change would appear to rest on altering the underlying normative framework that made it possible for those acts to pass as acceptable in the first place. As Celermajer has suggested:

> one of the main tasks of transitional mechanisms is to alter the normative framework of the society in question in order to move it from one in which certain types of violations and relationships of disrespect and inequality were normalized to one oriented towards equal respect for human rights.[19]

The ritual element in exceptional institutions is vital in this context because it is the only one that explicitly addresses itself to this 'normative framework' or to what Celermajer has elsewhere referred to as the 'moral grammar' of the political

17 Andrew Schaap, *Political Reconciliation* (London and New York: Routledge, 2005), 94–98.

18 Celermajer 2013, 290.

19 Ibid, 288.

community.[20] Because it operates at the level of the symbolic rather than the juridical, ritual has the capacity to generalize rather than to personalize injustice. It places the burden of responsibility for wrong-doing on the political community as a whole, encouraging citizens to recognize their complicity in the injustice and address the exclusions embedded in the political culture.

Celermajer's special interest in political apologies as transformative rituals stems, to a large degree, from their capacity to enact change at this deeper level of public culture or national identity. As she points out, 'political apologies tend not to be for single aberrant, "out of character" acts on the part of the State, but on the contrary for systematic acts that emerge from what the State was or is.'[21] When representatives of the people say sorry for past injustices, they are not apologizing for specific acts of wrong-doing but for the identity of the nation that made those acts possible. A political apology properly understood is, then, a kind of exemplary judgment *upon* the political community *by* the political community that is, at once, a signifier of and a catalyst for transformation. In the ritual of apology, the nation simultaneously recognizes that its identity was constituted through exclusion and promises to reconstitute itself on the basis of the new normative framework of universal respect. More so than criminal tribunals and reparative gestures, therefore, both of which are still closely tied to the juridical task of assessing specific acts, the ritual of political apology both heralds *and* enables a transformation at the level of political identity. To say sorry, according to Celermajer, is to establish a 'break in the chain of events and the self same identities informed by the past.'[22] As an admission of wrong-doing it does not simply foreshadow but actually enacts a 'constitutional shift in identity.'[23]

Exactly how well this defense of political apologies applies to other transformative rituals remains to be seen. While Celermajer's focus on political apology as a 'pure or unmixed form of ritual performance' is readily justified from a methodological point of view, it is not clear that it is without political consequence.[24] Might this focus on political apologies not blind us to some of the morally adverse consequences that attend other ritual forms in transitional settings? At the very least, however, Celermajer gives us good reasons for taking transitional justice rituals seriously. In the face of Trouillot's well-known claim that political apologies are 'destined to be abortive rituals' because they make false assumptions about the continuity of historical collectivities, she calls us to think more carefully about what they are and how they might work as instruments of transformation.[25] Indeed, by

20 Danielle Celermajer, 'The Apology in Australia: Recovenanting the National Imaginary,' in Barkan, Elazar and Alexander Karn (eds.), *Taking Wrongs Seriously; Apologies and Reconciliation* (Stanford: Standford University Press, 2006), 162.

21 Danielle Celermajer, 'Apology and the Possibility of Ethical Politics,' *Journal for Cultural and Religious Theory,* Vol 9, No 1 (2008), 14–33, 26.

22 Ibid, 25.

23 Ibid, 26.

24 Celermajer 2013, 288.

25 Trouillot, 171, 185.

insisting that we treat political apologies as *sui generis*, Celermajer goes beyond the common, purely formal, objection that an apology is quintessentially a personal gesture and allows us to attend more specifically to its efficacy as a transformative ritual. Her argument that performativity can shape, rather than simply reflect, normativity suggests that political apologies don't 'merely' symbolize political transformation, but do some of the work of political transformation.

However, Trouillot's skepticism remains useful to the extent that it keeps us alert to the ways in which these 'transformative rituals' fall short of revolution. As he rightly points out, such rituals invariably appeal to the 'soul of the nation' in ways that encourage a certain kind of mystification. Rather than focus attention on the way existing social, economic and political arrangements have been structured by the injustice in question, they displace that injustice on to a symbolic non-site – 'the national soul' – where it becomes available for erasure. This double process of displacement and erasure is particularly apparent in the case of administrative purges and political apologies, but, explicitly or implicitly, all exceptional institutions evoke the idea of a 'stain on the nation's soul' that will, through their ministrations, be 'flushed out' or 'washed away.' The capacity for these kinds of purification rituals to encourage citizens to reflect on the 'constitution' of the political community, in the broadest sense of that term, would thus seem fairly limited. Even if we concur with Celermajer that performativity can create normativity, it remains unclear whether it encourages the necessary *reflexivity*. Constituted as participant-spectators in these rituals of purification, citizens may reasonably assume they are on the other side of history, where the past has ceased to have any relevance. Trouillot's insistence that the current wave of public apologies is but the 'ritual overflow' of our political 'inability to face structures of inequality' may not, therefore, be entirely wide of the mark.[26]

While Celermajer is by no means unaware of this problem, it is not clear that she has an adequate answer to it. As she herself has noted, there is an 'inescapable ambiguity' that surrounds the work of rituals like political apologies. Thus, in each instance where it is offered, it remains

> unclear whether the apology's particular approach to 'dealing with the past' involves the preservation of the past, even as we alter our relationship to it, or if, when we apologise, we imagine that the future is a blank sheet, untainted by the violations of the past. Is the process one which seals the past, with the words of apology functioning like the final wax seal stamped with care to terminate any dialogue with the past? Or can the process of apology and reconciliation involve a more complex transformation in which the memory of the violation is not buried, but rather brought into the present to transform the relationship that perpetrators and victims have with their own past and future, and with each other?[27]

26 Ibid, 184.
27 Celermajer 2008, 17.

Much of Celermajer's work on political apology plays in this space of ambiguity. Though acutely sensitive to the risks political apologies pose to our ongoing 'dialogue with the past,' she refuses to dismiss them out of hand simply because they can, in certain cases, become complicit in the work of erasure. And yet there are moments when she gives the distinct impression that it is possible to escape this 'inescapable ambiguity' after all. Hence in her, admittedly quite brief, analysis of Chancellor Willy Brandt's famous *kniefall* before the monument to the Warsaw Ghetto Uprising, she seems to endorse the possibility not simply that such acts 'draw a line under' the past but that they might also 'delete it.'[28]

The risk that arises from the deployment of ritual in exceptional institutions is, then, that it will blur the distinction between the *finality of judgment*, according to which we determine, once and for all, that what 'we' did was unjust, and the *finality of the injustice*, according to which there is nothing more for the political community to do, no 'legacy issues' to resolve. As should already be abundantly clear, systemic wrongs, like Nazism or apartheid, are not erased through the ritualized performance of negative judgment. They embed themselves in the social, economic and political fabric of states in ways that put a lie to the possibility of a wholly new start. The illusion of the 'clean break' is not, of course, confined to transitional societies. As Connerton shows, even in revolutionary situations citizens can struggle to acknowledge, let alone rectify, injustices that have shaped the 'present arrangements' of society, such as its distribution of property and its institutions of sovereignty.[29] However, the risk of forgetting the legacy of the injustice seems to be far greater in transitional situations where rituals of purification are apt to be used as a kind of 'time engineering' that contains the injustice as a problem by displacing it to the past.[30] *Contra* Celermajer, transformative rituals may, by their very nature, incline towards a 'washing off' rather than a 'working through,' disabling the work of transformation rather than facilitating it.

Conclusion

The impact of transformative rituals in transitional justice settings would seem to be highly ambiguous. Such rituals could be regarded as valuable to the extent that they provide the public with an opportunity to take itself as an object of critical interrogation. To the extent that they allow judgment to be passed on the political community as a whole, they make citizen-spectators cognizant of the fact that there are issues *they* need to address. Such transformative rituals can, however, also endanger (or prematurely arrest) the very processes of communal self-reflection that they set in motion. Instead of encouraging citizens to repeatedly return to the questions that arise whenever the State commits an

28 Celermajer 2013, 303.
29 Connerton, 9.
30 Magdalena Zolkos, 'Jean Amery's Concept of Resentment at the Crossroads of Ethics and Politics,' *The European Legacy*, Vol 12, No 1 (2007), 23–38, 29.

injustice in the name of the people – how did this happen? What does it say about 'us' as a political community? What do 'we' need to do to insure that it never happens again? – they can work to relieve themselves of their newly acquired responsibility by creating the illusion that the polity has now been purified. A state that has been 'cleansed' of its 'sins' is a state that need not trouble itself about the past anymore. It can happily ignore the protests of victims on the grounds that their grievances have already been dealt with. This is not to say that transformative rituals do not have their place. But if the injustice is not to enjoy a healthy afterlife beyond the exceptional institution, we will have to constantly remind ourselves of the ways in which such rituals fall short of revolution.

7 Promoting reconciliation and protecting human rights

An underexplored relationship

Nasia Hadjigeorgiou

The United Nations was correct in asserting that the absence of war 'can only create a space in which peace can be built.'[1] This chapter examines the challenges that exist in filling this space and, particularly, in reconciling previously warring groups in ethnically divided societies. First, it argues that reconciliation can only be achieved when members of different ethnic groups rehumanize and start trusting each other. It then makes the case that reconciliation and human rights do not coexist in an easy relationship; rather, the connections between them are varied and often contradictory. On the one hand, human rights are indeed positively connected to reconciliation. On the other, the two terms can also be at odds with each other: human rights protection can undermine reconciliation, while the language of reconciliation sometimes derails the process of protecting human rights. In addition to these positive *and* negative connections between the two terms, it is also possible that human rights and reconciliation remain completely unconnected. While the former is well suited in inducing *legal and institutional* changes, it is *social and psychological* changes that the latter requires.

These conclusions about a nuanced relationship between human rights and reconciliation directly challenge the UN orthodoxy. The long-standing assumption of the international community has been that there is an exclusively positive connection between the two terms and that reconciliation in ethnically divided, post-conflict societies always 'requires that past human rights violations be addressed.'[2] This is often treated as a self-evident truth and no attempts have been made to explain it in any more detail. It is merely sufficient, it seems, to reiterate that 'United Nations human rights personnel can play a leading role [. . .] in helping to implement a comprehensive program for national reconciliation.'[3] Challenging the orthodoxy about the relationship between reconciliation and human rights is not only an exercise of theoretical importance. It can have

1 'Report of the Panel on United Nations Peace Operations' (New York: United Nations, 2000), para. 3 ('Brahimi Report').

2 Ibid, para. 24.

3 Ibid, para. 41.

profound practical implications on how human rights are used in post-conflict societies themselves. I will refer to four situations which will be Northern Ireland, Bosnia and Herzegovina, Cyprus and South Africa. These conclusions have implications for ongoing ethnic conflicts in the Middle East and elsewhere.

Defining 'reconciliation' and 'human rights'

The frequent repetition of the term 'human rights' in connection with 'reconciliation' in UN reports confirms the expectation that they both have important roles to play in peacebuilding operations. For example, the High-Level Panel on Threats, Challenges and Change refers to the importance of 'local capacity-building for human rights and reconciliation,' which 'can greatly benefit long-term peacebuilding.'[4] Similarly, the Brahimi Report argues that 'a mission well accomplished' is one where the population of the post-conflict country has been given the opportunity 'to build and hold on to peace, to find reconciliation, to strengthen democracy, to secure human rights.'[5] Despite such references, however, the UN has not satisfactorily defined either reconciliation nor human rights. I will be using a definition of reconciliation that emphasizes the importance of *meaningful cooperation* between the members of previously warring groups. In order for this meaningful cooperation to be achieved, I argue, it is necessary for people to start rehumanizing and trusting each other. I will also suggest that peacebuilders have adopted a rather narrow definition of the term 'human rights' as only referring to the protection granted by *legal* bodies, such as domestic and international courts. Both of these definitions have, at least by implication, been accepted and relied on by UN peacebuilders in practice. Yet little attention has been paid to the fact that the narrow and legalistic understanding of human rights is often unhelpful in promoting the broader objectives of reconciliation.

The term 'reconciliation' has been subject to various different definitions. For example, McEvoy *et al.* conceptualize reconciliation as the need to respect the rights of others and argue that this definition is practically important because it provides a discourse and vocabulary in which political conflicts can be framed.[6] Arguably, however, this understanding of reconciliation is too restrictive because it ignores the fact that not every single political conflict can be expressed in rights terms. Moreover, in the likely scenario where the parties are not in agreement as to what each competing right actually entails, expressing the political conflict in rights terms only rephrases, rather than successfully resolves, the problem. Finally, this definition should be avoided for the purposes of this chapter because of its unsuitability in answering the question at hand: since our objective is to clarify

4 High-Level Panel on Threats, Challenges and Change, 'A More Secure World: Our Shared Responsibility' (New York: United Nations, 2004), para. 229.

5 Brahimi Report, xv.

6 Lesley McEvoy, Kieran McEvoy and Kirsten McConnachie, 'Reconciliation as a Dirty Word: Conflict, Community Relations and Education in Northern Ireland,' *Journal of International Affairs*, Vol 6, No 1 (2006), 81–106.

the relationship between rights and reconciliation, any analysis becomes circular if reconciliation itself is defined as the respect of other people's rights.

A more appropriate definition of reconciliation therefore focuses not on the *rights* of others but on the importance of promoting *meaningful cooperation* between the previously warring parties. Two important distinctions should be made in order to clarify this definition of reconciliation. The first is between meaningful cooperation and inter-group harmony because, despite the numerous hurdles in achieving the former, this is a more modest aim than the arguably utopian goal of achieving the latter.[7] As Govier and Verwoerd put it, a 'realistic goal in contexts of reconciliation is not total harmony; nor is it a state of blissfully enduring unity.'[8] In order for harmony to exist there must be a compatibility of the groups' needs and interests, but competitive politics in divided societies operate by highlighting precisely this lack of compatibility. Moreover, had such compatibility existed it is unlikely that the society would have become ethnically divided and resorted to war in the first place. Separate groups, characterized by such distinct identities, needs and interests, do not have to be assimilated in order for reconciliation to be achieved. Reconciliation does not require the elimination of differences, but the ability to live with these differences through cooperation.

The second distinction that must be made is between meaningful cooperation and mere coexistence among members of different ethnic groups. If people are living next to each other without communicating, cooperating or having common goals, wishing that they did not have to mingle with the other group at all, there is no real reconciliation.[9] It is just a brief pause before the negative perceptions of each group resurface and potentially result in even more violence. If the UN is right that post-conflict states need a 'society-wide system of values [. . .] to put a premium on peace, to desire peace, to seek peace and to stand for peace,' then reconciliation has to mean more than simple coexistence.[10] Rejecting this minimalist definition, however, does not mean that meaningful cooperation has to stem from altruistic goals of loving one's enemy. It could result from the simple understanding that, unless the members of different ethnic groups reconcile, the alternative will be catastrophic for all of them.[11]

7 See: Yaacov Bar-Siman-Tov, 'Dialectics between Stable Peace and Reconciliation,' in *From Conflict Resolution to Reconciliation*, edited by Yaacov Bar-Siman-Tov (Oxford: Oxford University Press, 2004), 61–80.

8 Trudy Govier and Wilhelm Verwoerd, 'Trust and the Problem of National Reconciliation,' *Philosophy of the Social Sciences*, Vol 32, No 2 (2002), 178–205, 185.

9 See: Roger Mac Ginty, 'Everyday Peace: Bottom-up and Local Agency in Conflict-Affected Societies,' *Security Dialogue*, Vol 45, No 6 (2014), 548–564.

10 United Nations, 'Proceedings of the United Nations Department of Public Information's International Encounter for European Journalists on the Question of Palestine' (London: United Nations, 1993).

11 Charles Villa-Vicencio, 'Reconciliation,' in *Pieces of the Puzzle: Keywords on Reconciliation and Transitional Justice*, edited by Charles Villa-Vicencio and Erik Doxtader (Cape Town: Institute of Justice and Reconciliation, 2004), 3–9.

Meaningful cooperation occupies the middle ground in the spectrum between inter-group harmony and mere coexistence. Relationships of meaningful cooperation only become possible when members of different ethnic groups start trusting each other; in other words, when they form a confident expectation that one will not act in a manner which will take advantage of the other's vulnerability.[12] This expectation is unlikely to be popular, especially in the early stages of the peacebuilding process, but what is needed is not absolute trust. Rather, members of different ethnic groups must be comfortable enough with each other in order to form working relationships that can lead to functioning societies. Ideally, in the long term, this will produce a virtuous cycle whereby improved cooperation between the ethnic groups will result in better functioning societies, thus leading to higher levels of trust, which will in turn encourage even more cooperation.

The question remains: how is trust to be built in the first place? In conflict and post-conflict societies, levels of trust have been undermined due to a process of dehumanization. It is because of the problems created by ***dehumanization*** that ***rehumanization*** plays such an important part in reconciliation efforts. Rehumanization, on which trust relies, requires that the hurdles that prevent former enemies from being perceived as people are removed.[13] During the conflict, negative stereotyping, propaganda against and fear of the other side usually make people view members of the opposing group – the 'others' – as less than human. The 'others' are perceived as parts of a homogeneous unit and the possibility that there are those among them that are feeling scared, victimized or ashamed of the actions of their fellow group members is often wholly dismissed. Illustrative of this are the reactions of members of different ethnic groups in Bosnia and Herzegovina when they were asked who was to blame for the war.[14] Most of them expressed the belief that, while atrocities had been carried out by all sides, the ones committed by the 'others' were premeditated, while those committed by their own people were just individual excesses. As such negative stereotyping of the 'other' becomes more common, the individuality of the stereotyped group's members is lost and their dehumanization becomes easier.[15] This

12 Ibid.

13 Arie Nadler, 'Reconciliation: Instrumental and Socioemotional Aspects,' in *The Encyclopedia of Peace Psychology*, edited by Daniel J. Christie (New York: Wiley-Blackwell, 2012), 536–540.

14 Dinka Corkalo *et al.*, 'Neighbors Again? Intercommunity Relations after Ethnic Cleansing,' in *My Neighbor, My Enemy: Justice and Community in the Aftermath of Mass Atrocity*, edited by Eric Stover and Harvey M. Weinstein (Cambridge: Cambridge University Press, 2004), 143–161.

15 Jodi Halpern and Harvey M. Weinstein, 'Empathy and Rehumanization after Mass Violence,' in *My Neighbor, My Enemy: Justice and Community in the Aftermath of Mass Atrocity*, edited by Eric Stover and Harvey M. Weinstein (Cambridge: CUP, 2004), 303–322; see also Marlene C. Fiol and Edward J. O'Connor, 'Managing Intractable Identity Conflicts,' in *The Encyclopedia of Peace Psychology*, edited by Daniel J. Christie (New York: Wiley-Blackwell, 2012), 937–940.

stereotyping, portraying whole groups of people as less than human, predatory and unreasonable in their personal and political relationships, is the biggest hurdle to meaningful cooperation. At the heart of reconciliation, therefore, there is a need to challenge negative stereotypes and begin the process of rehumanization; it is the contribution of human rights to this rehumanization and trust-building process that I seek to examine in more detail here.

Even in the most favorable conditions the processes of rehumanization and building inter-ethnic trust are time-consuming; reconciliation does not occur naturally, it needs effort and time and is rarely the result of a linear process.[16] While, for example, positive attitudes between individuals from different groups might develop in the workplace, social pressures might prevent them from materializing in their personal lives.[17] Further, such positive attitudes might increase or decrease depending on a number of external factors, such as economic crises or spoilers. Consequently a number of reconciliation methods, bottom-up and top-down, and spanning different periods of time, have to be used. Each method has its strengths and weaknesses and might work with some people but not with others, so peacebuilders on the ground should use a combination of these. The specific combination of reconciliation methods that should be used in each context depends, among others, on the kind of conflict, the resources available and the cultures of the groups involved.[18]

The definition of reconciliation as meaningful cooperation is not expressly included in UN reports, but it is broadly in line with the organization's stated objectives in post-conflict countries.[19] Similarly, although official documents never define human rights, they do refer to the ways in which they expect them to contribute to peace operations; through these references, a narrow definition of *legal human rights* emerges.[20] Illustrative of the UN's tendency to primarily focus on the legal protection of human rights, rather than emphasizing their moral attributes, is *An Agenda for Peace*, which refers to the need to 'identify and support structures which will tend to consolidate peace' and uses the monitoring of elections and the protection of human rights as examples.[21] Elsewhere in the report

16 Daniel Bar-Tal and Gemma Bennink, 'The Nature of Reconciliation as an Outcome and as a Process,' in *From Conflict Resolution to Reconciliation*, edited by Yaacov Bar-Siman-Tov (Oxford: Oxford University Press, 2004), 11–38.

17 Jennifer Todd *et al.*, 'Does Being Protestant Matter? Protestants, Minorities and the Remaking of Ethno-religious Identity After the Good Friday Agreement,' *National Identities*, Vol 11, No 1 (2009), 87–99.

18 Bar-Tal and Bennink, 'The Nature of Reconciliation.'

19 See: para. 56 of the UN 'Agenda for Peace.'

20 UN Secretary-General, 'Rule of Law and Transitional Justice in Conflict and Post-Conflict Societies' (New York: United Nations, 2004), para. 7.

21 UN Secretary-General, 'An Agenda for Peace: Preventive Diplomacy, Peacemaking and Peace-Keeping: Report of the Secretary-General Pursuant to the Statement Adopted by the Summit Meeting of the Security Council on 31 January 1992' (New York: United Nations, 1992), para. 55. The emphasis on structures is also apparent in UN

there are also mentions of professionals who can help in peacebuilding operations; these include human rights monitors and electoral officials – in other words, those who are concerned with the implementation of legal provisions.[22] A similar emphasis on the legal, rather than moral, characteristics of human rights is found in the Brahimi Report, which recommends that the Office of the High Commissioner for Human Rights should increase its peacebuilding efforts by creating 'model databases for human rights field work.'[23]

Several divided societies around the world have adopted mechanisms for the protection of legal human rights as part of their peacebuilding operations. For example, peacebuilders in South Africa have relied on the Truth and Reconciliation Commission (TRC) and the Commission on Restitution of Land Rights,[24] while those in Bosnia and Herzegovina have been focusing on the International Criminal Tribunal for the Former Yugoslavia (ICTY). Differently still, peacebuilding efforts in Cyprus have been predominantly affected by the European Court of Human Rights (ECHR).[25] At the same time the constitutional or supreme courts in all three jurisdictions have produced human rights case law that has also contributed, whether positively or negatively, to reconciliation efforts. These institutions became part of the UN peacebuilding toolbox at different points in time and each contributes to the protection of human rights in diverse ways.[26] Moreover, some of them (most notably the ICTY) are concerned not with the protection of human rights *per se* but with addressing international crimes. While international human rights and international criminal law are distinct areas of law,[27] they share a common objective in that they are both responses to an increasingly urgent demand to safeguard values, such as human dignity.[28] Therefore, despite differences between them, all of these societies offer examples of attempts to protect human rights through *legal* mechanisms.

The emphasis on legal protections should not obscure other ways in which human rights can contribute to reconciliation. For instance, there does exist some

Secretary-General, 'Rule of Law and Transitional Justice in Conflict and Post-Conflict Societies,' para. 2.

22 UN Secretary-General, 'An Agenda for Peace,' para. 52.

23 'Brahimi Report,' para. 244. Also see para. 324 of the same report for a similar comment.

24 The Promotion of National Security and Reconciliation Act [34 of 1995]. See also: Restitution of Land Rights Act [22 of 1994].

25 Nikos Skoutaris, 'Building Transitional Justice Mechanisms Without a Peace Settlement: A Critical Appraisal of Recent Case Law of the Strasbourg Court on the Cyprus issue,' *European Law Review*, Vol 35, No 5 (2010), 720–733.

26 For instance, the process at the ICTY is instigated by the prosecutor, while at the ECHR by the victim.

27 Darryl Robinson, 'The Identity Crisis of International Criminal Law,' *Leiden Journal of International Law*, Vol 21 (2008), 952–963.

28 See: ICTY in *Kunarac* ICTY T. Ch. II 22.2.2001, para. 467. See also: Ruti G. Teitel, 'Transitional Justice Genealogy,' *Harvard Human Rights Journal*, Vol 16 (2003), 60–94.

literature on the importance of moral rights in relation to peace education,[29] and there have been some small-scale grassroots attempts to apply these theoretical findings in practice.[30] Nevertheless, the overwhelming attention and resources of peacebuilders have been directed towards the protection of human rights through legal mechanisms. Therefore, while the UN's implied definition of reconciliation is rather broad, the opposite applies to human rights, which have been understood to (mostly) operate within the rather narrow realm of the law. In turn, this variance in the ambit of the definitions of the two terms has had important ramifications for the relationship between them.

The dual relationship with reconciliation: assessing rights' strengths and weaknesses

Despite the UN's expectation that there is a positive association between human rights and reconciliation, few attempts have been made to explain this in any more detail. I will argue here that the former can indeed contribute to the promotion of the latter, but that this positive connection only presents one facet of the relationship in question. In addition to this it is also possible that human rights and reconciliation are negatively connected in the sense that one might undermine, rather than promote, the other. This possibility complicates the relationship between them and makes peacebuilding operations even harder to plan and execute; but ignoring it is to the peril of divided societies themselves.

The most obvious positive connection between human rights and reconciliation stems from the fact that protecting the former sends a clear message that the war is truly over. On the one hand, this legitimizes the new state of affairs and pushes members of all ethnic groups to work and cooperate towards its success. In addition to its symbolic significance, however, the protection of human rights can also contribute towards reconciliation in more practical ways by making post-conflict societies more secure. It has been argued, for example, that protecting civil and political rights, such as the liberty and security of the person, contributes to freedom from fear among the population.[31] While reconciliation does not happen automatically after people's fears have been alleviated, the Brahimi Report is right that 'a relatively less dangerous environment [. . .] is a fairly forgiving one.'[32]

29 Lesley McEvoy and Laura Lundy, 'In the Small Places: Education and Human Rights Culture in Conflict-Affected Societies,' in *Judges, Transition, and Human Rights*, edited by John Morison, Kieran McEvoy, and Gordon Anthony (Oxford: Oxford University Press, 2007), 495–514; Felisa Tibbits, 'Understanding What We Do: Emerging Models for Human Rights Education,' *International Review of Education*, Vol 48, Nos 3/4 (2002), 159–171.

30 Sara Clarke-Habibi, 'Transforming Worldviews: The Case of Education for Peace in Bosnia and Herzegovina,' *Journal of Transformative Education*, Vol 3 (2005), 33–56.

31 James Spigelman, 'The Forgotten Freedom: Freedom from Fear,' *International and Comparative Law Quarterly*, Vol 59 (2010), 543–570.

32 Brahimi Report, para. 25.

An additional contribution of human rights is that they provide the tools to the victims of the conflict to demand that they are compensated for what has been done to them.[33] Especially when such remedies are accompanied by meaningful apologies on behalf of the State, they can pave the way for a more reconciled society.[34] Finally, arguments have been made that punishing perpetrators of human rights violations can contribute to reconciliation, not only because this provides a sense of closure to the victims but also because it makes the public feel more confident that such atrocities will not be repeated.[35]

In order for human rights to promote reconciliation in these positive ways it is necessary that certain conditions are satisfied. Even in best-case scenarios, human rights protections do not, on their own, result in reconciled populations. It is important they are delivered by a body that the public considers legitimate, that members of all ethnic groups are engaged and familiar with its most important findings, and that these are accompanied by a positive public campaign.[36] An assessment of the ICTY provides evidence why these conditions are indeed necessary for the promotion of reconciliation. The ICTY cost the international community $1,585m[37] between 1993 and 2009; the expectation was that this would in turn 'contribute to the restoration and maintenance of peace' in the Balkans.[38] Indeed, in terms of numbers the tribunal has produced some positive results: overall, 161 individuals have been indicted and 74 of them have been found guilty of violations of international criminal law.[39]

Nevertheless, this has not resulted in a more reconciled Balkan population. Surveys in the region suggest that only a tiny percentage of people trust the ICTY (7.6 per cent in Serbia and 3.6 per cent in the Serb part of Bosnia and Herzegovina) and that the majority of Serbs consider it biased against them.[40] This profound hostility is coupled with a lack of knowledge about the institution itself: there is the misconception that it unfairly and overwhelmingly indicts Serbs, and the majority of the Serb population considers it 'the greatest danger to national security.'[41] A sizable number of people polled (19 per cent) believe that Serbia

33 Dinah Shelton, *Remedies in International Human Rights Law* (Oxford: Oxford University Press, 2006), Chapters 13 and 14.

34 Patricia Lundy and Bill Rolston, 'Redress for past harms? Official apologies in Northern Ireland,' *The International Journal of Human Rights*, Vol 20, No 1 (2016), 104–122.

35 Gary Jonathan Bass, *Stay the Hand of Vengeance: The Politics of War Crimes Tribunals* (Princeton and Oxford: Princeton University Press, 2000), 305.

36 Aoife Duffy, 'A Truth Commission for Northern Ireland?' *International Journal of Transitional Justice*, Vol 4, No 1 (2010), 26–46.

37 Robert Cryer, Hakin Friman, Darryl Robinson and Elizabeth Wilmshurst, *An Introduction to International Criminal Law and Procedure* (Cambridge: Cambridge University Press, 2010), 135.

38 Preamble of United Nations Security Council Resolution 827 (1993).

39 Key figures of the cases of the ICTY, www.icty.org/sid/24 [accessed 12 January 2015].

40 Mikro Klarin, 'The Impact of the ICTY Trials on Public Opinion in the Former Yugoslavia,' *Journal of International Criminal Justice*, Vol 7 (2009), 89–96, 91–92.

41 Ibid, 89.

should not cooperate with the ICTY no matter the cost, while only 15 per cent believe it is important to do so for reasons of justice and reconciliation.[42] These statistics should have been expected considering there has been no public campaign that addresses the Balkan population, explains the purpose of the ICTY and presents the tribunal's findings in a neutral way. As a result, rather than the ICTY's decisions being perceived as attempts to punish certain individuals for violations of international criminal law, they have been portrayed as unwarranted attempts by the international community to collectively punish the defendants' ethnic groups as a whole. If such outcomes are to be avoided, peacebuilders must identify and work towards achieving those conditions which promote, rather than undermine, the reconciliation-promoting potential of human rights.

In the presence of these conditions, human rights can support reconciliation efforts in divided societies in two additional ways. The first stems from the fact that human rights are popularly associated with ideas such as dignity and respect of the person.[43] Adhering to and respecting these ideas can contribute to the rehumanization of members of the other ethnic group and ultimately lead to reconciliation. The second is based on the notion that human rights can challenge dominant narratives that present one group's identity as diametrically opposed to the other's. By highlighting the concerns that members of various ethnic groups have in common, human rights advocates reject perceptions of unavoidably conflicting interests between them. An example of this is the foundation of the Northern Ireland's Women Coalition, the members of which, Protestant and Catholic alike, building on their common experiences, worked towards the protection of women's rights.[44] Nevertheless, while these are important ways in which human rights can contribute to reconciliation, expressions such as 'dignity,' 'respect of the person' and 'common interests between the ethnic groups' do not frequently find their way to courts, which is where the legal protection of fundamental interests takes place.[45] Although human rights language can contribute to reconciliation, therefore, the extent of its contribution should not be exaggerated.

Moreover, if the language of human rights can lead to reconciliation, the reverse is also true since references to reconciliation have often been (ab)used in such a way so as to prevent robust human rights protections. This danger, identified by McEvoy *et al.* when analysing the conflict in Northern Ireland, usually arises when the powerful group in the society argues that the ethnic conflict exists because of a lack of reconciliation rather than due to human rights abuses.[46] Attempts by the weaker party to label the problem as one of non-compliance with human rights

42 Ibid, 93.
43 Bertrand Ramcharan, 'Human Rights and Human Security,' *Disarmament Forum*, Vol 3 (2004), 39–47, 45.
44 Robin Whitaker, 'Debating Rights in the New Northern Ireland,' *Irish Political Studies*, Vol 25, No 1 (2010), 23–45.
45 See: August and Another v Electoral Commission and Others (CCT8/99) [1999] ZACC 3.
46 Generally McEvoy, McEvoy and McConnachie.

law are often dismissed as being too divisive. Instead, attention is being focused on using the language of inter-ethnic cooperation and reconciliatory values. These values, however, can be abused and be detrimental to overall peacebuilding attempts, especially where they crowd out other activities that could have led to the remedying of past injustices in the country. This is what happened in Bosnia and Herzegovina, where shortly after the end of the war the leaders of the different ethnic groups committed to allow refugees to return to their homes and made vague political promises to this effect. This general talk of sustainable return (which in Bosnia was equated with reconciliation[47]) appeased the international community and stopped it from demanding more robust strategies for the remedying of displaced people.[48] Thus, while attempts for the remedying of displaced people began in 1996, by 2000, the first time the international community systematically started collecting statistics, only 12 per cent of applications by displaced people had been dealt with.[49] It took another half a decade for peacebuilders to abandon the language of reconciliation and replace it with actions that actually enforced human rights and resulted in the return of displaced people's properties.[50]

An additional limitation of human rights is that they can be abused by judges seeking to justify nationalist practices with which they personally agree. A tendency to view domestic courts separately from the larger institutional context in which they operate has resulted in the mistaken assumption that the judiciary is always progressive and independent.[51] Nevertheless, this is particularly misleading in relation to issues that have to do with ethnic identities, which deeply affect people's perceptions of what is right, whether they have had legal training or not.[52] Illustrative of the dangers of ethnically biased case law is the statistical evidence

47 Leopold Von Carlowitz, 'Resolution of Property Disputes in Bosnia and Kosovo: The Contribution to Peacebuilding,' *International Peacekeeping*, Vol 12, No 4 (2005), 547–561, 558.

48 Ayaki Ito, 'Politicisation of Minority Return in Bosnia-Herzegovina: The First Five Years Examined,' *International Journal of Refugee Law*, Vol 13, Nos 1/2 (2001), 98–122.

49 Office of the High Representative, 'Statistics: Implementation of the Property Laws in Bosnia and Herzegovina' (Sarajevo: Office of the High Representative, 31 May 2000), on www.ohr.int/plip/pdf/PLIP5.00.PDF [accessed 10 June 2014].

50 See: Charles Philpott, 'Though the Dog Is Dead, the Pig Must Be Killed: Finishing with Property Restitution to Bosnia Herzegovina's IDPs and Refugees,' *Journal of Refugee Studies*, Vol 18 (2005), 1–24.

51 Erik G. Jensen, 'The Rule of Law and Judicial Reform: The Political Economy of Diverse Institutional Patterns and Reformers' Responses,' in *Beyond Common Knowledge: Empirical Approaches to the Rule of Law*, edited by Erik G. Jensen and Thomas C. Heller (Stanford: Stanford University Press, 2003), 336–381.

52 See: Constitution of the Republic of Cyprus, Article 133(1)(1) for the Supreme Constitutional Court and Article 153(1)(1) for the High Court of Justice; Constitution of Bosnia and Herzegovina, Article VI(1)(a) and (b). See also: Sujit Choudhry and Richard Stacey, 'Independent or Dependent? Constitutional Courts in Divided Societies,' in *Rights in Divided Societies*, edited by Colin Harvey and Alex Schwartz (Oxford: Hart Publishing, 2012), 87–121.

gathered by Gibson and Gouws in South Africa, which suggests that an intolerant judgment of the Constitutional Court increases intolerant public attitudes in relation to the same issue from 58.3 per cent to 75 per cent.[53] An intolerant judgment, according to Gibson and Gouws, is one based on the idea that someone is not like us and therefore does not deserve our support; for instance, a court renders an intolerant judgment if it refuses to protect the civil liberties of an unpopular, or highly disliked by the majority, group of people. Such intolerant judgments are problematic in themselves, but they become even more dangerous when they are couched in human rights language, which provides them with additional legitimacy and undermines reconciliation attempts even further.

This limitation of human rights can arguably be dealt with through a good vetting procedure and adequate training for the judiciary.[54] Human rights, however, also suffer from other – unavoidable – deficiencies. Perhaps the most important among them is that they make black-and-white distinctions between perpetrators and victims and thus often fail to reflect the complex terrain of a post-conflict society. They ignore, for example, that someone can, at the same time, be both a victim and a perpetrator of human rights violations and that there are those who committed violations yet, in the eyes of the people, acted justly.[55] An example of such an ambivalent figure is Winnie Mandela, who suffered greatly as a victim in the hands of the apartheid regime but was also allegedly responsible for human rights violations herself; violations which some members of the South African community considered necessary responses to the regime's actions.

Moreover, the language of human rights often clouds the fact that there are different types of perpetrators in a conflict.[56] For instance, in most conflict situations there are those who give the orders for human rights violations to be committed and others who execute the orders. Another part of the population falls into the category of people who were not actively involved in culpable acts but were nevertheless benefiting from these acts and therefore simply failed to stop or report them. These subtle distinctions between the different levels of culpability are lost when someone is labelled with the generic term 'perpetrator.'[57] Coupled with the fact that human rights are morally loaded concepts, with perpetrators always being presented as villains and those diametrically opposed

53 James L. Gibson and Amanda Gouws, *Overcoming Intolerance in South Africa: Experiments in Democratic Persuasion* (Cambridge: Cambridge University Press, 2003), 173.

54 This has happened in South Africa, for example, with the South African Judicial Education Institute Act [No 14 of 2008].

55 Tristan Anne Borer, 'A Taxonomy of Victims and Perpetrators: Human Rights and Reconciliation in South Africa,' *Human Rights Quarterly*, Vol 25 (2003), 1088–1116.

56 Ibid.

57 Mark Osiel, 'Who are Atrocity's "Real" Perpetrators, Who Its "True" Victims and Beneficiaries?' *Ethics and International Affairs*, Vol 28, No 3 (2014), 281–297.

to them being the disempowered victims,[58] human rights trials might polarize, rather than bring together, those ethnic groups that have different perceptions for who is to blame for the conflict.

A similar limitation of human rights exists in relation to victims. Prosecutions of human rights violations tend to only deal with an arbitrarily narrow segment of injustices caused during a conflict, either because these are deemed more important than others or due to evidentiary reasons. However, decisions to only prosecute specific types of violations often mean that those who suffered by unjust policies in other ways are not formally considered victims. This changes the way different types of harms caused by the conflict are portrayed and, as a result, affects people's perception of whether someone should be blamed for them. For example, the TRC in South Africa condemned violations of the right to life and freedom from torture, but did not deal with the more general discriminatory practices of the apartheid regime in relation to housing or education.[59] This narrow understanding of the harm caused by the regime made the general discriminatory practices less condemnable and those who committed or acquiesced to them less likely to apologize for their actions. Illustrative of this is the fact that 77 per cent of black South Africans consider apartheid to be a factor that has influenced land inequality in the country today, but only 34 per cent of white South Africans agree.[60] This difficulty of human rights to accurately describe the victims' experiences during a conflict risks polarizing members of ethnic groups rather than encouraging them to trust and cooperate with each other.

Promoting reconciliation through non-legal tools

Despite the UN's expectations of a positive connection between reconciliation and human rights, it transpires that often one undermines rather than promotes the other. Nevertheless, perhaps the most important observation about the relationship between the two terms is that in the majority of cases they are not connected at all. As Philpott put it, '[t]hough reconciliation encompasses core commitments of the liberal tradition, such as human rights, it is a far more holistic concept.'[61] In order for rehumanization and trust to develop in an ethnically divided, post-conflict society, which is what reconciliation requires, it is necessary for people to challenge some deeply held beliefs about their identity and that of the 'other.' While, therefore, reconciliation does not require the abandonment

58 Kieran McEvoy and Kirsten McConnachie, 'Victims and Transitional Justice: Voice, Agency and Blame,' *Social and Legal Studies*, Vol 22 (2013), 489–513; David Kennedy, 'The International Human Rights Movement: Part of the Problem?' *Harvard Human Rights Journal*, Vol 15 (2002), 101–126.

59 See: The South African Promotion of National Unity and Reconciliation Act [No 34 of 1995].

60 James L. Gibson, *Overcoming Historical Injustices: Land Reconciliation in South Africa* (Cambridge: Cambridge University Press, 2009), 46.

61 Daniel Philpott, 'An Ethic of Political Reconciliation,' *Ethics and Intentional Affairs*, Vol 23, No 4 (2009), 389–407, 390.

of ethnic identities, it does involve the re-evaluation of people's attitudes and perceptions. It is difficult, however, to see how such *psychological* changes can be the result of the *legal* protection of human rights.[62] Even where human rights are implemented successfully, which is not always the case, their enforcement will result in an amendment to the law, a change to the relevant procedures or a reform of an institution. Such changes might be necessary and beneficial for the societies under discussion because, for example, they promote the more effective functioning of different state institutions. They do not, however, automatically result in psychological changes *per se*.[63] In order for the legal protection of human rights to lead to social and eventually psychological changes, it must be supplemented by other peacebuilding strategies.

Illustrative of this is the ECHR decision of *Aziz* v *Cyprus*, which condemned the 50-year disenfranchisement of Turkish Cypriots in the Republic of Cyprus as a violation of the right to vote and freedom from discrimination.[64] The decision was swiftly enforced and the Cypriot electoral law was amended to allow the applicants and those in a similar position to vote.[65] In theory this legislative amendment, which treated Greek and Turkish Cypriots as equal citizens of the republic, should have contributed to the reconciliation efforts that are underway in the divided island. However, the legal change was not accompanied by any public debate about the issue, leaving most Greek Cypriots unaware of the amendment and its implications. Moreover, the new law was introduced without any popular discussion about the reasons why Turkish Cypriots had been disenfranchised in the first place. While the equal right to vote could have made a contribution to reconciliation, in the absence of a communication strategy to supplement the court's decision its positive effects remained marginal.

This is not to argue that changing a state's formal practices cannot eventually influence the politicians' and public's opinions and promote reconciliation. Gibson and Gouws provide statistical evidence that a hypothetical decision of the South African Constitutional Court to allow an unpopular party to protest would be likely to increase levels of 'grudging tolerance' in the population.[66] However, it is unclear what the long-term impact of such a decision would be on the people and whether tolerant attitudes usually take root or are ephemeral, especially when these judicial decisions are not accompanied by other reconciliation-promoting

62 For the contrary view see: Robert Sloane, 'The Expressive Capacity of International Punishment,' *Stanford Journal of International Law*, Vol 43 (2007), 39–94.

63 See: Colin Harvey, 'Contextualised Equality and the Politics of Legal Mobilisation: Affirmative Action in Northern Ireland,' *Social & Legal Studies*, Vol 21, No 1 (2012), 23–50.

64 *Aziz v Cyprus* (2005) European Human Rights Reports, Vol 41(2005), 11.

65 O π ερί Άσκησης του Δικαιώματος του Εκλέγειν και Εκλέγεσθαι απ ό Μέλη της Τουρκικής Κοινότητας π ου Έχουν Συνήθη Διαμονή σε Ελεύθερο Έδαφος της Δημοκρατίας (Προσωρινές Διατάξεις) Νόμος του 2006 (2(I)/2006) [The Law Concerning the Right to Vote and be Elected Members of the Turkish Community that Permanently Reside in the Unoccupied Areas of the Republic, Law of 2006 (2(I)/2006)].

66 Gibson and Gouws, Overcoming Intolerance in South Africa: Experiments in Democratic Persuasion, (Cambridge: Cambridge University Press, 2003), 171.

measures on the ground. Moreover, even if changes in laws and institutions are sometimes followed by a change in popular attitudes, this tends to be a fortuitous side-effect rather than a necessary consequence of mobilizing human rights. Promoting reconciliatory attitudes within a population requires legal and institutional amendments, changes in political and social attitudes and the rethinking of perceptions concerning the 'other.' Yet a human rights decision is considered as having been successfully implemented as soon as the legal and institutional amendments have been put into place. The success of human rights lawyers therefore arrives well before – and irrespective of whether – the social and psychological changes have taken place and the population has been reconciled. Finally, relatively few issues that have to do with inter-ethnic reconciliation can be put in legal language and be heard by the courts, and it is rare that judicial decisions are published broadly enough to become known to the public. Since the contributions of human rights to reconciliation tend to be indirect and sporadic, it is better to supplement them with other peacebuilding and reconciliation-promoting tools.

The limited power of human rights to *automatically* result in the social and psychological changes that are needed for reconciliation is not in itself a weakness, as long as it is acknowledged. If this happens, the implementation of human rights will promote legal and institutional changes while other peacebuilding tools will be used to support reconciliation efforts more directly. The problem arises from the fact that, in practice, peacebuilders have not acknowledged this limitation. The absence of 'legal humility'[67] and the expectation that 'a bit more human rights can never make things worse'[68] have resulted in an overemphasis on their protection. This has shifted attention away from other peacebuilding strategies that could have addressed psychological grievances and promoted reconciliation more effectively. An illustrative example of this is the tendency in many post-conflict societies to assume that the protection of the right to property is in itself sufficient to promote reconciliation among the displaced population.[69] The legal protection of the right to property is indeed the most appropriate tool for the transfer of the property title. It is ill-suited, however, for the task of cultivating reconciliatory ideas, such as that the occupier of the refugee's property might have been a victim of forced displacement himself or that his actions could have been motivated by necessity rather than hatred. The problem of displacement is both a legal and a psychological one; if peacebuilders seek to address it only by relying on the legal protection of human rights, different ethnic groups might return to their houses but this will likely result in mere coexistence rather than meaningful cooperation with each other.[70]

67 Kieran McEvoy, 'Beyond Legalism: Towards a Thicker Understanding of Transitional Justice,' *Journal of Law & Society*, Vol 34, No 4 (2007), 411–440, 425.

68 Kennedy, 124.

69 Theunis Roux, 'Land Restitution and Reconciliation in South Africa,' in *Justice and Reconciliation in Post-Apartheid South Africa*, edited by Francois Du Bois and Antje Du Bois-Pedain (Cambridge: Cambridge University Press, 2008), 144–171.

70 Charles Philpott, 'Though the Dog is Dead, the Pig must be Killed: Finishing with Property Restitution to Bosnia-Herzegovina's IDPs and Refugees', *Journal of Refugee Studies*, Vol. 18, No. 1 (2005), 1–24.

Acknowledging that, in addition to the positive and negative relationship between human rights and reconciliation, the two are often not connected at all can fundamentally change the strategies adopted by peacebuilders in the societies under discussion. This analysis suggests that protecting legal human rights, strengthening the judiciary and making governmental institutions more efficient is important. It is also necessary for peacebuilders to focus on the – often-ignored – people on the ground. An example where this happened, albeit to a limited extent, is in Bosnia and Herzegovina, where the international community funded enterprises that were jointly run by members of different ethnic groups.[71] Among the most successful projects was the creation of a coffee and cake shop in the Bosnian city of Drvar, which became the first place to not be characterized in ethnic terms and as a result was frequented by members of all ethnic communities.[72] It is steps such as this that can supplement the protection of human rights and can most effectively promote reconciliation among victims and perpetrators.

Conclusion

The UN's expectation that reconciliation and human rights are positively connected is accurate. It is, however, also subject to several conditions. Human rights must be interpreted by judges and other officials who are positively predisposed to reconciliation efforts. Moreover, a public campaign is required that will reliably inform the people of important legal decisions and promote a reconciliatory dominant narrative. Even if these conditions are satisfied, peacebuilders must acknowledge that the protection of human rights, if narrowly understood as legal tools, can also have negative consequences for reconciliation. The simple distinctions made between perpetrators and victims are not always – or even often – representative of what happened during a conflict. As a result, and especially because labelling an individual as a human rights violator can be perceived as an attack on his entire ethnic group, the legal protection of human rights might result in further polarization.

Equally important to acknowledging the positive *and* negative connections between reconciliation and human rights is the realization that the two might not be connected at all. Human rights, as the UN has understood the term, seem to result in legal, procedural and institutional changes to an ethnically divided society. If this is to be transformed to a reconciled one, psychological changes must also take place. These are most effectively induced not through legal tools such as human rights but by adopting peacebuilding strategies that directly address the people on the ground. The best peacebuilding recipe, therefore, is to take human rights with a pinch of salt and balance any positive contributions

71 Huma Haider, '(Re)Imagining Coexistence: Striving for Sustainable Return, Reintegration and Reconciliation in Bosnia and Herzegovina,' *International Journal of Transitional Justice*, Vol 3, No 1 (2009), 91–113.

72 Ibid, 106.

they are likely to make to reconciliation with the unavoidable dangers and limitations that accompany them.

8 Human rights as acts of faith

Universal jurisdiction and the Law of Historical Memory in Spain

Barry Collins

The rise and fall of Baltasar Garzón, the campaigning Spanish judge, dramatically drew international attention to Spain's struggle with the legacy of Francoism. Garzón, who throughout his career displayed a crusading attitude to human rights, was deeply involved in many high-profile cases. He played a key role in the prosecution of Basque militants during the 1980s and 1990s and, in 1994, sought the prosecution of a government interior minister who had been involved in an assassination campaign against Basque militants (the infamous GAL case). He was also instrumental in the development of Spain's Law of Universal Jurisdiction (LOPJ), although his attempt to extradite the former Chilean dictator, Augusto Pinochet, from the United Kingdom in 1998 proved unsuccessful.[1] This was the first time that a head of state had been arrested on the basis of universal jurisdiction. The campaigning judge obtained a more successful result for universal jurisdiction in 2005, when Adolfo Scilingo, a former Argentine military officer, was convicted for crimes against humanity committed during Argentina's military dictatorship. Such cases were crucial to the definition of human rights in modern Spain, and they made Garzón a household name.

However, his fall from high office was equally dramatic. In 2008 he began investigating 22 cases involving the disappearances of more than 100,000 people between 1936 and 1951. His action was highly controversial and, as a result, he became the subject of virulent press criticism. He was accused of undermining the principles that had enabled the transition from dictatorship to democracy. Additionally, Spain's 1977 amnesty law, which exempted from prosecution 'all crimes of a political nature' committed under the Franco dictatorship from 1939–75, hampered his investigation.[2] In response Garzón, citing recent

1 Re: *Pinochet*, Spanish National Court (*Audiencia Nacional*), Criminal Division, Case 19/97, 4 November 1998.

2 Law of Amnesty (*Ley de Amnistía*) (Law 46/1977), *BOE*, 248, 17 October 1977. See further: Angela M. Guarino, 'Chasing Ghosts: Pursuing Retroactive Justice for Franco-Era Crimes against Humanity,' *Boston College International and Comparative Law Review*, Vol 33 (2010), 61–85.

jurisprudence of the European Court of Human Rights, argued that the amnesty did not apply to crimes against humanity.[3]

In 2010, soon after launching his investigations, Garzón was prosecuted and suspended for malpractice. He was suspended initially as a result of a legal action initiated by a right-wing organization called *Manos Limpias* (Clean Hands), a trade union associated with the neo-Fascist right, and accused of a judicial malpractice known as prevarication. It was alleged he changed the legal criteria surrounding indictable offenses in order to sidestep the 1977 amnesty law, and that by doing so had attempted to pervert the course of justice. Garzón appealed to the Supreme Court (*Tribunal Supremo*), alleging the prosecuting judge, Luciano Varela, had a prejudicial involvement with the plaintiffs. In a separate case he alleged that five of the seven Supreme Court judges who were likely to judge him had a partial interest in the outcome of the case.

In 2012 he was cleared of abusing his powers in relation to his investigation of Franco-era crimes.[4] In the meantime, two other legal actions alleging malpractice were brought against him. One of these led to his conviction for unlawfully authorizing wire-taps in a prominent corruption case (the *Gürtel* case) involving the Popular Party (*Partido Popular*). It should be noted that, although other judges in the case also ordered wire-taps, he was the only one to be prosecuted and despite the fact that the public prosecutor had said there were no grounds for criminal proceedings, Garzón was stripped of his judicial powers for a period of 11 years.

A *New York Times* editorial described the decision as a 'miscarriage of justice' and a 'chilling verdict' that was '. . .enormously damaging to the prospects of fair and impartial justice.'[4] Amnesty International described his trial as a 'blow to human rights.'[5] Garzón's removal from judicial office demonstrated to many observers that there were certain issues still off limits in Spanish society, particularly in relation to the 1977 amnesty law.

In contrast to the zeal with which the suspension of Garzón was pursued, Spanish courts have routinely thwarted attempts to investigate historical human rights abuses within the country. It is hard to avoid the conclusion that Garzón's investigation into Franco-era atrocities touched a raw nerve within the Spanish legal and political establishment, for which he paid a high price. Ironically his previous activities as an activist judge did not attract such hostility, and his close involvement with Spain's LOPJ, although controversial, did not lead to political

3 The European Court of Human Rights held in 2009, as a general principle, that an amnesty law is generally incompatible with states' duty to investigate acts of torture or barbarity. *Ould Dah v France* (dec.), no.13113/03, ECHR (2009).

4 'A Chilling Verdict in Spain,' *New York Times*, 10 February 2012, www.nytimes.com/2012/02/11/opinion/a-chilling-verdict-in-spain.html [accessed 20 November 2016].

5 'Spain: Trial of Judge Baltasar Garzón a blow to human rights,' Amnesty International, www.amnesty.org/en/latest/news/2012/01/spain-trial-judge-baltasar-garz-n-blow-human-rights/ [accessed 20 November 2016].

(or indeed judicial) persecution. This points us towards an interesting comparison between the two. In this chapter I will discuss some contrasting features of these two aspects of human rights law and practice in Spain, and examine what they tell us about human rights discourse and the field of politics.

Spain's Law of Universal Jurisdiction

The universal jurisdiction law was adopted in 1985.[6] It allowed Spain to prosecute crimes of terrorism, genocide and other war crimes under international conventions, wherever these were committed, as long as there were no proceedings against the alleged perpetrators in their own countries or in another international forum. The LOPJ offers, in theory at least, considerable flexibility in the prosecution of international crimes. This has been of particular interest to those seeking redress for historical wrongs. In the absence of political initiatives that address historical atrocities, universal jurisdiction laws may be the only available course of action. However, as this essay will explore, the exercise of universal jurisdiction in the Spanish context has been fraught with inconsistency, raising interesting questions about the value of law as a means of pursuing historical justice.

Before examining in detail the Spanish experience, it is worth recalling the exercise of universal jurisdiction in Belgium, which played a pioneering role in developing the concept. Belgium in 1993 adopted a law that allowed domestic courts to prosecute individuals for war crimes. The law was extended in 1999 to include prosecutions for genocide and crimes against humanity.[7] The statute was broadly worded and allowed prosecution for crimes wherever committed. There was also no need to show a connection between the crimes alleged and Belgium. The high water mark of the Belgian universal jurisdiction law was a 2001 prosecution of four Rwandans who were convicted of war crimes.[8] Some controversial, but ultimately inconsequential, cases then ensued, including cases lodged against Ariel Sharon for his involvement in the massacres committed in Sabra and Shatila in Lebanon in 1982 and a case against Yasser Arafat for terrorist activity. In total almost 30 lawsuits were initiated in the Belgian courts against various world leaders and senior officials. In 2000 the court issued an arrest warrant against Abdoulaye Yerodia Ndombasi, the Democratic Republic of Congo's foreign affairs minister. The Democratic Republic of Congo challenged the warrant before the International Court of Justice, arguing it violated the immunity of their officials from

6 Organic Law of Judicial Power, *Ley Orgánica del Poder Judicial* (Organic Law 6/1985), 14 Boletín Oficial del Estado, 157, 2 July 1985 (hereafter referred to as LOPJ).

7 Act of 16 June 1993 Concerning the Punishment of Grave Breaches of the Geneva Conventions of 12 August 1949 and their Additional Protocols I and II of 18 June 1977. This law was modified by the Act of 10 February 1999 Concerning the Punishment of Grave Breaches of International Humanitarian Law to include crimes against humanity and genocide.

8 Verdict of Assize Court of Brussels, Decision of 8 June 2001, *Jura Falc.* (2003–04), 247 (also known as the *Butare Four* case).

criminal prosecution.[9] Although the court did not consider the validity of universal jurisdiction by national courts as a general principle, it found, by drawing on customary international law, that Belgium had violated its legal obligations towards the Democratic Republic of Congo. Consequently it called on Belgium to rescind the arrest warrant. State officials, it declared, were entitled to immunity from prosecution by national courts of other jurisdictions to ensure the effective performance of their functions. This immunity extended to war crimes and crimes against humanity. In an important dissenting judgment, Judges Buergenthal, Higgins and Kooijmans insisted that this immunity is a procedural rather than a substantive one; one that only applied during the period while they were performing their official function. It did not permanently exonerate them from all criminal responsibility (crucially, international criminal tribunals recognize no such immunity).[10] In 2003 a case was lodged against George H.W. Bush, Dick Cheney and Colin Powell for the bombing of a bomb shelter during the 1991 Gulf War that killed some 400 civilians. Following this, Belgium faced immense diplomatic pressure from the United States and other allies to change its law. In 2003 Belgium replaced its Law of Universal Jurisdiction with a far more limited Law on Extra-Territorial Jurisdiction, which required the victim of an alleged crime to be a Belgian resident of three years' standing in order to make a claim.[11] With hindsight, the Belgian's Law of Universal Jurisdiction seems to have over-reached itself in its ambition; an ambition that foundered on the practicalities of international *realpolitik* and the practice of customary international law.[12]

The Spanish LOPJ followed a somewhat similar trajectory to that in Belgium. This legislation initially gave Spain's courts jurisdiction over crimes committed outside Spain when such crimes could, under Spanish law, be classified as genocide and terrorism, or any other crime that, according to international treaties or conventions, must be prosecuted in Spain.[13] This wide definition of jurisdiction, which did not require that either the accused or the applicant be a Spanish citizen, led to some interesting litigation in the 1990s. In the hands of activist judges, such as Garzón, the Spanish courts used the LOPJ to launch international prosecutions in Spain for numerous human rights violations around the world. Prosecutions were directed against military officers who committed atrocities in the Guatemalan civil war, against Jiang Zemin, former Chinese president, for

9 Arrest warrant case (No 1), judgment of 14 February 2002, *ICJ Reports* (2002), 14.
10 Ibid (Joint separate opinion of Judges Higgins, Kooijmans and Buergenthal), para. 74.
11 Law of 5 August 2003 on Serious Violations of International Humanitarian Law.
12 See: Noora Arajärvi, 'Looking Back from Nowhere: Is There a Future for Universal Jurisdiction over International Crimes?' *Tilburg Law Review*, Vol 16 (2011), 5–29; Roozbeh B. Baker, 'Universal Jurisdiction and the Case of Belgium: A Critical Assessment,' *ILSA Journal of International and Comparative Law*, Vol 16 (2009), 141–167; M. Halberstam, 'Belgium's Universal Jurisdiction Law: Vindication of International Justice or Pursuit of Politics?' *Cardozo Law Review*, Vol 25 (2003), 247–267; Kingsley Chiedu Moghalu, *Global Justice: The Politics of War Crimes Trials* (New York: Greenwood, 2006).
13 Organic Law of Judicial Power, *Ley Orgánica del Poder Judicial* (Organic Law 6/ 1985), 14 Boletín Oficial del Estado 157, 2 July 1985, Article 23.4.

genocide in Tibet, and against Israeli general Dan Halutz and defense minister Binyamin Ben Eliezer for the killing of civilians in Gaza. In 2008 some 40 senior Rwandan officials were indicted for crimes against humanity committed in the aftermath of the Rwandan genocide. In 2009 Judge Garzón considered filing charges against US officials for the use of torture in Guantánamo Bay, including Alberto Gonzales, the former attorney-general.

One notable success of the legislation (and indeed of Garzón) was the prosecution and imprisonment of Scilingo, the former Argentine naval officer who had participated in the torture and murder of political detainees during the Argentine dictatorship.[14] The 1985 law, which allowed for prosecutions for genocide and terrorism, made no mention of crimes against humanity. The law provided for the prosecution of crimes which according to international treaties had to be prosecuted in Spain; but there was no particular treaty obliging Spain to prosecute crimes against humanity. The Spanish National Court (*Audiencia Nacional*) held that 'the universality of prosecution of crimes against humanity was beyond question, particularly if exercised by international tribunals.'[15] This analysis was upheld by the Supreme Court, which declared that the crimes in question were identical in their nature and gravity to genocide, crimes against peace, and war crimes. A second case involving a former Argentine officer, Ricardo Miguel Cavallo, also had a successful outcome. Cavallo was extradited from Mexico to Spain in 2000 on charges of genocide and terrorism committed during the Argentine dictatorship. In 2005 the Argentine Supreme Court declared that a previous law guaranteeing immunity for crimes committed during the dictatorship was unconstitutional; in 2008 Spain consequently extradited Cavallo to Argentina, where he was convicted of the offenses and sentenced to life imprisonment.

The broad approach to the definition of universal jurisdiction, which is evident in the Scilingo case, indicates the readiness of the Spanish courts to embrace an expansive concept of universal jurisdiction for crimes against humanity, even though this concept was not expressly incorporated into the original 1985 statute. However, with the exception of the Cavallo and Scilingo cases, most of the cases taken under the Spanish LOPJ proved entirely unworkable. In genocide cases involving Guatemala and Alberto Fujimori, the former Peruvian president, the Spanish courts adopted a 'necessity of intervention' test, by which the Spanish court could not intervene if an investigation was already taking place at the national level.[16] In 2009, in response to international pressure, the Spanish parliament

14 See: Christian Tomuschat, 'Issues of Universal Jurisdiction in the Scilingo Case,' *Journal of International Criminal Justice*, Vol 3 (2005), 1074–1081 and Richard Wilson, 'Spanish Supreme Court Affirms Conviction of Argentine Former Naval Officer for Crimes Against Humanity,' *American Society of International Law Insights*, No 12 (2008): www.asil.org/insights/volume/12/issue/1/spanish-supreme-court-affirms-conviction-argentine-former-naval-officer [accessed 20 November 2016].

15 See Tomuschat 1079.

16 Beth Van Schaack and Ronald Slye, *International Criminal Law and its Enforcement* (New York: Foundation Press, 2007), 120.

sought to limit the scope of the LOPJ by limiting universal jurisdiction to cases where: the alleged perpetrator was in Spain; there were Spanish victims; and there was a relevant link between the perpetrator to Spain. Additionally, the new law provided that a case must be dismissed if proceedings on the same facts had been lodged before any other domestic or international court.[17] Further international pressure, particularly from China, led to a second, more substantial, restriction. It was introduced by the conservative *Partido Popular* government in 2014 and, among other modifications, provided that the exercise of universal jurisdiction must be legitimated and justified by the existence of an international treaty that provides for or authorizes it.

As Alija Fernández points out, though, universal jurisdiction is not typically imposed by international treaties (with the exceptions of the Convention against Torture and Other Cruel, Inhuman or Degrading Treatment or Punishment (CAT) and the International Convention for the Protection of All Persons from Enforced Disappearance (CPED)). Additionally, as she notes, there are no equivalent treaties providing for universal jurisdiction in relation to genocide, crimes against humanity and war crimes, apart from the 1949 Geneva Conventions.[18] The limitations created by the 2014 legislation not only required that the more politically contentious indictments (including those against China) had to be withdrawn. Universal jurisdiction was removed from the Spanish legal system for all practical purposes, although formally still maintained on the statute books.

While it is true that the LOPJ enjoyed a couple of remarkable successes, the exercise of universal jurisdiction in Spain typically involved the issuing of writs that were never likely to lead to an actual prosecution. Indeed, the strength of the LOPJ usually lay not in actual court outcomes but in the field of public opinion, as it drew international attention to particular human rights abuses. In this sense the LOPJ projected a global image of Spain as a campaigning nation for human rights on the global stage. This was notwithstanding Spain's failure to prosecute the perpetrators of its own domestic atrocities.

During the high point of the LOPJ there was, of course, an unavoidable irony evident in the fact that the Spanish legal system, which had consistently failed to deal with the atrocities committed by the Franco regime, could enable judges to show flexibility in the pursuit of human rights abuses committed overseas. The indictments could be unpredictable and inconsistent, but they also created the

17 Law Modifying the Organic Law of Judicial Power (Ley Orgánica 1/2009, de 3 de noviembre, complementaria de la Ley de reforma de la legislación procesal para la implantación de la nueva Oficina judicial, por la que se modifica la Ley Orgánica 6/1985, de 1 de julio, del Poder Judicial), 1/2009, BOE 266, 4 November 2009, Article 23.4. See further: José Elías Esteve Moltó, 'Causes and Initial Effects of the Spanish Organic Law 1/2009; Reforming the Principle of Universal Jurisdiction in Spain,' *Spanish Yearbook of International Law Online*, Vol 16 (2010), 19–53.

18 Rosa Ana Alija Fernández, 'The 2014 Reform of Universal Jurisdiction in Spain: From All to Nothing,' *Zeitschrift fur Internationale Strafrechtsdogmatik*, Vol 13 (2014), 717–727, 719.

remarkable anomaly whereby Argentine suspects could be prosecuted in Spain for committing war crimes in Argentina but Spanish suspects who had committed equivalent crimes in Spain could not. It should not be forgotten, however, that the divisions of the Franco era (and indeed of the civil war) continue to fracture the Spanish political landscape. Although the Socialist Party (PSOE) government of José Luis Rodriguez Zapatero in 2007 made important strides in addressing Spain's past through the Law of Historical Memory (which will be further examined below), it is notable that no Spanish government since the transition to democracy – socialist or otherwise – has sought to repeal the 1977 amnesty law. Indeed, the Spanish left in the post-Franco period (from the government of Felipe González onwards) can be accused of having made a Faustian pact: forgetting the past as the price of power. The Spanish political establishment, and indeed the Supreme Court, was quite willing to tolerate Garzón's quixotic pursuit of human rights claims under the LOPJ, but ruthlessly unforgiving when he sought to bring the same human rights principles to bear on the political situation in Spain.

Debates around universal jurisdiction tend to be polarized. On the one hand, opponents of the principle, such as Henry Kissinger, have argued that universal jurisdiction is a new concept that undermines state sovereignty and is not authorized by existing human rights instruments. Kissinger argues that universal jurisdiction fails to take account of processes of national reconciliation, in which amnesties for perpetrators are made as part of a conflict-resolution process.[19] A more sophisticated argument was made by Goldsmith and Krasner, who charged the defenders of universal jurisdiction (in particular the drafters of the 2001 Princeton principles on universal jurisdiction) with a dangerous idealism, accusing them of underestimating the political interests at stake in international criminal prosecutions.[20] Goldsmith and Krasner observe that 'because relevant constituencies cannot hold courts exercising universal jurisdiction accountable for the negative consequences of their rulings, the courts themselves will invariably be less disciplined and prudent than would otherwise be the case.'[21]

The counter-argument, however, holds that crimes against humanity transcend the national context. Kenneth Roth argues that Kissinger's argument is simply an excuse for impunity and that universal jurisdiction has precedents in, for example, the Eichmann trial, the torture convention of 1984 and the Geneva Conventions of 1949.[22] (It is perhaps no coincidence that Garzón also considered

19 Henry A. Kissinger, 'The Pitfalls of Universal Jurisdiction,' *Foreign Affairs*, Vol 86 (2001), 90–91.

20 Jack L. Goldsmith and Stephen D. Krasner, 'The Limits of Idealism,' *Daedalus*, Vol 132 (2003), 47–63. See also Christiane Hohn, 'Comment on Jack Goldsmith & Stephen D. Krasner, The Limits of Idealism,' *Eyes on the International Criminal Court*, Vol 1, Issue 1 (2004), 99–113.

21 Goldsmith and Krasner, 51.

22 Kenneth Roth, 'The Case for Universal Jurisdiction,' *Foreign Affairs*, Vol 80 (2001), 150–155.

Kissinger a potential target for prosecution under the LOPJ on account of his involvement in the clandestine activities of Operation Condor in Latin America.) Goldsmith and Krasner's claim that universal jurisdiction ignores the domestic political scenarios in which human rights abuses take place is countered by Orentlicher's observation that 'societies do not deliberate in isolation. A fundamental feature of law and norm-generating activities is the participation of national communities in transnational processes.'[23] It can be argued that universal jurisdiction, despite the inconsistencies of its application, enables juridical intervention in the pursuit of human rights in situations where the political will is lacking. Indeed, from this perspective, it can also be argued that remoteness of universal jurisdiction from its political consequence enables judges the freedom to act unhindered by the machinations of interested political actors.

While the remoteness of universal jurisdiction indictments from political consequence is claimed as both a strength and weakness of the remedy, there is a deeper issue at stake about what the concept of universal jurisdiction means for human rights discourse. This separation of human rights discourse from the political field recalls Wendy Brown's description of human rights discourse as something of an anti-politics: 'a pure defense of the individual against immense and potentially cruel or despotic machineries of culture, state, war, ethnic conflict, tribalism, patriarchy, and other mobilizations or instantiations of collective power against individuals. . . .'[24] Brown here invokes the idea of human rights discourse as a free-floating normative discourse, disconnected from debates and consequences within the boundaries of the *polis*. However, such depoliticization of human rights discourse also begs Brown's question: 'what kind of politicization do those who intervene on behalf of human rights set in motion against the powers they oppose? Do they stand for a different formulation of justice? What relation do they have to principles or projects of collective justice?'[25] This is the question that snaps at the heels of universal jurisdiction: how does universal jurisdiction relate to questions of justice within the *polis*?

At the heart of any attempt to theorize universal discourse lies an opposition between two conceptions of human rights. Brown's description of a humanitarian 'anti-politics' stands in contrast to a more mundane conception of human rights as a tool to be employed to make legal and political claims within a political society. It is the former version that is more often engaged in universal jurisdiction, and this is certainly consistent with the Spanish experience. This is a conception of human rights as a global normative project, one which bears little relation to the collective implementation of justice. Human rights discourse operates in this ideological register as a system of faith. To oppose it appears unthinkable, at least

23 Diane Orentlicher, 'Whose Justice? Reconciling Universal Jurisdiction with Democratic Principles,' *Georgetown Law Journal*, Vol 92 (2004), 1057–1134 1066.

24 Wendy Brown, 'Human Rights as the Politics of Fatalism,' *South Atlantic Quarterly*, Vol 2, No 3, Spring (2004), 451–463 453.

25 Ibid.

in a liberal world-view, as to do so would appear to deny the unquestionable status of human rights as a global system of humanitarian values.

A useful way to think about the humanitarian (or anti-political) concept of human rights discourse is to examine its relation to the concept of the human. Universal jurisdiction is a jurisdiction of last resort, to be invoked when all other avenues for pursuing justice in the municipal legal system have failed. As such it is concerned with victims of human rights abuses whose suffering is excluded from recognition by political society. Does the concept of the victim here not also echo Giorgio Agamben's notion of *homo sacer* as the human being whose exclusion from the *polis* is such that he is stripped of all characteristics but 'bare life'? Drawing on the example of Nazi concentration camps, Agamben conceives of *homo sacer* as stripped of all rights, occupying a space of exception outside of legal-political concepts and defined outside the boundaries of humanity.[26] Such global humanitarianism removes the political context of the relationship between state and citizen. This denies to the victim of human rights violation any other political subjectivization other than that of victim. As Žižek observes '. . .paradoxically, in Agamben's version, I am deprived of my human rights at the very moment at which I am reduced to a human being in general and thus become the ideal bearer of those universal human rights which belong to me independently of my profession, sex, citizenship, religion, ethnic identity etc. . . .'[27] According to Žižek, such a 'post-modern,' 'anti-essentialist' description of *homo sacer* constructs the bearer of human rights by the 'political practices which materialize citizenship.'[28]

There is, as Jacques Rancière points out, a curious resonance between the transcendent humanitarianism found in the humanitarian conception of human rights and the conception of human rights as the product of reified political practice described by Agamben. Both conceptions in effect depoliticize human rights, situating the discourse of human rights more properly in the domain of ethics than in that of politics: 'Far from being pre-political, universal human rights designate the precise space of politicization proper; what they amount to is the right to universality itself, the right of the political agent to assert its radical non-coincidence with itself.' Rancière warns that, if we try to conceive of political rights without reference to the universal, we run the risk of 'losing politics itself . . . reducing politics to a post-political play of particular interests.'[29] The depoliticization of human rights discourse reframes political questions as a simple ethical opposition between good and evil, taking them out of the context of the

26 Giorgio Agamben, *Homo Sacer – Sovereign Power and Bare Life* (Redwood City: Stanford University Press, 1998).

27 Slavoj Žižek, 'Against Human Rights,' *New Left Review*, Vol 34 (2005), 115–131, 127. See also Slavoj Žižek, 'Weclome to the Spiritual Kingdom of Animals,' *The Meaning of Rights: The Philosophy and Social Theory of Human Rights*, edited by Costas Douzinas and Conor Gearty (Cambridge: Cambridge University Press, 2014) 298–318.

28 Slavoj Žižek, *The Universal Exception* (London: Bloomsbury, 2007), 244.

29 Jacques Rancière, 'Who is the Subject of Human Rights?' *South Atlantic Quarterly*, Vol 2, No 3 (2004), 297–310.

relationship between state and citizen. This denies to the victim of human rights violations any other political subjectivization other than that of victim.

Rancière also makes an interesting observation about what happens to human rights when they are conceived of as the rights of those who have no rights; who are not part of the *polis*. He notes that:

> When [human rights] are no use, one does the same as one does with old clothes. One gives them to the poor. Those rights that appear to be useless in their place are sent abroad, along with medicine and clothes, to people deprived of medicine and clothes and rights. . . . They become humanitarian rights, the rights of those who cannot enact them, the victims of the absolute denial of right. For all this they are not void. . . . The void is filled by somebody or something else. . . . If those who suffer inhuman repression are unable to enact human rights that are their last recourse, then somebody else has to inherit their rights in order to enact them in their place.[30]

This, of course, describes precisely the role of universal jurisdiction. When the victims of repression in other parts of the world have little recourse to justice in their own legal systems and are excluded from political society, it typically falls to those of other countries to speak on their behalf; to act for them. Most universal jurisdiction indictments are issued in Europe, notwithstanding the fact that the perpetrators in question are rarely likely to face European legal sanction. In this process a psychic circuit is completed; Europe, through demonstrating its commitment to human rights, receives a mirror image of itself as committed to a global, normative system of humanitarian values (as opposed to, for example, being the inheritor of a legacy of violent global colonialism). In this sense Europe's declaration of commitment to human rights, or its claim to be the home of human rights, reinforces an ideological self-image of the continent as a reservoir of global civilization and humanitarian values.

However, in the case of Spain's LOPJ another image is also revealed; that of a country in denial of its own violent and tragic past. Spain's adoption of such a broadly conceived universal jurisdiction law, when examined in the light of the country's failure to challenge the legal immunity of the perpetrators of Franco-era abuses, looks like a kind of overcompensation. Spain's incapacity to confront its past is the truth of its universal jurisdiction law. In psychoanalytical terms, this could be described as the sender receiving back his own message in its inverted (true) form.[31]

This is illustrated by Argentina's 2013 request under its own universal jurisdiction law for the arrest of former officials of the Franco regime for crimes against

30 Ibid, 307.

31 Jacques Lacan, seminar on 'The Purloined Letter,' translated by Jeffrey Mehlman, in *The Purloined Poe: Lacan, Derrida, and Psychoanalytic Reading*, edited by John P. Muller and William J. Richardson (Baltimore: Johns Hopkins University Press, 1987), 28–54.

humanity, including a former Civil Guard captain who is alleged to have tortured and beaten to death a detainee in 1968. The Spanish National Court rejected the extradition claim in Spain for crimes committed in the country between 1936 and 1977.[32] The court noted that the facts of the case did not indicate genocide (for which there is no statute of limitations) and that the allegation of torture was barred by a ten-year statute of limitations. In a further irony the court invited the Argentinian magistrate to initiate proceedings in Spain, a somewhat disingenuous request given the 1977 amnesty law and the experience of the Garzón debacle.

The Law of Historical Memory

However, the claims of human rights victims that are made within the *polis*, rather than in a global appeal to humanitarian values, operate in a different register as these are intimately connected both to political context and legal consequence. In Spain, for example, the campaign to document and commemorate the tens of thousands of victims of the Francoist repression, who lie in unmarked graves across the country, has been of necessity linked to an attempt to redefine the political reality and to challenge the 'pact of forgetting' that has characterized the transition to democracy. The number of people assassinated during the Francoist repression between 1936 and 1975 is a matter of some dispute, but estimates vary from 150,000[33] to 400,000.[34] Notable among the civil society organizations campaigning for historical memory has been the Association for the Recovery of Historical Memory (*Asociación para la Recuperación de la Memoria Histórica* (ARMH)), which collects testimonies about the disappeared, identifies their places of execution and has conducted more than 150 exhumations.[35] The campaign led to the Spanish Law of Historical Memory (*Ley de la Memoria Histórica*), which was passed by the government of José Luis Rodríguez Zapatero in 2007.[36]

The law provided for: the recognition of the victims of violence on both sides of the Spanish Civil War and of Franco's regime; a condemnation of the Francoist dictatorship; a prohibition of political events at the Valley of the Fallen; the removal

32 Case 62/2013, National Court (*Audiencia Nacional*), Criminal Division, Decision of 24 April 2014.

33 Julián Casanova, Francisco Espinosa, Conxita Mir, Francisco Moreno Gómez. *Morir, matar, sobrevivir. La violencia en la dictadura de Franco* (Barcelona: Editorial Crítica, 2002), 8. Another widely quoted figure is that of 200,000 deaths, estimated by historian Paul Preston in Paul Preston, *The Spanish Holocaust* (London: Harper Press, 2012), 493.

34 Michael Richards, *A Time of Silence: Civil War and the Culture of Repression in Franco's Spain, 1936–1945* (Cambridge; Cambridge University Press, 1998), 11.

35 See: Joanna Bourke and Francesc Torres, *Dark is the Room where we Sleep/ Oscura es la Habitación donde Dormimos* (Barcelona: Actar, 2007). See further: Michael Humphrey, 'Law, Memory and Amnesty in Spain,' *Macquarie Law Journal*, Vol 13 (2014), 25–40.

36 Law of Historical Memory (Ley de Memoria Histórica / La Ley por la que se reconocen y amplían derechos y se establecen medidas en favor de quienes padecieron persecución o violencia durante la Guerra Civil y la Dictadura), Law 52/2007, Boletín Oficial del Estado, 310, 31 October, 2007.

of Francoist symbols from public buildings and spaces; state assistance in the tracing, identification and exhumation of victims of Francoist repression; a formal rejection of the legitimacy of laws passed and trials conducted by the Francoist regime; the granting of Spanish nationality to surviving members of the International Brigades; the provision of financial aid to the victims and descendants of the victims of the Franco regime; and the granting of the right of return and citizenship to those who left Spain under Franco and their descendants. The law was passed despite vociferous opposition by the *Partido Popular*, which argued it would reopen wounds and undermine the political consensus that has defined Spanish political reality since 1975. This consensus, known as the pact of forgetting (*el pacto del olvido*), meant that questions about the legacy of Francoism were suppressed to facilitate the creation of a multi-party democracy. In practice this meant that the Francoist narrative about the civil war and the post-war repression remained largely unchallenged at an official level. It also meant that the thousands of victims of the repression remained undocumented and their disappearance shrouded in mystery. The Spanish historical memory campaign has also had a significant international human rights dimension, including representations to the United Nations Human Rights Commission. Among the results of these interventions was a report by a UN working group on forced or involuntary disappearances, which recognized the 'significant, if tentative, steps . . . taken to secure truth, justice and reparation and to preserve memory in the context of the enforced disappearances committed during the civil war and the dictatorship.'[37]

However, the historical memory law has been criticized by the ARMH as a 'low-cost' law because it did not place a duty on local authorities to participate, merely encouraged them to assist.[38] Additionally the law did not overturn the 1977 amnesty and did nothing to challenge the impunity of perpetrators. The law has faced a further blow since the 2011 election of the *Partido Popular*, which has largely withdrawn government support for the campaign for historical memory. The UN working group report noted the 'deep frustration at the administrative hurdles and [relatives'] difficulty in accessing the information they need to clarify the fate and whereabouts of their loved ones.'[39] It also noted the limited scope of the Historical Memory Act and the lack of any budget for its implementation; the continued applicability of the Amnesty Act as interpreted by the courts; impunity in all the cases of enforced disappearance; the fact that there is no separate offense of enforced disappearance; the lack of any law on access to information; the difficulty in accessing the archives; and the lack of any national plan on the search for disappeared persons.[40]

37 Report of the Working Group on Enforced or Involuntary Disappearances, United Nations Human Rights Council, 2 July 2014, 1. www.ohchr.org/EN/Countries/ENACARegion/Pages/ESIndex.aspx [accessed 18 November 2016].

38 James Badcock, 'UN tells Spanish Government it Must Atone for its War Crimes,' *Newsweek*, 21 August 2014, www.europe.newsweek.com/un-tells-spanish-government-it-must-atone-francos-crimes-265603?rm=eu [accessed 18 November 2016].

39 Ibid, 1.

40 Ibid, 16

The struggle surrounding the historical memory law situates human rights in an antagonistic political context. In this case, human rights are a site of contest, of argument about what kind of society Spain should be and how it should deal with its history. This contest is a reminder of the radical potential contained in human rights to transform the political community.

An interesting way to conceptualize the transformative capacity of human rights discourse can be found in a conception of how political struggle involves an effort to allow the excluded particular (what Žižek calls 'the part of no part'[41]) to occupy the place of the universal. Žižek describes this as the capacity of the particular to sometimes behave, in Rancière's words, as a *singulier universel*.[42] This can be illustrated by the occupation of the place of the universal by those who are historically excluded from power. Demands for inclusion by those excluded may be entirely compatible with the universalism of modern constitutionalism, but may simultaneously be deeply threatening to the political status quo underpinning the legal order. The demand made by the African National Congress during apartheid for equal rights for non-white South Africans, for example, was, at one level, a recognizable and simple demand for political rights in the liberal legal tradition. As such it had an irresistible force and logic within that legal tradition. However, it was also a demand whose realization would require a complete transformation of political society and the dismantling of white minority rule. In the example of historical memory in Spain, the demand for equal recognition of those murdered by the Franco regime is, on the face of it, a moderate political demand that fits easily within liberal legal discourse. It is a demand for inclusion and for the historical recognition of the victims of Francoist repression as equal members of Spanish political society. As such it is a demand whose moral claim, from a liberal legal (or human rights) perspective, is difficult to resist. On the other hand, it is also a demand that fundamentally challenges the broader historical narrative that has underpinned Spain's foundation as a democracy and a constitutional monarchy. The Law of Historical Memory also raises difficult questions about the legitimacy of the state's foundation, about the collusion of the Catholic Church in the commission and concealment of atrocities and about the complicity of Spaniards in the *pacto del olvido*: the institutional denial of mass murder. It is clear that this mode of human rights discourse, which is rooted firmly in the *polis*, has a transformative dimension not evident in the same way in the LOPJ.

Faith, law and memory

The disappearance of tens of thousands of Spaniards during the Franco years was an attempt to erase not just the political opponents of the regime but the memory of the republic itself. Does this not recall the Roman punishment of *damnatio memoriae*? This punishment, which was used against those who brought discredit

41 Slavoj Žižek, 'A Leftist Plea for Eurocentrism,' *Critical Inquiry*, Vol 24 (1998), 988–1009, 988.

42 Ibid.

to Rome, erased every trace of the victim's existence. A *damnatio memoriae* required that all statues and coins depicting the convicted person had to be removed and their name erased wherever written.[43] If the condemned person was a citizen they were retrospectively stripped of their citizenship, which sometimes meant erasing the person from legal documents, contracts and marital documents – from the public record itself. (It also means it is a very difficult phenomenon for historians to research, for the obvious reason that there are so few traces of the condemned.)

This is a useful way to think about the debate surrounding the Law of Historical Memory. At stake in this debate is not just the gradual fading of personal memories about the disappeared, but the more general principle that, in a democracy, former political dissidents cannot be erased from political society. Many of the executions committed under the Franco regime were planned and carried out after a legal process. Many were convicted under a 1939 law which declared that all those who had been a member of a popular front from 1934 onwards, and all those who had opposed or shown 'grave passivity' towards Franco's military coup, could be convicted of military rebellion.[44] Unlike the repression of Stalin or Hitler, this was not a general annihilation of a class of people based on some abstract category, nor was it an arbitrary spree of mass killing. It was, in the words of one researcher, 'constant, regular and methodical. It was not arbitrary in character, even though it often seemed so. The repression was frightful, but it was also selective and rational.'[45]

The continuing failure of Spain to document the disappeared in effect erases them from their historic place in the *polis*. The Law of Historical Memory, despite its failure to address the 1977 amnesty, plays an important role in addressing this *damnatio memoriae*, at the very least by restoring the integrity of public records. Ironically this act of restoring the public record is an act of restoring the political community to itself by reminding the people of its already fractured nature. This aspect of the historical memory law is a thoroughly political activity, as it seeks to effect a transformation within the *polis* despite the continuing impunity of the perpetrators.

By contrast, as this chapter has argued, Spain's LOPJ has operated in a very different way. Spain's pursuit of international human rights violators appears, on the best reading, to have been a noble, though not always fruitful, endeavor. A less generous reading of the LOPJ would see it as a law that distracted attention away from Spain's failure to address its own bloody past. Instead, Spain's universal jurisdiction is perhaps best understood as having been a loud public declaration of faith in human rights. However, it was not so much an expression of faith in the capacity of law to end impunity but in abstract humanitarianism as a value that transcends the political field.

43 Eric Varner, *Multilation and Transformation: Damnatio Memoriae and Roman Imperial Portaiture* (Leiden: Brill, 2004).

44 Law of Political Responsibilities (*Ley de Responsabilidades Políticas*), *BOE*, 44, 13 February 1939.

45 Josep Solé i Sabaté, *La Repressió Franquista a Catalunya* (Barcelona: Edicions 62, 2003) p. 268, quoted in Stanley G. Payne, *The Franco Regime, 1936–1975* (Madison: University of Wisconsin, 2011), 223.

9 The right to historical truth and historical memory versus historical revisionism and denialism

A human rights analysis

Kalliopi Chainoglou

Denial of genocides, negationism, trivialization of historical atrocities and claims to historical truth and historical memory often challenge the orthodox understanding of historical events. Such interpretations may result in historical revisionism and reshape historical memory[1]. During the past few decades there has been an increasing tendency to address such claims by reference to international human rights law and before international human rights judicial bodies. This chapter assesses the role of international judicial mechanisms when examining historical revisionism cases and laws against the denial of historical atrocities, and addresses how historical memory is mediated through the human rights judicial route. The analysis below compares and contrasts the approaches endorsed by the United Nations Human Rights Committee and the European Court of Human Rights and questions their suitability as courts of history and memory.

The interpretation and reinterpretation of historical facts can be at times highly politicized; this is not only related to the particularities of historiographic methodology, which may allow for empirical manipulation,[2] but also to the political or societal factors which aim to target historical memory at a particular moment. As Karl Schlogel has pointed out, 'the discourse about the past is in many cases only the encoded and masked form of a contemporary political debate, a proxy struggle, conducted in a historical costume.'[3]

1 Harris O'Boyle and Colin Warbrick, *Law of the European Convention on Human Rights* (Oxford: Oxford University Press, 2014), 626.

2 See: Michal Kopecek, *Past in the Making, Historical Revisionism in Central Europe after 1989* (Budapest: Central European University Press, 2013).

3 Karl Schlogel, 'Places and strata of memory: Approaches to Eastern Europe,' Eurozine (2008), www.eurozine.com/articles/2008-12-19-schlogel-en.html [accessed 21 September 2016].

It is also observed that states, especially those going through transitional periods, are often characterized by moves to forge a more authentic or 'official' past.[4] In certain cases states have matched their version of 'official past' with institutionalized forgetfulness and adoption of amnesty laws.[5]

While national narratives are expected to serve narrow ideological ends, the recovery of historical memory can be a painful, contradictory, messy or disturbing process that can entail forgetting.[6] However, despite the accepted plurality in approaches to historical memory,[7] the construction of historical narratives often – if not teleologically – stumbles on techniques illegitimate to historical discourse that ultimately lead to historical revisionism. Such techniques may include presenting known forged documents as genuine; inventing reasons for distrusting genuine documents; logical fallacies; manipulating statistical series to support the given point of view, etc. From this perspective the advancement of historical views can be an attempt to dress reconstruction or denial of historical events into the guise of trustworthy academic discourse. Yet historical revisionism is not limited to dubious discursive practices but often amounts to hate speech and incitement to discrimination, hostility or violence. The question that arises then is to what degree does historical revisionism actually constitute hate speech and to whom is the apology or the affirmative active action to truth owed?[8]

Legislative control over the collective memory and the criminalization of historical revisionism has resurfaced in national legal orders during the past few decades. This has not come as a surprise, given the millennium trend for transitional justice and post-conflict reparatory mechanisms.[9] A significant number of states have adopted a spate of laws, the so-called 'memory laws,' punishing the

4 This is the case for the Central and Eastern European states which have been committed to the construction of new national narratives; reflected in the emergence of new memorial sites across the region. See: Istvan Pogany, 'International Human Rights Law, Reparatory Justice and the Re-ordering of Memory in Central and Eastern Europe,' *Human Rights Law Review*, Vol 10, No 3 (2010), 397–428.

5 See for example *Margus v Croatia*, Application No 4455/10, Grand Chamber judgment of 27 May 2014.

6 See for example, Renata Uitz, *Constitutions, Courts and History: Historical Narratives in Constitutional Adjudications* (Budapest: CEU Press, 2005), 242.

7 See: Stiina Loytomaki, *Law and Politics of Memory: Confronting the Past* (Abingdon: Routledge, 2014).

8 See: Uladzislau Belavusau, *Historical Revisionism in Comparative Perspective: Law, Politics and Surrogate Mourning* (Budapest: European University Institute, 2013) 6. The author questions the construction of the 'victim' – for example, is it the intention of such laws to establish a 'legal fiction of second and third generation of traumatized victims' when considering the Holocaust atrocity in modern times? Another related issue would be the claim for insulting the reputation of deceased political figures. Such has been the case of *Dzhugashvili* v *Russia*, Application No 41123/10, Decision of Admissibility, 9 December 2014, which stemmed from Stalin's grandson suing a Russian newspaper for insulting Stalin's memory.

9 See: Dustin N. Sharp, 'Emancipating Transitional Justice from the Bonds of the Paradigmatic Transition,' *International Journal of Transitional Justice* (2014), 1–20.

denial of historical events.[10] Such laws may penalize the denial of the Holocaust, genocide or crimes against humanity, or even criticisms and negative comments concerning political figures in particular countries (for example Kemal Ataturk[11]) as expressed via public statements, publications or through posts on the internet.

'Memory laws' are often met with criticisms from legal scholars and groups of history militants.[12] These laws are deemed to contribute, in effect, to the shaping of the collective memory of historical facts, including facts of past violence.[13] A related aspect of the laws is that they form the basis of 'mnemonical security' whereby certain historical remembrances are made secure by means of law by delegitimizing or criminalizing others. The potential for the securitization of historical memory is obvious: it tends to reproduce a sense of insecurity among its contesters.[14]

Other criticisms of 'memory laws' are based on the grounds that the laws are deemed unduly restrictive of the freedom of expression as they can practically lead to the imposition of historical dogmas and stagnation in historical debate, which is incompatible with the normative content and the scope of the freedom of expression. The application of such 'memory laws' is also considered damaging to academic freedom; academics and scholars of history may subject themselves to self-censorship for fear of criminal prosecution.[15] In addition, despite the purported role of 'memory laws' in protecting the national identity or the identity of the group affected by the historical event, the laws can be pivotal to disparaging the 'national narrative.'[16]

10 See for example laws punishing the Holocaust denial in France, Germany, Italy, Lichtenstein, Romania, Russia, Austria, Slovakia and Belgium, and laws punishing the denial of atrocities committed by the communist regimes in Poland, Hungary, Slovakia, the Czech Republic and Lithuania.

11 For example, cases against Turkey have been brought on the grounds of violations of freedom of expression under article 10 ECHR concerning a law that prohibited 'insulting the memory of Ataturk.' See: *Cengiz and Others* v *Turkey*, Application Nos 48226/10 and 14027/11, judgment of 1 December 2015.

12 Robert A. Kahn, 'Does it matter how one opposes memory bans? A commentary on Liberte Pour L'Histoire,' *Washington University Global Studies Law Review*, Vol 15 (2015), 55–92.

13 See for example the Law of Historical Memory of Spain adopted in 2007. See: Michael Humphrey, 'Law, Memory and Amnesty in Spain,' *Macquarie Law Journal*, Vol 13 (2014), 25–40.

14 Maria Mälksoo, 'Memory must be defended: Beyond the politics of mnemonical security,' *Security Dialogue*, Vol 46, No 3 (2015), 221–237.

15 See: Alfred de Zayas and Aurea Roldan Martin, 'Freedom of Opinion and Freedom of Expression: Some reflections on General Comment No 34 of the UN Human Rights Committee,' *Netherlands International Law Review*, Vol 59 (2012), 425–454, 445.

16 See: Antoon De Baets, 'Conceptualising Historical Crimes,' *Historein*, Vol 11 (2011), 59–68; Pierre Nora, *History, Memory and the Law in France* (2011), at: www.lph-asso.fr/index.php?option=com_content&view=article&id=159%3Apierre-nora-qlhistoire-la-memoire-et-la-loi-en-france-1990–2008q&catid=53%3Aactualites&Itemid=170&lang=en [accessed 18 September 2016].

Furthermore, as a result of these memory laws, legal scholars have become involved in a complicated process entailing judicial pitfalls as the legal exclusion of untruthful writings, in the form of historical revisionist narratives, has to be examined on the assumption of the identification of facts (*vis-à-vis* the expression of opinions). As a consequence, legal professionals and judges find themselves in the 'uncomfortable' position of deliberating on what constitutes a true historical fact and thus essentially legislating on history.[17]

The picture that emerges is one where the right to historical truth and the right to historical memory conflict with historical revisionism and denialism under the wider umbrella of the exercise of the freedom of expression and intellectual freedom in a democratic state.[18]

In the UN system, denial of historical atrocities are covered by article 19 (freedom of expression)[19] and article 20(2)[20] (prohibition of hateful incitement) of the International Covenant of Civil and Political Rights (ICCPR).[21] The

17 See: Alfred de Zayas and Aurea Roldan Martin, 448. See also *Dzhugashvili* v *Russia*, para. 33, where the court noted that: 'It is not the court's role to arbitrate the underlying historical issues, which are part of a continuing debate between historians. A contrary finding would open the way to a judicial intervention in historical debate and inevitably shift the respective historical discussions from public forums to courtrooms.'

18 Another perspective could be that historical revisionism or denialism is affecting the collective memories and thus the narrative within which culture is developed. 'Culture consists of narratives which occupy our public space. These narratives form part of what we consider "heritage" and are lived, remembered and sustained through the individual. In this light, the engagement in cultural life entails how these narratives are created, interpreted, sustained and lived, shaping a form of collective memory.' In this way, revisiting history could have serious implications as to the enjoyment of cultural rights, the right to participate in cultural life etc. See: Pok Yin S. Chow, 'Culture as Collective Memories: An Emerging Concept in International Law and Discourse on Cultural Rights,' *Human Rights Law Review*, Vol 14, No 4 (2014), 611–646, 636. On the relationship between culture, heritage and human rights see Andreas J. Wiesand, Kalliopi Chainoglou, Anna Sledzinska, and Yvonne Donders (eds.), *Culture and Human Rights: The Wroclaw Commentaries* (Berlin/Boston: de Gruyter, 2016).

19 Article 19: 1. Everyone shall have the right to hold opinions without interference.

2. Everyone shall have the right to freedom of expression; this right shall include freedom to seek, receive and impart information and ideas of all kinds, regardless of frontiers, either orally, in writing or in print, in the form of art, or through any other media of his choice.

3. The exercise of the rights provided for in paragraph 2 of this article carries with it special duties and responsibilities. It may therefore be subject to certain restrictions, but these shall only be such as are provided by law and are necessary:

(a) For respect of the rights or reputations of others;
(b) For the protection of national security or of public order (ordre public), or of public health or morals.

20 Article 20(2): Any advocacy of national, racial or religious hatred that constitutes incitement to discrimination, hostility or violence shall be prohibited by law.

21 GA Res 2200A (XXI, 21 UN GAOR Supp. No 16, 52, UN Doc 1/6316 (1966) 999 UNTS 171. The ICCPR entered into force 23 March 1976 and has 168 state parties.

Human Rights Committee (HRC), which is the body monitoring the implementation of ICCPR by its state parties, has examined a number of complaints on alleged violations of the above provisions concerning memory laws and denial of historical facts.[22] The HRC's approach is that any restriction on the right to freedom of expression must cumulatively meet the following conditions: it must be provided by law; it must address one of the aims set out in paragraph 3 (a) and (b) of article 19; and it must be necessary to achieve a legitimate purpose.

The most controversial case heard by the HRC is *Faurisson* v *France*[23]. In this case the author was an academic who had argued that there had been no gas extermination chambers in Nazi death camps. He was convicted under a law (the Gayssot Act) which criminalized contesting the existence of the category of crimes against humanity as defined in the London Charter of 1945. The HRC considered the impugned statements on a content basis and held that the penalty in question was not a violation of article 19 as the denial of the existence of the Holocaust was 'the principle vehicle for anti-Semitism' and that 'the statements made by the author, read in their full context, were of a nature as to raise or strengthen anti-Semitic feelings.'[24] According to this doctrine, Holocaust denial results in anti-Semitism and could be equated to advocacy to hatred that constitutes incitement to discrimination, hostility or violence.[25]

Throughout the text of the decision of the HRC and the individual opinions of the HRC members in this case it is evident that the broadly formulated crime of denial could have been found in violation of the ICCPR provisions.[26] What stopped the HRC from concluding so was the fact that it chose to focus on the content of the speech and hence deem that the restriction was necessary, in that it 'served the respect of the Jewish community to live free from fear of an atmosphere of anti-Semitism' and that it 'was intended to serve the struggle against racism and anti-Semitism.'[27] The *Faurisson* approach, therefore, provides for memory laws to be compatible with the ICCPR provisions while imposing on the author of the complaint the burden of proof to undermine the necessity of the said restriction.[28]

22 See: Alfred de Zayas and Aurea Roldan Martin, 425.

23 Communication No 550/1993, *Faurisson* v *France*, UN Doc CCPR/C/58/D/550/1993 (1996), Admissibility Decision of 19 July 1995, http://hrlibrary.umn.edu/undocs/html/VWS55058.htm [accessed 18 September 2016].

24 Ibid, para. 9.6.

25 See for example *Faurisson* v *France*, Individual opinion by Rajsoomer Lallah, para. 4 and Individual opinion by Prafullachandra Bhagwatim.

26 See for example *Faurisson* v *France*, Individual opinion by Elizabeth Evatt, David Kretzmer, Eckart Klein, paras. 4 and 9.

27 *Faurisson* v *France*, para. 9.7. See also Jeroen Temperman, 'Laws Against the Denial of Historical Atrocities: A Human Rights Analysis,' *Religion & Human Rights*, Vols 2–3 (2014), 151–180.

28 *Faurisson* v *France*, para. 9.7.

Almost a decade later the HRC deviated from its original position in *Faurisson* v *France*,[29] opting for a more contextual approach. In 2011 it issued General Comment (GC) No 34 whereby it clarified the relationship between the ICCPR provisions and the memory laws:

> Laws that penalize the expression of opinions about historical facts are incompatible with the obligations that the Covenant imposes on States parties in relation to the respect for freedom of opinion and expression. The Covenant does not permit general prohibition of expressions of an erroneous opinion or an incorrect interpretation of past events. Restrictions on the right of freedom of opinion should never be imposed and, with regard to freedom of expression, they should not go beyond what is permitted in paragraph 3 or required under article 20.[30]

The essence of this paragraph is that generic-content memory laws will *a priori* be deemed in violation of the ICCPR provisions.[31] This view has been upheld also by the UN Rapporteur on the Promotion and Protection of the Right to Freedom of Opinion and Expression, who has commented that:

> historical events should be open to discussion. . . . By demanding that writers, journalists and citizens give only a version of events that is approved by the Government, states are enabled to subjugate freedom of expression to official versions of events.[32]

The GC is instrumental in that it also sets the threshold for the violation of article 19 when concerning memory laws: the mere dissemination of opinions on historical facts, even if they are historically dubious or historically wrong, are permissible as long as they do not lead to incitement to discrimination or violence

29 See: Temperman, 151–180.

30 Human Rights Committee, General Comment No 34: Article 19, Freedoms of Opinion and Expression (CCPR/C/GC/34, adopted at its 102nd session, Geneva, 11–29 July 2011), para. 49 (footnotes omitted).

31 Michael O'Flaherty, 'Freedom of Expression: Article 19 of the International Covenant on Civil and Political Rights' and the Human Rights Committee's General Comment No 34, *Human Rights Law Review*, Vol 12 (2012), 627–54, 653; Michael O'Flaherty, 'International Covenant on Civil and Political Rights: interpreting freedom of expression and information standards for the present and the future – critical perspectives,' in *The United Nations and Freedom of Expression and Information*, edited by Tarlach McGonagle and Yvonne Donders (Cambridge: Cambridge University Press, 2015) 55–88.

32 See also UN Special Rapporteur on the Promotion and Protection of the Right to Freedom of Opinion and Expression, Report of the Special Rapporteur to the General Assembly on Hate Speech and Incitement to Hatred, A/67/357, 7 September 2012, para. 55.

and they do not threaten the coexistence of a community. The position of the HRC here is thus in favor of drawing the line between activities contrary to the ICCPR and the mere dissemination of opinions including the non-conformist historical ones. It is the purpose of the HRC to impose the obligation on states to define carefully the elements of the crimes of 'incitement to racial hatred, discrimination or violence' and 'hate speech' when adopting memory laws, particularly laws with penalties, as they have to be very narrow and specific and frame their scope unambiguously in order to be compatible with the ICCPR. Furthermore, because restrictions on the freedom of expression may put in jeopardy the right itself, the HRC requires that '[w]hen a state party invokes a legitimate ground for restriction of freedom of expression, it must demonstrate in specific and individualized fashion the precise nature of the threat, and the necessity and proportionality of the specific action taken, in particular by establishing a direct and immediate connection between the expression and the threat.'[33] That means states are discouraged from adopting memory laws while they are encouraged to prosecute historical denialism cases under laws mirroring article 20(2) ICCPR; furthermore, states are expected to substantiate their context-based approach by advancing evidence of the likelihood of harm caused by the speech acts in terms of discrimination, hostility or violence.

Even though the HRC's approach is understandable for a UN body, it still fails to address the implications of the compatibility between the ICCPR provisions and the legal instruments of other international organizations, such as the European Union and its EU framework decision on combating certain forms and expressions of racism and xenophobia.[34]

For more than 60 years the European Commission of Human Rights and the European Court of Human Rights (ECtHR) have offered rich case law on cross-cutting issues challenging European societies. Since the adoption of the European Convention on Human Rights and Fundamental Freedoms (ECHR), the member states of the Council of Europe (CoE) have come to see their obligations expanding, despite the original intentions of the founding fathers of the CoE. Such has been the imprint of the ECtHR on member states' domestic legal orders that scholars have questioned whether the ECtHR has 'exceeded its legitimate role of interpretation and transgressed into the realm of policy-making.'[35]

While it is, to a certain extent, true that the ECtHR has interpreted human rights provisions in a widening range of contexts and has developed universally acknowledged standards which are cited and applied by both domestic and other supranational judicial bodies, at the same time the ECtHR has maintained

33 GC para. 35.

34 Council Framework Decision 2008/913/JHA of 28 November 2008 on combating certain forms and expressions of racism and xenophobia by means of criminal law, *Official Journal of the European Union*, L 328/55, 6 December 2008.

35 Alastair Mowbray, 'The Creativity of the European Court of Human Rights,' *Human Rights Law Review*, Vol 5, No 1 (2005), 57–79, 57.

through its lengthy experience with denials of genocides and historical revisionism cases a restrictivist approach. In this section we examine the ECtHR's approach on the right to historical truth against the arguments of historical revisionism and denialism.[36]

As there is no equivalent to article 20(2) ICCPR in the ECHR, the ECtHR examines cases on the right to historical memory and the right to seek historical truth on the merits of article 10 (freedom of expression); therefore the court examines if an interference in the freedom of expression exists, if this interference is prescribed by law and pursues one or more legitimate aims, and, finally, if it is necessary in a democratic society to achieve these aims.[37]

Through its case law the ECtHR has accepted that there is a category of 'clearly established historical facts' such as the Holocaust[38] whose revision or negation would be removed from the protection scheme of article 10 pursuant to article 17 (abuse of rights),[39] the so-called 'guillotine' provision.[40] Article 17 was originally conceived as an institutional safeguard against the threats posed to the ECHR's underlying values, thus conferring legitimacy to the actions of public authorities which necessarily limit certain rights in the name of the 'greater stability of the country as a whole.'[41] Throughout the jurisprudence the ECtHR has extended the applicability of article 17 on cases of concrete expressions constituting hate speech (i.e. expressions inciting ethnic hatred, anti-Semitism or

36 Paolo Lobba, 'Holocaust Denial Before the European Court of Human Rights: Evolution of an Exceptional Regime,' *European Journal of International Law*, Vol 26, No 1 (2015), 237–253.

37 *National Union of Rail, Maritime and Transport Workers* v *the United Kingdom*, Application No 31045/10, para. 98, ECHR 2014. See generally, European Court of Human Rights Factsheet, *Hate Speech* (2016), www.echr.coe.int/Documents/FS_Hate_speech_ENG.pdf [(accessed 18 September 2016].

38 See: *Chauvy* v *Others*, Application No 64915/01, para. 69. See also Hannes Cannie and Dirk Voorhoof, 'The Abuse Clause and Freedom of Expression in the European Human Rights Convention: An Added Value for Democracy and Human Rights Protection?' *Netherlands Quarterly of Human Rights*, Vol 29, No 1 (2011), 54–83. See also *Lehideux and Isorni* v *France*, Application No 24662/94, judgment of 23 September 1998, para. 47. See: Olivier de Schutter, *International Human Rights Law: Cases, Materials, Commentary* (Cambridge: Cambridge University Press, 2014), 423–426.

39 Article 17: 'Nothing in this Convention may be interpreted as implying for any state, group or person any right to engage in any activity or perform any act aimed at the destruction of any of the rights and freedoms set forth herein or at their limitation to a greater extent than is provided for in the Convention.'

40 See: David Keane, 'Attacking Hate Speech under Article 17 of the European Convention on Human Rights,' *Netherlands Quarterly of Human Rights*, Vol 25, No 4 (2007), 641–663.

41 *Seurot* v *France*, Application No 57383/00, Judgment of 18 May 2004; *Zdanoka* v *Latvia*, Grand Chamber, Application No 58278/00, judgment of 16 March 2006, para. 99; *Refah Partisi (The Welfare Party) and others* v *Turkey*, Grand Chamber para. 99.

Islamophobia[42]), which may be insulting to particular individuals or groups.[43] The court's approach on the application of article 17 has now matured as it also pays regard to acts intended to humiliate or negate the dignity of the victims of serious violations of human rights through attacks on their memory.[44] While certain writers have expressed their concern over the paternalistic application of article 17[45] and more recent case law has affirmed that it should be applicable 'only on an exceptional basis and in extreme cases,'[46] one should not dismiss the wider political and social context within which statements and opinions are expressed across European societies.

The ECtHR has, in fact, been faced more frequently than any other judicial body with cases concerning historical revisionism and genocide denial. This has occurred despite the original foundational, conceptual and procedural failures that come with the Council of Europe and the functioning of the court. In this light,the ECtHR has introduced the element of a lapse of time between the historical events in question and the alleged violation. For example, in *Lehideux and Isorni* the court said that, while remarks about traumatic historical events were always likely to reopen the controversy and bring back memories of past sufferings, a lapse of time of some 40 years made it inappropriate to deal with them with the same severity as ten or 20 years previously.[47] In *Monnat* v *Swizerland* the court held that:

> the historical events discussed in the program in issue had occurred more than 50 years previously. Even though remarks such as those by the applicant are always likely to reopen the controversy among the public, the lapse of time

42 *Molnar v Romania*, Application No 16637/06, decision of 23 October 2012, para. 23; *WP and Others* v *Poland*, Application No 42264/98, decision of 2 September 2004, *Panel Ivanov* v *Russia*, Application No 35222/04, decision of 20 February 2007, *Hizb Ut-Tahrir and Others* v *Germany*, Application No 31098/08, decision of 12 June 2012; *Norwood* v *UK*, Application No 23131/03, decision of 16 November 2004; *M'Bala M'Bala* v *France*, decision of 20 October 2015.

43 See for example *Gunduz* v *Turkey*, Application No 35071/97, judgment of 4 December 2003, para. 41.

44 See for example *Orban and Others* v *France*, Application No 20985/05, judgment of 15 January 2009, para. 52; *Lehideux and Isorni*, paras. 43 and 55; *Witzch* v *Germany*, Application No 7485/03, decision of 13 December 2005; *Leroy* v *France*, Application No 36109/03, judgment of 2 October 2008, paras. 27 and 43.

45 Hannes Cannie and Dirk Voorhoof, 83.

46 *Paksas* v *Lithuania*, Application No 34932/04, judgment of 6 January 2011, para. 87; *Fatullayev* v *Azerbaijan*, Application No 40984/07, judgment of 14 December 2010.

47 Lehideaux and Isorni para. 55. See also *Editions Plon* v *France*, Application No 58148/00, judgment of 18 May 2004, final judgment of 18 August 2004, para. 53, ECHR 2004-IV; *Vajnai* v *Hungary*, Application No 33629/06, judgment of 8 July 2008, para. 49, ECHR 2008; *Orban and Others*, para. 52; *Smolorz* v *Poland*, Application No 17446/07, para. 38, judgment of 16 October 2012; *Hachette Filipacchi Associés* v *France*, Application No 71111/01, judgment of 14 June 2007 para 47; ECommHR, *De Becker* v *Belgium*, Application No 214/56, judgment of 9 June 1958.

> makes it inappropriate to deal with such remarks, 50 years on, with the same severity as ten or 20 years before. That forms part of the efforts that every country must make to debate its own history openly and dispassionately.[48]

In a more recent case, *Perincek* v *Switzerland*,[49] the court upheld the time element test. This case concerned the criminal conviction of Dogu Perincek, chairman of the Turkish Workers' Party, when he publicly denied the Armenian genocide 'as a great international lie.' Article 261 bis § 4 of the Swiss criminal code establishes criminal liability 'for any person who publicly. . . denies, grossly trivializes or seeks to justify a genocide or other crimes against humanity.'[50] Originally, the Chamber of the ECtHR ruled that the application of the Swiss law breached article 10 on freedom of expression of the ECHR; in 2015, the Grand Chamber of the ECtHR issued the final judgment on merits and upheld the previous ruling of the court. By assessing whether the application of the Swiss law constituted interference with the freedom of expression under the ECHR, the court took into consideration whether there was a 'pressing social need' and whether it was 'proportionate to the legitimate aim pursued' and referred to the content and the context the statements were made in. In this case the lapse of time between the applicant's statements and the tragic events was considerable (about 90 years); the ECtHR reaffirmed the time element test and ruled that 'whereas events of relatively recent vintage may be so traumatic as to warrant, for a period of time, an enhanced degree of regulation of statements relating to them, the need for such regulation is bound to recede with the passage of time.'[51] Even though the court deems the lapse of time element a reliable test repeatedly through its case law, one cannot disregard the fact that statutory limitations are not applicable to war crimes and crimes against humanity. Furthermore, it allows room for speculation that the judgments of the court are highly politicized as they respond to what is deemed unacceptable in the present – i.e. Holocaust denial *vis-à-vis* less acknowledged crimes such as the Pontian genocide[52] – yet cannot

48 Application No 73604/01, judgment of 21 September 2006, para. 64.
49 Application No 27510/08, Grand Chamber judgment of 15 October 2015.
50 Para. 32.
51 Para. 250.
52 The Greek genocide was the systematic extermination of the 1.5 million Greek subjects of the Ottoman Empire before, during and after the First World War (1914–1923). It was conducted by successive governments of the Ottoman Empire and it included massacres, forced deportations and death marches, summary expulsions, rape, forced conversion to Islam, arbitrary executions, and destruction of Christian Orthodox cultural, historical and religious monuments. See: Constantinos Fotiadis (ed.), *The Genocide of the Pontus Greeks* (Athens: Herodotus, 2004); Harry Tsirkinidis, *At Last We Uprooted Them: The Genocide of Greeks of Pontos, Thrace, and Asia Minor, through the French Archives* (Thessaloniki: Kyriakidis Bros, 1999); Albert Wuarin, *The Martyrdom of the Pontus and International Public Opinion* (Geneva: J. Delfino 1922); George N. Shirinian (ed.), *The Asia Minor Catastrophe and the Ottoman Greek* (Bloomingdale, IL: Asia Minor and Pontos Hellenic Research Center, 2012).

or does not wish to set the threshold on other categories of historical facts that can be subjected to denialism in the future. Following this line of reasoning, historical atrocities which will be played down with the passage of time may be acceptable in 20 or 50 years in terms of freedom of expression. In this sense, the ECtHR is not willing to acknowledge whether impugned statements may 'have a differing impact in different places or at different moments in time.'[53]

More to the point, even though the court accepts that there is such a special category of historical facts which falls directly within the scope of article 17, one wonders whether this is a *numerus clausus* list, what set of historical events can be considered 'clearly established' and whether the court is justified in shielding particular forms of speech from scrutiny under article 10 ECHR when applying this problematic time element test. While in *Lehideux* the court referred to a general category of 'clearly established facts'; in a subsequent case the court referred to the denial of 'crimes against humanity.' In *Garaudy* v *France*,[54] by questioning the reality, extent and seriousness of the Holocaust, the applicant had, in effect, sought to rehabilitate Nazi policies. The court deemed such acts incompatible with the ECHR values and ideals, and rejected the applicant's invocation of freedom of expression for purposes contrary to the text and the spirit of the ECHR. The court held that:

> There can be no doubt that denying the reality of clearly established historical facts, such as the Holocaust, as the applicant does in his book, does not constitute historical research akin to a quest for the truth. The aim and the result of that approach are completely different, the real purpose being to rehabilitate the Nationalist-Socialist regime and, as a consequence, accuse the victims themselves of falsifying history. Denying crimes against humanity is therefore one of the most serious forms of racial defamation of Jews and of incitement to hatred of them. The *denial or rewriting of this type of historical fact undermines the values on which the fight against racism and anti-Semitism are based and constitutes a serious threat to public order. Such acts are incompatible with democracy and human rights because they infringe the rights of others.* Their proponents indisputably have designs that fall into the category of aims prohibited by article 17 of the Convention. [emphasis added]

In *Orban* v *France* the court referred additionally to statements pursuing the aim of justifying war crimes such as torture or summary executions and in

53 See: Jeroen Temperman, 'Laws Against the Denial of Historical Atrocities: A Human Rights Analysis' (2014), Research paper, 1–27, 22, at: https://papers.ssrn.com/sol3/papers.cfm?abstract_id=2712706 [(accessed 4 October 2016].

54 Application No 65831/01, inadmissibility decision of the ECtHR (Fourth Section) of 24 June 2003. See also European Audiovisual Observatory, *Political Debate and the Role of the Media: The Fragility of Free Speech* (Strasbourg: European Audiovisual Observatory, 2005); Anne Weber, *Manual on Hate Speech* (Strasbourg: Council of Europe Publishing, 2009).

Janowiec v *Russia*[55] the court reaffirmed its 'constant position' that 'a denial of crimes against humanity, such as the Holocaust,' along with war crimes as held in *Orban*, 'run counter to the fundamental values of the Convention and of democracy, namely justice and peace.'[56] This again brings up the issue of (non-)applicability of article 17 to historical facts that may not currently fall within our contemporary and common understanding of war crimes and crimes against humanity. Even though it is understood that the court's approach is premised on endorsing European shared values, ignoring the reality of the heterogeneity of European societies and allowing for restrictive measures against other types of denialism not to fall under article 17 can only feed further historical revisionism discourses, which dispute the reality of past sufferings and express disdain towards the victims, and re-set the values of tolerance and respect for human rights.

Compared with the HRC's (former) approach in *Faurisson*, the ECtHR had also shown a preference for a content-basis examination of the speech act in question. Naturally the different wording from the ICCPR and ECHR allows the court not to scrutinize in much detail whether the impugned statements amount to 'incitement.'[57] This is perhaps best illustrated in the case of *Hans-Jurgen Witzsch* v *Germany*,[58] where the applicant had sent a private letter to a history professor and had denied the existence of gas chambers and mass killings by the Nazi regime. The letter was submitted to the police who then informed family members of people who had died in a concentration camp. Even though the impugned statements were made in private correspondence (and not before a larger audience), the very act of writing this letter had, in effect, amounted to the offense of disparaging the dignity of the deceased.

However, the necessity principle employed by the ECtHR in its jurisprudence indirectly and increasingly provides for a context-based analysis; that is, an assessment as to the likelihood of future adverse acts – for example, whether the impugned statements engendered a risk or danger to society or whether it was likely to become one.[59] As the court admitted in *Perincek*: 'the court's assessment of the necessity of interferences with statements relating to historical events has

55 *Janowiec and Others* v *Russia*, Application Nos 55508/07 and 29520/09, judgment of 16 April 2012, para. 165.

56 See also Ireneusz C. Kaminski, 'The Katyn massacres before the European Court of Human Rights,' *East European Politics and Societies and Cultures*, Vol 29, No 4 (2015), 784–810.

57 See for example *X* v *Germany*, Application No 9235/81, admissibility decision of 16 July 1982; *Hans-Jurgen Witzsch* v *Germany*. Application No 41448/98, admissibility decision of 20 April 1999.

58 *Hans-Jurgen Witzsch* v *Germany*, Application No 7485/03, admissibility decision of 13 December 2005.

59 See for example *Arslan* v *Turkey*, Application No 23462/94, Grand Chamber judgment of 8 July 1999; *Surek and Odzemir* v *Turkey*, Application Nos 23927/94 and 24277/94, Grand Chamber judgment of 8 July 1999. See also Temperman, 1–22.

also been quite case-specific and has depended on the interplay between the nature and potential effects of such statements and the context in which they were made.'[60]

The ECtHR has examined a number of cases brought by people who had been convicted in Turkey following statements on the 1915 events. In *Güçlü v Turkey*[61] the applicant publicly stated that the events of 1915 and the following years had amounted to genocide and that Turkey needed to come to terms with this and engage in an open debate on the issue. The court found that this statement had clearly concerned a debate on a question of public interest and that debate by definition consisted in the expression of divergent points of view. It was the court's opinion that the applicant had sought to provoke a debate on historical and political questions; it was further noted that the expression of such opinions, even if they did not match those of the public authorities and could offend or shock others, was entitled to protection under article 10 of the ECHR. The court held that there was a breach of article 10.[62] In *Dink v Turkey*[63] the applicant, a Turkish-Armenian writer, had been convicted of denigrating 'Turkishness' (Türklük), a criminal offence under former article 159 of the Turkish Criminal Code. Examining that conviction under article 10 of the ECHR, the court noted that, when expressing his resentment at attitudes which in his view amounted to denial of the incidents of 1915 and the following years, the applicant had conveyed his opinions on an issue of indisputable public concern in a democratic society. The court emphasized it was essential in democratic societies that debates surrounding historical events of certain gravity should be able to take place freely. What is noteworthy is that the ECtHR reaffirmed that it was an integral part of freedom of expression to seek historical truth, and acknowledged therein the court's limits in not arbitrating on an underlying historical matter forming part of an ongoing public debate. In this light, the applicant's statements were neither gratuitously offensive nor insulting, and had not fostered disrespect or hatred. Hence, the court concluded that there was no pressing social need to find the applicant guilty of denigrating 'Turkishness.'[64] Furthermore, the ECtHR upheld the state's positive obligation to protect individuals against attacks when exercising their freedom of this expression.

Finally, in *Akcam* v *Turkey*[65] the applicant, a history professor involved in research and publication on the historical events of 1915 concerning the Armenian population in the Ottoman Empire, published an editorial opinion in a bilingual Turkish-Armenian newspaper criticizing the prosecution of the late editor, Hrant

60 *Perincek*, para. 220.
61 Application No 27690/03, Chamber judgment of 10 February 2009.
62 Paras. 33–42. Cited in *Perincek*, para. 221.
63 Application Nos 2668/07, 6102/08, 30079/08, 7072/09 and 7124/09), Chamber judgment of 14 September 2010.
64 Ibid, para. 135. Cited in *Perincek*, paras. 221–222.
65 Application No 27520/07, judgment of 25 October 2011.

Dink, of that newspaper for the crime of 'denigrating Turkishness' under article 301 of the criminal code. The court considered whether the applicant could claim to be a victim of violation of article 10 as no prosecution had been initiated against him. In this regard the ECtHR held that article 301 constituted an interference with the applicant's freedom of expression as he was forced into self-censorship in fear of prosecution under the domestic law, given the fact that he was involved in generating content concerning the Armenian question which was targeted by article 301. To assess whether article 301 was overly broad or vague, the court referred to whether the law was sufficiently clear to enable individuals to regulate their conduct and to reasonably foresee the consequences of their actions. As article 301 was applicable to legitimate statements that offend, shock and disturb, and which are already protected under article 10 of the ECHR, it was found to be in violation of article 10 ECHR.

It should be mentioned that the ECtHR has recognized a new dimension to the freedom of expression and the right to historical truth, which is the right to access to original documentary sources. In *Kenedi* v *Hungary*[66] the applicant, a historian, was refused access to documentation concerning the communist era in Hungary. The court found violations of a number of ECHR provisions, including article 10, as 'access to original documentary sources for legitimate historical research was an essential element of the exercise of the applicant's right to freedom of expression.'[67] Although the ECtHR refrained from stipulating a general right to access to documents, what the judgment does clarify is that, once access on the national level is ordered (in this case by a court), such access should be effective and be given within a reasonable time. This principle is under guise in the more recent *Janowiec* judgment, where the court deduced, albeit from article 3 of the ECHR, an obligation of states to provide past crimes' victims with 'information and uncover relevant facts.'[68]

The international community has come a long way since the adoption of the Universal Declaration on Human Rights. Since 1948 international human rights law has greatly expanded and domestic legal orders have accordingly been largely influenced by the transformative impact of international human rights standards. While European societies have endorsed this transformative culture of human rights, the current increase in incidents of hate speech as well as censorship is a sound reason to be wary.

Memory, historical truth and history are redefined in a context which is not devoid of political interests and social needs. Memory laws have spread throughout Europe during the past few years; such laws may encode state-approved interpretations of historical facts, yet they raise questions as to the protection of the freedom of expression and how historical memory is mediated through the

66 Application No 31475/05, Chamber judgment of 26 May 2009, final judgment of 26 August 2009.

67 Ibid, para. 43.

68 *Janowiec and Others* v *Russia* paras. 163, 164, 166.

human rights judicial route. The implications of memory laws for the protection of the dignity and the rights of the victims of denied historical atrocities and the promotion of the right to historical memory and historical truth cannot be overlooked.

This overview of the case law of the HRC and the ECtHR indicates that the existing human rights instruments may not be the appropriate ones for resolving issues concerning claims to historical memory, and the existing human rights bodies may not consistently address denials of historical facts. Both the HRC and the ECtHR have now adopted a context-based approach when examining statements denying historical facts; yet for the CoE the Holocaust denial, as opposed to the denial of other historical facts, is clearly out of the limits of the protection of the freedom of expression. This remains an uncharted area for historical revisionism claims and denial of historical atrocities. Both the HRC and ECtHR are struggling in their role as courts of memory; this may have negative implications for the victims of historical atrocities. What can international and European human rights judges offer to victims of disputed historical memory, such as members of the Armenian or Pontian community?[69] Perhaps it is time to admit that the progression of the human rights agenda has exceeded the intentions and capacities of the universal and European human rights judicial bodies. Admittedly there is still limited understanding and knowledge about how to source memory and historical truth within human rights law while guaranteeing the universality, the interdependence and the indivisibility of human rights; and how to insure that memory and history do not become an excuse for the denial of fundamental human rights, either individual or collective, at national, regional and international level.

69 Carole Lyons, 'Just Fatherlands? Judging the Shoa in Strasbourg,' in *Europe's Justice Deficit*, edited by Dimitry Kochenov, Grainne de Burca and Andrew Williams (Oxford: Hart, 2015), 381–400.

Part III

Questions of faith

10 Misplaced faith?

Implementing Spain's 2007 Reparation Law[1]

Georgina Blakeley

The Reparation Law, popularly known as the Law of Historical Memory, represented at the time of its approval a flawed but real step forward in the struggle to gain reparation and public recognition for the victims of the Spanish Civil War and Francoist dictatorship. Whatever the law's initial strengths might have been, however, this chapter argues that it has been emptied of content given the lack of political will for its implementation. In particular it focuses on how two limitations within the law – the definition of memory as a private matter and the refusal to nullify Francoist-era rulings – explain its lack of implementation, underpinned by the State's view of its role in transitional justice as discretionary. This chapter concludes that just as the law has become emptied of content, the State also risks being emptied of its legitimacy and authority as victims are forced to place their faith in other levels of governance, such as the autonomous communities, supranational organizations such as the European Union and the United Nations and other nation states (for example, Argentina).

The Reparation Law

The Reparation Law was a long time in the making and its final passage through the Spanish Congress was a turbulent one. Nevertheless, once approved on 26 December 2007 the law represented a qualitative leap forward in Spain's reluctant reckoning with the past. Reparation and recognition, rather than truth or justice, were the focus of the law, with six of its 22 articles dealing with reparatory measures such as improving existing compensation payments to victims (articles 5–9) or

1 This article follows Aguilar, Balcells and Cebolla in referring to the Law of Historical Memory as the Reparation Law. Although Aguilar *et al.* do not specify why they choose this terminology, it is used here as it more accurately denotes the law's content: Paloma Aguilar, Laia Balcells and Hector Cebolla, 'Determinants of Attitudes Towards Transitional Justice: An Empirical Analysis of the Spanish Case,' Estudio/Working Paper No 243 (2009). Center for Advanced Study in the Social Sciences, Madrid: Instituto Juan March de Estudios e Investigaciones, 3.

defining new categories of victims eligible for compensation (article 10).[2] The first four articles include the aim of the law (article 1), a statement of general public recognition (article 2), a statement of the illegitimacy of Francoist-era courts and rulings (article 3) and, in article 4, the right to obtain a declaration of personal reparation and recognition. Four articles (11–14) relate to identifying and finding the bodies of the disappeared and the role of the public authorities in this process. Article 15 concerns the removal of Francoist symbols from public places, article 16 refers to the Valley of the Fallen, and article 17 concerns the elaboration of a census detailing buildings and public works carried out by forced labor. Article 18 improves existing legislation relating to the concession of Spanish nationality to those who fought in the International Brigades by no longer requiring them to renounce their current nationality. The remaining four articles (19–22) concern the acquisition and preservation of documents relating to the civil war and Francoist dictatorship and the right to access public and private archives.

The strengths of the law were its symbolic value, its recognition for the first time of the victim status of those who suffered during the civil war and Francoism, the widespread societal acceptance it seemed to acquire and the mere fact that such a law existed and had been passed by the majority of political parties. The PSOE government at the time, however, was disappointed that approval was only secured by voting on each article of the law in turn, in light of remaining disagreements, rather than voting on the law in its entirety.[3] Whatever the law's initial strengths, though, it has become emptied of content given the lack of political will to ensure its implementation. Clues to the reasons behind this failure can be found in two weaknesses apparent in the law at the time of its approval. The historical memory movement and the PSOE's main negotiating partners – the left-wing IU/ICV coalition and the nationalist parties, principally the ERC, the CiU and the Basque PNV – criticized the law for both defining memory as a private matter and for failing to nullify Francoist-era rulings. Each of these weaknesses testifies to the reluctance of the different branches of the State – executive, legislature and judiciary – to assume their responsibilities in the areas of truth and justice for the victims of the civil war and Francoism.

Private memories

The first weakness is that the law frames memory as a private matter. The PSOE government attached much importance to protecting each individual's right to their personal and family memory. Article 1 states that the aim of the law is 'to recognize and extend rights to those who suffered persecution or violence, for reasons of politics, ideology or religious belief, during the civil war and the

2 Georgina Blakeley, 'Evaluating Spain's Reparation Law,' *Democratization*, Vol 20, No 2 (2013) 240–259, 4.

3 Ibid, 8–10.

dictatorship, to promote their moral reparation and the recovery of their personal and family memory.' Article 4 details the right to obtain a declaration of personal reparation and recognition. To some extent this private focus is understandable, given the extent to which Republican memories were silenced during the Francoist dictatorship, even within the private sphere of the family. It also denoted the State's reluctance to impose any kind of official 'truth' about the past. This private focus, in addition, chimed with the socialist government's broad ethical agenda based on the extension of rights relating to gay marriage, disability, gender parity, new territorial rights and environmental and animal rights. In the second plenary discussing the reparation bill, the PSOE spokesperson, José Andres Torres Mora,[4] argued that the bill was 'coherent with the politics of recognition and extension of rights followed by this government throughout this legislature,' thereby placing the Reparation Law firmly within the socialists' overall legislative agenda, which some commentators have labelled Spain's 'second transition.'[5]

The privatization of memory, however, denotes an approach to dealing with the past that is grounded on notions of personal guilt and innocence. This approach contrasts with that advocated by one of the main associations of the historical memory movement, the Association for the Recovery of Historical Memory (ARMH), which has articulated a discourse of universal human rights, rather than individual victimhood, and defines Francoist crimes as crimes against humanity. It is telling that human rights are only referred to three times in the law and only in the preamble. Moreover, the preamble only refers to violations of human rights but not to the category of victim of these human rights violations.[6]

The extent to which memory is framed as a private issue also denotes an absence of state responsibility. One area where there were significant changes between the draft bill and the final law related to the central state's responsibility in ensuring the implementation of various aspects of the law. These changes were an acknowledgement that the central state was not, in the view of some, assuming sufficient responsibility. The central state's role was strengthened in the final law in various aspects, including: educating its citizens about the civil war and the dictatorship; assuming a proactive role *vis-à-vis* the mass civil war graves; and responsibility for the removal of Francoist symbols.[7]

4 Diario de Sesiones del Congreso de los Diputados, No 296. Sesión del 31/X/2007, www.congreso.es/public_oficiales/L8/CONG/DS/PL/PL_296.PDF 1463.

5 See for example, Bonnie Field (ed.), *Spain's 'Second Transition'? The Socialist Government of José Luis Rodrigo Zapatero* (London: Routledge, 2010).

6 'Casos Cerrados, Heridas Abiertas. El desamparo de las víctimas de la Guerra Civil y el franquismo en España. Resumen ejecutivo' (Madrid: Sección española de Amnistía Internacional, 2012), 15.

7 For more detail about the changes between the draft and final law, see Georgina Blakeley, 'Politics as usual? The Trials and Tribulations of the Law of Historical Memory in Spain,' *Entelequia. Revista Interdisciplinar*, Vol 7 (2008), 315–330.

A law only on paper?

Although progress was made in implementing the law during the final years of the socialist administration, even then progress on the location of mass graves, the exhumation of bodies or the removal of Francoist symbols often depended on the will of local and regional governments which, particularly when in the hands of the right-wing PP, remained hostile to the implementation of some aspects of the law. The victory of the PP in the 2011 general elections transferred this local and regional intransigence to the national stage.

Under the cover of the economic recession, the PP in effect repealed the law by withdrawing its funding. The first cuts came in the 2012 budget when the €6.2m allocated by the last Socialist executive was slashed to €2.5m, destined exclusively for the opening of graves. Even this proved to be a chimera, as the associations waited in vain for the call for grants which was never published in the Boletín Oficial del Estado (BOE). In 2013, and again in 2014, no central state funds were allocated to the tasks of the historical memory movement.[8]

The PP government also failed to act with regard to the Valley of the Fallen, disregarding the report of the Committee of Experts which was asked to study the issue under the previous socialist government. One of its chief proposals was to move Franco's remains to another place as 'the only way of assigning a different meaning to the monument and to provide some solace to the children and grandchildren of those Republicans who were buried in the mausoleum without their consent.'[9] Although the PP government was already in power when the report was presented, the Basque Socialist MP Ramón Jáuregui asked Mariano Rajoy, the prime minister, to not simply 'put it in a drawer.'[10] Yet Rajoy, it seems, did just that. In this case it is more difficult to attribute inaction to a lack of funding. On 17 May 2013 the government published in the BOE a public invitation to tender worth €286,485 to restore the facade of the basilica of the Valley of the Fallen which had deteriorated severely. In response Jáuregui asked the government if it would adopt any of the recommendations of the Committee of Experts. The government replied in writing that: 'With regard to actions pertaining to completely changing the meaning of the Valley of the Fallen as proposed in the report of the experts' commission, it is necessary to point out that this would require the maximum consensus in order not to reopen unnecessary wounds.'[11]

As part of the austerity programme in 2012 the PP government also closed the Office of Assistance to Victims of the Civil War and Dictatorship, created in 2008. The functions of this office, such as the development of graves maps,

8 Natalia Junquera, 'Bronca en el Congreso por la memoria histórica,' *El País*, 18 December 2013.

9 Natallia Junquera, 'El Gobierno dice que cambiar el Valle de los Caídos "reabriría heridas,"' *El País*, 6 August 2013.

10 Ibid.

11 Ibid.

were transferred to the División de Derechos de Gracia y Otros Derechos (the Pardons' Office). This nomenclature pinpoints why the State has failed to implement the Reparation Law effectively. Its inaction is much less to do with financial difficulties and more to do with how it perceives its role with regard to historical memory. The State regards any action concerning truth, justice and reparation as discretionary, rather than a mandatory part of its constitutional and international obligations. This voluntary approach is long-standing. Iosif Kovras highlights how early reparations to widows and orphans were granted to certain victims' groups 'not as an acknowledgement of their suffering or their contribution to a noble cause but to comfort the disaffected,' which leads him to conclude that such reparations were framed as 'acts of benevolence – not justice.'[12] Javier Chinchón Alvarez, likewise, argues that all measures adopted in relation to the past 'are afforded as a matter of grace and not obligation.'[13] He notes, for example, that the Supreme Court has admitted that the historical memory law implies nothing more than 'the mere collaboration with private persons (and) the contribution of public powers in the desired reparation of the victims of the civil war and the dictatorship that followed.'[14] Alicia Gil adds that the task of gaining compensation or recognition 'as a matter of grace' is made even more difficult as it is the victims' responsibility to provide evidence to support any claims they make.[15]

This shortcoming applies to the right to request a declaration of reparation and personal recognition from the Pardons' Office, which requires citizens to complete a form and provide evidence of the facts leading them to request a certificate of recognition and moral restitution. The obligation placed on the victims to provide evidence might explain why few citizens have chosen to gain recognition. The Spanish government's historical memory website continues to claim that more than 950 people have already gained a declaration, yet this website is no longer updated. In a personal request for information (22 July 2014) the Ministry of Justice stated that 1,628 declarations of reparation and personal recognition had been issued to date, yet this is still a low figure in the face of even the most conservative estimates of the number of victims to whom such a declaration might apply.

In response to criticisms of his government's inactivity, Alberto Ruíz-Gallardon, then justice minister, declared in December 2013 that the government was

12 Iosif Kovras, 'Explaining Prolonged Silences in Transitional Justice: The Disappeared in Cyprus and Spain,' *Comparative Political Studies*, Vol 46, No 6 (2013), 730–756, 742.

13 Javier Chinchón Alvarez, 'The challenges posed to the recent investigation of crimes committed during the Spanish Civil War and Francoism,' in *The Role of Courts in Transitional Justice*, edited by Jessica Almqvist and Carlos Espósito (London: Routledge, 2012), 132–158, 137.

14 Ibid.

15 Alicia Gil, 'Spain as an example of total oblivion with partial rehabilitation,' in *The Role of Courts in Transitional Justice*, 103–131, 131.

fulfilling its obligations under the law and was managing the map of graves. He added that 27 new locations had been added in 2013, bringing the number to 2,382. Although recognizing that the recession had cut funding, he claimed that, since 2006, associations had received €25m and that most of the requests to locate and exhume bodies were made as soon as the law was passed, such that the location and exhumation of the most important graves had already been carried out by 2011.[16] This is a deeply cynical statement: it fails to clarify that of those €25m, €20m corresponded to the period 2006–2011 under the socialist governments. Moreover, the historical memory associations claim that, of the 2,382 mass graves identified, less than 400 had been opened, thereby directly disputing the government view expressed in 2012 by Fernando Román, the Secretary of State for Justice, that 'the work to carry out the law has been almost finished.'[17]

The gaps left by the State in terms of education are filled sometimes by the activities of the historical memory associations. Rubin notes the 'focus on public education' at many of the excavation sites where exhumations occur.[18] Exhumations and the processes that accompany them, including interviewing relatives and the reburial of victims, contribute to teaching citizens about the civil war and the Francoist dictatorship. This educative function helps in 'constructing a proper relationship to the past, one citizen at a time.'[19] And yet it can be problematic when citizens are left to substitute for the State's shortcomings. Rubin argues that, 'in order to be successful, transitional justice programs require the authority, organization and juridical power that can only come from a state-directed enterprise,' not the least because 'NGOs cannot provide the sort of official state recognition of past wrongs and continued suffering so highly valued by the relatives of victims.'[20]

The United Nation's special envoy for the promotion of truth, justice and reparation criticized the State's inaction. Pablo de Greiff insisted on the need for the government to have a 'state policy' to provide reparation for the victims of Francoism and criticized the State for leaving the responsibility of finding and opening civil war graves in the hands of the families, claiming that 'the model of

16 Diario de Sesiones del Congreso de los Diputados, No 167, Sesión del 18/XII/2013, www.congreso.es/public_oficiales/L10/CONG/DS/PL/DSCD-10-PL-167.PDF [accessed 30 January 2015], 16.

17 When Gaspar Llamazares asked who would take responsibility for carrying out the Reparation Law given the closure of the Office of Assistance to Victims of the Civil War and Dictatorship, the Secretary of State for Justice, Fernando Román, replied that 'El desarrollo está prácticamente concluido' ('The work is almost finished'). Natalia Junquera, 'La Promesa que Rajoy sí cumplió,' *El País*, 5 October 2013.

18 Jonah S. Rubin, 'Transitional Justice against the State: Lessons from Spanish Civil Society-Led Forensic Exhumations,' *The International Journal of Transitional Justice*, Vol 8 (2014), 99–120, 111.

19 Ibid.

20 Ibid, 119–120.

privatization of the exhumations makes it easier for state institutions to maintain their indifference.' In fact, during the ten days he spent in Spain interviewing government members, judges and victims, what he found particularly striking was 'the immense distance' between state institutions and victims. He stressed that 'never in his 20 years of experience has he come across anything like this.'[21]

The distancing of the State from its responsibilities to provide truth, justice and reparations results from the State's view of its role as discretionary rather than obligatory and, hence, memory work in Spain is essentially privatized. With regard to the mass civil war graves, Ferrándiz argues that the 2007 law actually legalizes 'a human rights outsourcing system whereby the State would provide (limited) assistance and funding while transferring the responsibility for the research, exhumations and identifications, and the overall management of the executed bodies to the historical memory associations and victims' relatives.'[22] The Reparation Law continues 'to treat exhumations as a private, individual right' despite making available limited state funds to help historical memory organizations carry out their activities.[23] This discretionary nature of the state's role in transitional justice is also evidenced by the fact that the UN's envoys noted that the treatment of victims 'depends enormously on the political party which is in government in each place.'

Some politicians argue that the extraordinary cuts the Spanish government had to make in light of the global financial crisis justify the cuts to funding for the historical memory movement. Surely, this argument goes, present problems, not past problems, should attract government money. This is a valid claim, but two points can be considered in relation to it. The first axiomatic point to make is that political will always drives how much money there is to allocate (for example through tax policies) and where it is allocated. Arguments about a lack of money are, therefore, usually political rather than practical ones.[24] Second, past problems are also often present problems. Victims often continue to bear the consequences of their or their relatives' past mistreatment, particularly when this goes unacknowledged publicly or truths remain silenced.

In addition to the location and exhumation of the bodies of thousands of victims in unmarked graves, which has received considerable public attention

21 Natalia Junquera, 'El relator de la ONU insiste: España debe juzgar los crímenes del franquismo,' *El País*, 3 February 2014.

22 Francisco Ferrándiz, 'Exhuming the defeated: Civil War mass graves in 21st-century Spain,' *American Ethnologist*, Vol 40, No 1 (2013), 38–54, 45.

23 Rubin (2014), 107.

24 For example, it was recently revealed that the Spanish Ministry of Defence doubled its catering budget for planes which carry Spanish royals, ministers and other senior officials. According to the Boletín Oficial del Estado, the annual budget for 2014 was increasing to €133,000 from €65,000 the year before. *20 Minutos*, 'El Gobierno gastará el doble en el catering de los aviones que llevan a los reyes y a los ministros,' 24 July 2014. www.20minutos.es/noticia/2201270/0/ala-45-defensa/catering-contratros-boe/ministros-autoridades [accessed 30 August 2014].

since the formation of the ARMH in 2000, other issues are only just coming to light and around which victim collectives are beginning to coalesce. These include: the 'stolen children,' a label which refers to those children who were forcibly taken from their Republican parents and adopted by childless Francoist sympathizers in what has now become recognized as a sophisticated, profit-making 'child trafficking network';[25] polio victims who suffered a kind of 'social apartheid' under Francoism, where regime sympathizers were able to avail themselves of the vaccination while others were excluded;[26] and Basque victims of human rights abuses committed by the police between 1960 and 1978.[27] The people in these and other victim collectives continue to live with the consequences of past human rights abuses as they feel 'silenced in the past and forgotten in the present.'[28] The past is not so easily decoupled from the present.

Judicial shortcomings

Another weakness of the Reparation Law, for many historical memory associations and some of the PSOE's negotiating partners, was its failure to nullify Francoist-era rulings despite European precedents. The right-wing CDU government in Germany passed the Law to Nullify Unjust National-Socialist Sentences on 25 August 1998, which 'declared the entire apparatus of Wehrmacht "justice" as unjust, null and void,'[29] while in Austria laws have been passed that annul unjust sentences passed during the German occupation.[30] There was evidence that annulment had societal support, with 50.4 per cent of Spaniards agreeing in one survey that 'democracy should annul the political trials that took place under Francoism'; this compared with only 19.3 per cent against.[31] Instead, and only after intense pressure from its negotiating partners, the PSOE declared Francoist-era rulings 'illegitimate,' but was at pains to stress that this had no legal effect. Moreover, the Reparation Law is silent on the possibility of any judicial investigation into crimes committed during the civil war and the Francoist

25 Rafael Escudero, 'Road to Impunity: The Absence of Transitional Justice Programs in Spain,' *Human Rights Quarterly*, Vol 36, No 1 (2014), 123–146, 127–8.

26 Montse Armengou And Ricard Belis, 'Polio: Crónica de una negligencia,' 2014. www.ccma.cat/tv3/alacarta/programa/Version-en-castellano-del-documental-Polio-cronica-de-una-negligencia/video/4900033 [accessed 14 June 2014].

27 XabierEsnaola. 'Las víctimas del franquismo reclamen justicia tras el recurso de Urquijo,' *El País*, 20 June 2014.

28 Armengou and Belis.

29 Douglas Carl Peifer, 'The Past in the Present: Passion, Politics and the Historical Profession in the German and British Pardon Campaigns,' *The Journal of Military History*, Vol 71, No 4 (2007), 1107–113, 1125.

30 Aguilar, Paloma, Laia Balcells and Hector Cebolla 'Determinants of Attitudes Towards Transitional Justice: An Empirical Analysis of the Spanish Case,' Centre for Advanced Study in the Social Sciences, Estudio/Working Paper 243 (Madrid: Instituto Juan March de Estudios e Investigaciones, 2009).

31 *Memorias de la Guerra Civil y el Franquismo*, Centro de Investigaciones Sociológicas (CIS), Estudio No 2760, April 2008.

dictatorship. The inactivity of the executive branch with regard to the Reparation Law is thus replicated in the judicial branch of the State, where the overriding tendency has been to claim that 'there exists no legal obligation to open a criminal investigation.'[32] This is unsurprising given Aguilar's assertion that half of the members of the Military Chamber of the Supreme Court, which is in charge of reviewing court-martial sentences, once belonged to the Juridical-Military Corps, whose members were required to participate in Francoist courts-martial. She writes: 'The members of this corps are likely to be reluctant to declare void sentences handed down during trials in which the corps participated.'[33]

The judiciary has thus proved intransigent when it comes to pursuing those cases brought before it relating to human rights abuses during the civil war and Francoism. Following the ruling in November 2008 that Court Five of the High Court, then under the responsibility of Judge Baltasar Garzón, did not have jurisdiction to take forward the case presented by four historical memory associations in 2006 to investigate 114,266 disappearances between 1936 and 1951, the responsibility to investigate these crimes was devolved to the regional courts. Since then Amnesty International notes 'a continuous tendency on the part of Spanish judges to archive these cases.'[34] According to Amnesty, of the 47 cases devolved to the regional courts at least 38 have been archived.[35] Moreover, Amnesty argues that this tendency to archive cases was strengthened by the Supreme Court decision 101 of 27 February 2012, which stated that it was legally impermissible to investigate disappearances with respect to which 'the right to know the historical truth is not part of the criminal process and can only be satisfied tangentially.'[36]

This Supreme Court decision was not actually directly related to the disappearances but concerned the case brought against Judge Garzón by the right-wing lobby group Manos Limpias and subsequently the right-wing Libertad e Identidad, which claimed that Garzón had knowingly and deliberately overstepped his powers by beginning an investigation into a number of disappearances.[37] Although Garzón was found not guilty, the Supreme Court's ruling in effect ended any hope of pursuing cases related to the civil war or the Francoist dictatorship through the Spanish courts because it reasoned that, at the time such crimes occurred, Spain had not codified nor had any knowledge of the applicability of international law relating to 'crimes against humanity' and, given the passage

32 Chinchón Alvarez, 157.
33 Aguilar (2013), 18.
34 *Casos Cerrados, Heridas Abiertas. El desamparo de las víctimas de la Guerra Civil y el franquismo en España. Resumen ejecutivo* (Madrid: Sección española de Amnistía Internacional, 2012), 3.
35 Ibid, 5.
36 Ibid, 4.
37 Although it lost the case, the Secretary-General of Manos Limpias, Miguel Bernad, was rewarded in December 2011 for his 'services in defense of the ideals of the movement' by being named 'Caballero de Honor de la Fundación Francisco Franco', 'El Franquismo agradece a Manos Limpios sus Servicios,' *Público*, 9 December 2011. www.publico.es/espana/franquismo-agradece-manos-limpias-servicios.html [accessed 14 June 2014].

of time, such crimes were now prescribed. Escudero argues that this amounts to a rejection by the State of 'the international legal doctrine that establishes a duty to investigate the destiny of the disappeared, even if it is not possible to punish those who are guilty because of amnesty or prescription.'[38]

The Supreme Court decision reveals its misunderstanding of the motives of Spanish activists in pressing the courts to act. The desire for justice is much less about punishing particular individuals and more about establishing truths and having these recognized publicly. María Servini, the Argentine judge currently investigating various Francoist crimes, noted that what struck her most when gathering testimonies was 'the fear and terror of each person in testifying.'[39] This fear results in part from the State's failure to legitimize alternative narratives about the civil war and Francoist dictatorship, such that many individuals fail to see their own private memories reflected in collective memories. Accordingly, many victims and victims' relatives look to courtrooms to establish for the historical record what actually happened. Rubin argues that 'Spanish activists and many relatives of the disappeared place particular emphasis on the power of criminal prosecution not only to reveal the truths but also to make such truths authoritative.'[40] This goes beyond what a truth and reconciliation commission can achieve as these often become 'an archive of information, rather than a tool of justice,' and they lack the authority of the law.[41] In contrast, legal testimony contains 'truth claims' and ultimately the law decides which truth claims carry authority. This quest for authority speaks volumes as it is the inactivity of the branches of the State – executive, legislature and judiciary – and their failure to supply this authority which motivates the quest for truth and justice on the part of many relatives and victims.

It is possible that the Spanish judiciary has gone beyond inactivity to active dissuasion. In 2013 the UN's envoys for the Working Group on Forced Disappearances – Jasminka Dzumhur and Ariel Dulitzky – asserted that no judge had undertaken investigations following Garzón's attempt in 2008 because of the 'dissuasive effect' of Garzón's trial and the subsequent Supreme Court verdict 101 in February 2012.[42] This Supreme Court ruling contradicts the recommendations of the UN, whose envoys concluded that the executive should 'assume its responsibility' and develop a 'national plan to locate the disappeared,' repeal the amnesty law and judge the more than 114,000 disappearances detailed by Garzón in his 2008 judgment. At a minimum the UN envoys requested the government to provide 'every judicial support' to any ongoing legal trial begun in other

38 Escudero, 124–125.

39 Àngeles Lucas, 'Servini: Si no creyera en la justicia universal, no estaría aquí,' *El País*, 23 May 2014.

40 Rubin (2014), 14.

41 Jonah, S. Rubin, 'Adjudicating the Salvadoran Civil War: Expectations of the Law in Romogaza,' *Political and Legal Anthropology Review*, Vol 32, No 2 (2008) 264–285, 268.

42 Natalia Junquera, 'Naciones Unidas reclama a España juzgar las desapariciones del franquismo,' *El País*, 30 September 2013.

countries, such as Argentina, in relation to these facts.[43] According to the UN, forced disappearance is 'a permanent crime which is not prescribed' despite the fact that the Supreme Court declared the argument about the permanence of the crime of forced disappearance as 'lacking in plausibility.'[44]

The UN's special envoy, Pablo De Greiff, reiterated these concerns. He repeated the request to repeal the amnesty law, saying that in reality 'this worked as a full stop law given that it had been used to archive nearly all the cases which come before the judiciary.'[45] He argued that in other countries where amnesty laws had not been annulled the courts had been able to interpret such laws in ways 'which have not prevented proceedings against those presumed to be responsible.' In Spain, however, he argued that the amnesty law 'is constantly invoked to prevent victims from gaining access to justice.'[46] De Greiff also spoke of his 'concern' about the National Court's refusal to carry out the extradition request from Argentina concerning two suspected Francoist torturers: José Antonio González Pacheco (Billy el Niño) and Jesús Muñecas Aguilar.[47]

Paloma Aguilar puts this 'continuous lack of judicial accountability' in Spain down to the judiciary's complicity with the Francoist regime, which included 'the direct involvement of the ordinary judicial system in the Francoist repressive machine.'[48] The fact that the role of the ordinary judiciary increased towards the end of the regime is noteworthy in explaining the judiciary's inactivity today. Aguilar highlights the 'exclusive participation' of the ordinary judiciary in the special Court of Public Order 'in which judges and prosecutors from 1963 to the end of 1976 took the lead in carrying out ideological and political repression, except in the case of terrorist offenses, which continued to fall under military jurisdiction.'[49]

Substituting the State?

The central state's failure to implement the 2007 Reparation Law explains the recourse of relatives of the disappeared and the historical memory movement to regional levels of government in Spain, to supranational levels of government in the form of the EU or the UN and other states. The executive has shown itself reluctant to implement the Reparation Law by stopping all funding to carry out any of its provisions. The legislature continues to reaffirm the validity of the 1977

43 Ibid.
44 Julio M. Lázaro, 'El Supremo Cierra la vía a la investigación penal de los crímenes del franquismo,' *El País*, 29 March 2012.
45 Natalia Junquera, 'El relator de la ONU insiste: España debe juzgar los crímenes del franquismo,' *El País*, 3 February 2014.
46 Ibid.
47 Ibid.
48 Aguilar, 5.
49 Ibid, 7.

amnesty law despite various proposals to modify it.[50] The judiciary has rejected and/or archived all cases brought before it and, following the 2012 Supreme Court decision, can now justify its decisions to do so on the jurisprudence of the court.[51]

The failure has also led to the appearance of 'different public memory policies in different regions of the country' depending on the party in power.[52] In the Canary Islands the regional government is attempting to cover the gaps that the PP government has left by establishing an internet site with all the available information about the disappeared during the civil war and Francoism on the island.[53] Catalonia's Democratic Memorial Project, an institution aimed at researching, disseminating and commemorating the Second Republic and the anti-Francoist struggle, has awarded grants to various historical memory projects since 2006.

The Andalusian government has been at the vanguard of promoting historical memory. The Law of Democratic Memory, approved on 26 January 2015, broadens the scope of the Reparation Law in various aspects.[54] In temporal terms it extends the time period covered to the Second Republic and a greater portion of the transition period, so that it extends from 14 April 1931 to 11 January 1982. The classification of victims is broadened to include collectives such as the 'stolen children' and those who suffered in Nazi concentration camps.[55] A greater and more proactive role for the state authorities is also envisaged with the Andalusian Vice-President, Diego Valderas (IU), arguing that, 'in Andalusia, democratic memory is elevated to the category of public policy.'[56] State commitment is also evident in the allocation of €10m to fund the initiative over the next five years.[57] The Andalusian law establishes a period of 18 months to remove Francoist symbols, after which the regional government assumes responsibility for their removal. Likewise a more proactive role is envisaged in the location and exhumation of graves. Also of significance is the inclusion of democratic memory as a subject in the curriculum for secondary schools, the Baccalaureate and adult continuing education. The law is also innovative in

50 The latest proposal came from the Parliamentary Mixed Group in June 2011. Much of the validity of the law comes from the fact that it was passed by the first democratic parliament (rather than the outgoing authoritarian regime, as has been the case with most Latin American amnesty laws for example), but this democratic legitimacy is compromised by the fact that the amnesty law precedes the 1978 Constitution which explicitly allows all acts prior to its approval to be ignored or not applied by any judge if such an act is considered unconstitutional; Escudero, 133.

51 El Tiempo Pasa (Amnestia Internacional) 8.

52 Ferrándiz, 45.

53 M. Dosantos, 'Canarias crea un portal en Internet de la memoria histórica', *El País*, 9 July, 2014.

54 Junta de Andalucía, *Proyecto de Ley de Memoria Democrática de Andalucía*, 2015.

55 Ibid.

56 Antonio Jesús Mora Caballero, '10 millones para aplicar la ley de Memoria Democrática,' *El País*, 20 January 2015.

57 Ibid.

attributing to the regional government the duty to denounce to judicial authorities the existence of evidence of crimes against humanity in the location and identification of bodies. This duty arises from the way in which the preamble of the 2015 law, which follows the recommendations of the UN special envoy, clearly defines crimes committed by Francoism as 'crimes against humanity' which, by their very nature, 'are imprescriptible and [. . .] are not covered by amnesty laws.'[58] This contradicts the 2012 Supreme Court resolution and stems from the long-standing Andalusian demand to the Spanish State to annul the guilty judgment against Blas Infante, seen as the father of Andalusian nationalism.

As regards supranational levels of government, this chapter has cited various UN reports urging the State to assume its responsibilities. Similarly, various cases have been brought to the European Court of Human Rights by victims' relatives. Most recently, in February 2014, a victims' delegation traveled to Brussels to speak to the President of the Petition Commission, Erminia Mazzoni, requesting the EU to press Spain to create a truth commission – as the UN has also urged. Nevertheless, despite support for victims' associations from these supranational organizations, none of them has pursued a legal case. When the ARMH submitted 64 cases of forced disappearance to the UN's Working Group on Enforced or Involuntary Disappearances in 2002, only two were deemed admissible, given that all the other cases dated from before the UN's foundation in 1945.[59] Similarly, the European Court of Human Rights has rejected all of the eight cases brought before it to date, citing as reasons that the alleged facts are prior to the ratification of the European Convention on Human Rights and that the cases were not brought to the court without undue delay.[60]

Given the above, perhaps the best hope for bringing a legal case relating to crimes during the civil war and Francoism lies with the Argentine legal system which could, in a neat twist of fate, use the principle of universal jurisdiction which Garzón utilized to such good effect in investigating crimes against humanity committed by the military junta in Argentina from 1976–1983.[61] María Servini, the Argentine judge, could declare her own court in Buenos Aires competent to investigate several crimes committed during Francoism if it can be proved that the Spanish State is unwilling to try these crimes itself. The prosecutor revealed that the case now has more than 100 victims and 47 volumes of evidence.[62] In October 2014 Servini requested the arrest and extradition to Argentina of

58 Junta de Andalucía, *Proyecto de Ley de Memoria Democrática de Andalucía*, 2015. www.juntadeandalucia.es/administracionlocalyrelacionesinstitucionales/cms/export/sites/default/comun/galerias/galeriaDescargas/portal/MemoriaHistorica/Proyecto_Ley_LMDA.pdf [accessed 30 January 2015].

59 Georgina Blakeley, 'Digging up Spain's Past: Consequences of Truth and Reconciliation,' *Democratization*, Vol 12, No 1 (2005), 44–59.

60 El Tiempo Pasa (Amnestia Internacional), 5.

61 Blakeley (2013), 10.

62 Àngeles Lucas, 'Servini: Si no creyera en la justicia universal, no estaría aquí,' *El País*, 23 May 2014.

20 former Francoist officials, including two former cabinet ministers, José Utrera Molina and Rodolfo Martín Villa, in order to question them over accusations of torture during the dictatorship.[63]

Even here, however, there are claims that the Spanish State is blocking attempts at justice. The Argentine authorities have twice requested information from Madrid – on 14 October 2010 and 13 December 2011 – with regard to whether or not Spain is investigating crimes committed during the civil war and Francoism. Amnesty International claims the two responses of the State have been erroneous. In its first response, on 6 May 2011, the State Public Prosecutor replied that Spain was investigating the cases resulting from the 2008 ruling that Garzón was not competent to take forward. This response was reiterated on 27 March 2012 when the Public Prosecutor also requested the cases be returned to Spain as it had preferential competence over them. According to Amnesty, however, Spain is not investigating these crimes nor does it have preferential competence as they are crimes of universal jurisdiction.[64] It remains to be seen how the State will respond to Servini's latest arrest and extradition orders.

Despite the Supreme Court's 101/2012 decision, Argentine pressure may still bear fruit. In April 2014 Spain's Public Prosecutor argued in response to an extradition request for Jesús Muñecas, an ex-Civil Guard captain accused of torturing Andoni Arrizabalaga for 22 days in 1968, that Argentina does not have the right to carry out the trial but that there is a possibility the trail could be held in Zarautz, where the alleged events are said to have occurred. This could be highly significant as the first summons of an individual accused of Francoist crimes.[65] The prosecutor was at pains to say the alleged crimes were prescribed under Spanish law but that a trial 'would give the victims the possibility of attending a proceeding being heard in a Spanish court of the facts committed under the dictatorship and, in some way, satisfy the desire for justice which has motivated them to present this case.'[66]

The search by victims and their relatives for alternative sources of authority to recognize their 'truth claims' risks not just rendering the Reparation Law meaningless but, more significantly, undermining the political authority of the State. This weakening might play out in various ways. Supranational bodies like the EU and the UN are unlikely to do much more than continue to condemn the inaction of the State to deal with its past; this may embarrass the State but will have few consequences beyond opprobrium. Regional governments will continue to exert pressure on the central state, not the least in Andalusia where

63 Jonathan Gilbert, 'Argentine judge orders arrest of Spanish ex-officials,' *New York Times*, 1 November 2014. www.nytimes.com/2014/11/02/world/americas/argentine-judge-orders-arrest-of-spanish-ex-officials.html [accessed 27 January 2015].

64 El Tiempo Pasa (Amnestia Internacional), 6.

65 Magdalena Martínez, 'Los impulsores del juicio contra Muñecas celebran su comparencia,' *El País*, 4 April 2014.

66 María Fabra, 'La Fiscalía propone un juicio al capitán Muñecas en España,' *El País*, 3 April 2014.

the regional government, using the principle of universal jurisdiction, has assumed the duty to report to the judicial authorities the existence of evidence of crimes against humanity in the location and identification of bodies. While this might not change the stance of the Spanish central authorities, such reporting might be used as evidence by other nation states to pursue legal cases and will, at the very least, continue to keep the past in the public sphere. Finally, the most significant impact might result from a legal finding against the Spanish State which, at the time of writing, is most likely to come from Argentina. This would be more than just embarrassing: such a ruling could have legal effects which Madrid would find difficult to ignore.

Conclusion

Even setting to one side the weaknesses that the Reparation Law had as a piece of legislation, the fact that its implementation has been hampered not just by a lack of funding but by a lack of political will to carry out its provisions means it has been emptied of content and thus lost perhaps its main strength – its symbolism. The executive branch of the State has been unable and unwilling to ensure the law is implemented.

The judicial branch has likewise failed to fulfill its functions. Some jurists had claimed that the law's declaration of the 'illegitimacy' of Francoist-era rulings could be used as valid proof in any requests to reopen cases which come before the Supreme Court, despite the socialist government's insistence that this declaration had no legal effect.[67] The law, however, has failed to open up new legal avenues, given the judiciary's tendency to archive cases related to the civil war and Francoist era. This tendency was strengthened following the 2012 Supreme Court ruling and is reinforced by the legislature's inaction *vis-à-vis* the 1977 amnesty law.

The inaction of the executive, legislative and judicial branches of the State underscores the discretionary nature of the State's role in transitional justice. Yet, by being intransigent in the short term, the State may be storing up problems for the future. I have noted elsewhere[68] the importance of the dynamic nature of democratization in the sense that one generation's successful pact can become another generation's unsuccessful compromise. To ignore the open-ended nature of political settlements is to ignore the fact that political strategies that silence elements of the past, 'while potentially effective for limited periods of time, may be destabilizing in the long term.'[69]

While the original transition pacts in the 1970s successfully established democracy and political conciliation, the inability of the various branches of the central state to adequately confront the past means it is unable to move beyond this narrow political agreement to achieve a broader social reconciliation.

67 Blakeley (2013), 9.
68 See: Blakeley (2005).
69 Ferrándiz, 39.

For a state to operate successfully as an 'imagined community,'[70] all of those who potentially belong to it must feel part of the common and shared tale which underpins such a community. Victims of the losing side of the civil war and Francoism are still waiting to be recognized as part of this national narrative.

70 Benedict Anderson, *Imagined Communities: Reflections on the Origin and Spread of Nationalism* (London: Verso, 1983).

11 Faith, justice and Catholic public memory

The politics of reconciliation in Australia and New Zealand

Dominic O'Sullivan

Since the early 1990s, reconciliation has influenced Australian political discourse to reflect a unique political/theological policy nexus in a jurisdiction where prevailing values and practices ordinarily position religious ideals beyond the political system's overt and immediate concern. In indigenous policy, the Catholic Church's own public memory has assumed particular influence as the Church responds to its historical acquiescence with public policies of un-Christian intent: the removal of indigenous children from their families and a general failure to confront colonialism's cultural and economic impact. On a national level, reconciliation is both public memory and practical politics. It requires acknowledgement of wrong-doing, sorrow and substantive resolve to settle conflict through the development of 'socially just' relationships. Reconciliation is a particular way of 'calling up' the past through acts of public memory which illuminate, in a liberal democracy, questions of relational justice. This chapter draws on New Zealand examples to contextualize its assessment of reconciliation as public memory in Australian policy discourse. The Treaty of Waitangi has provided the rationale and framework for successive New Zealand governments to say sorry for acts of aggression against Maori tribes. In New Zealand, sorrow is expressed through Acts of Parliament that serve not only as instruments of restitution but as symbols of public memory. Through the treaty, reconciliation is entrenched into New Zealand law and politics and, in contrast with Australia (which lacks a treaty with its indigenous peoples), certainty surrounds questions of apology, including that of who ought to apologize to whom and for what.

The memory of failure

Reconciliation proceeds on the assumption that public memory of historical failure is preliminary to the recognition of contemporary indigenous political rights. Public memory is not objective; it is created to suit particular purposes, and memorializing unjust acts against indigenous peoples is an essential step towards atonement. For example, in an address to the Aboriginal and Torres Strait Islanders, Pope John Paul II acknowledged the Catholic Church's historical failings towards Australia's indigenous peoples:

> The Church expresses deep regret and asks forgiveness where her children have been or still are party to these wrongs. Aware of the shameful injustices done to indigenous peoples in Oceania, the Synod Fathers apologize unreservedly for the part played in these by members of the Church, especially where children were forcibly separated from their families.[1]

Ecclesial failures were, however, interrupted by 'intermittent stirrings of a troubled conscience'[2] that, during the nineteenth and twentieth centuries, prompted occasional interventions in favor of indigenous rights so that religious and secular developments, beginning in the 1960s, could support the emergence of a two-fold public memory. First, this allows reconciliation to consider how the consequences of historic injustice might be addressed. Second, the memory of failure motivates the search for principles in both intellectual and missionary history to support restitution and relational justice in contemporary society. On the one hand, failure motivates attention to the constant religious truth of human dignity. On the other, the memorialization of prelates like John Polding, the first Archbishop of Sydney, who saw his advocacy for indigenous rights as an act of religious duty, is recalled to give particular purpose to contemporary public engagement. Similarly, the missionary priests Duncan McNab and Duncan McKillop saw themselves very much as religious, not political, activists. Their Church's magisterium had a particular contextual relevance that could never be made subservient to prevailing secular political aspirations of un-Christian intent: 'their Church did not require them to mask religious principle for the convenience of governments.'[3]

In New Zealand the presence of the first bishop, Jean-Baptiste Pompallier, at the signing of the Treaty of Waitangi is memorialized to explain a particular Catholic interest in the agreement as an instrument of reconciliation. In 1995 the New Zealand Catholic Bishops' Conference observed that:

> The Church was present in 1840, and is still present in 1995. Through its social teachings the Church seeks to ensure that the dignity of persons, and the common good of all, are reflected within the economic, social and political structures of society. Where there exist situations of conflict the Church seeks that social and economic life be directed toward just and peaceful solutions.[4]

1 John Paul II, 'Address to Aboriginal and Torres Strait Islanders,' in *Always the Same Spirit*, edited by Sandie Cornish (Homebush, NSW: St. Paul's, 1996), 28.

2 Eugene Stockton, 'Maverick Missionaries: An Overlooked Chapter in the History of Catholic Missions,' in *Aboriginal Australians and Christian Missions*, edited by T. Swain and D. Rose (Adelaide: Australian Association for the Study of Religions, 1988), 202.

3 Dominic O'Sullivan, *Faith Politics and Reconciliation: Catholicism and the Politics of Indigeneity* (Adelaide: The Australian Theological Forum, 2005), 253.

4 New Zealand Catholic Bishops' Conference, 'A Statement on the Treaty of Waitangi in Today's Perspective,' 1995. www.catholic.org.nz/news/fx-view-article.cfm?ctype=BSART&loadref=51&id=101 [accessed 5 October 2014].

Faith and memory are similarly important to wider Christian treaty discourses, as it was Anglican missionaries who drafted the agreement and translated it from English to Maori. While Pompallier offered no opinion on the treaty's wisdom, Anglican and Wesleyan missionaries actively promoted it to the Maori chiefs, which these churches presently accept as imposing a moral duty to advance a particular view of its contemporary significance. For example, the constitution of the Anglican Church in New Zealand, Aotearoa and Polynesia maintains that: 'by the Treaty of Waitangi, signed in 1840, the basis for future government and settlement was agreed. . . .'[5]

Sorrow in context

Since the Second Vatican Council (1962–1965), and in the context of concurrent political developments, Catholic interest in indigenous public policy is increasingly distinguished by a more deliberate public theology that is forthrightly and consistently advanced in sympathy with indigenous aspirations. However, for most of the twentieth century the Australian Church did not resist the break-up of families, even as Leo XIII insisted that it 'is a great and pernicious error' that 'the civil government should at its option intrude into and exercise intimate control over the family and the household.'[6] There were no religious grounds for setting aside this authoritative position of the Holy See and, instead, ecclesial practice was politically compliant with the imperial objectives of the British Crown. Religious failure has, then, become an obvious element in the memory of twentieth-century Catholic mission.

In 1869 Pius IX reminded the Australian bishops of a 'duty to the Aborigines,' which was emotively expressed, but inconsistently followed, in a Pastoral Letter suggesting that: 'White men have too often been apostles of Satan, have riveted his chains and confirmed his kingdom.'[7] The letter is drawn into Catholic public memory to justify the development of a public theology of reconciliation. However, it also contributes to the public memory of a Church that, more often than not, failed to recognize the connection between religious values and political decisions, as the subject did not receive further collective episcopal attention until 1971, after Paul VI's 'brief but positive greeting. . . to the Aborigines in Sydney.'[8]

> We know that you have a lifestyle proper to your own ethnic genius or culture – a culture which the Church respects and which she does not in any way

5 Constitution of the Anglican Church in New Zealand, Aotearoa and Polynesia, www.anglican.org.nz/CanonsReprint/English.pdf [accessed 25 May 2003].

6 Leo XIII, 'Rerum Novarum,' Vatican City (1891) www.ewtn.com/library/ENCYC/L13RERUM.TXT. 12 [accessed March 1998], 14.

7 The Bishops of Australia, 'The Bishops of Australia on Christian Duty to the Aboriginal People' (1869).

8 Christopher C. Prowse, 'Australia's Two Founding People's – Implications for Pastoral Directions,' *Australasian Catholic Record*, Vol 74 (1997), 604.

> ask you to renounce. . . . Society itself is enriched by the presence of different cultural and ethnic elements.[9]

Paul dismissed the assimilationist paradigm (whereby Australian public policy was directed to the gradual assimilation of indigenous peoples into the non-indigenous population) at the same time as it was gradually losing secular influence and credibility. Paul did not accept the narrowness of interpretation of the Church's theology that caused some prelates to minimize any relationship between religious objectives and political means. It was the diminishing of such a relationship that explained a missionary detachment from the full and immediate circumstances of people's lives that was common in the nineteenth and earlier twentieth centuries. It was a similar view that helped to explain the Australian Catholic Church's failure to intervene comprehensively, systematically and effectively in defense of indigenous children removed from their families from the early 1900s until the 1970s.

Reconciliation and memory

Memory brings the contemporary Church into the complex and still contested indigenous public policy domain, where reconciliation reflects a new-found religious certainty and rationale for Christian political engagement. Sacramentally, reconciliation requires the examination of personal conscience. The Church has tried to draw a theological parallel between the further sacramental understanding of reconciliation as the individual penitent correcting a relationship with God and public reconciliation, which involves a society correcting relationships among its members and, by extension, with God. Its presumption that memory is preliminary to atonement puts reconciliation at odds with Luhmann's (2002) secular perspective that 'memory's true function consists not in remembering but forgetting. Only by forgetting can a people reorient itself toward the future.'[10]

Reconciliation evokes a collective and public imperative. Religious language is employed to emphasize a transcendental significance beyond just private faith. Reconciliation is a religious call to human solidarity and to atonement for the failure to provide a public voice against un-Christian public policies. The connection between reconciliation as public theology and the penitent's sacramental intention of correcting a personal relationship with God is one that allows the Church to give substantive and practical interpretation to its place 'in but not of this world,' where sin is not simply a matter of private failing; it is structured into social and political organizations, resisted only by collective social conscience. Reconciliation proceeds as public theology because:

9 Paul VI, 'Speech to Indigenous Australians' (Sydney, 1970).

10 Barbara A. Misztal, 'Memory and Democracy,' *American Behavioral Scientist*, 48 (2005), 1320–1338, 1335.

> Christologically, God reconciles the world through Christ (Romans 5: 11). The death of Christ substitutes and atones for the sins of humanity, and marks the beginnings of a world that is not merely redeemed but transformed. Ecclesiologically, Christ reconciles disparate cultures, such as Jew and Gentile (Ephesians 2: 12–18). This is a kind of horizontal reconciliation. And, thirdly, Christ affects a cosmological reconciliation of all the universe (2 Corinthians 5: 11–21).[11]

Atonement for past errors is an affirmation of faith that allows the Church to prevent historical failure alone from defining its mission. Although serious, collective public failure, like personal failure, is not beyond resolve and one need not give up hope of an authentic religious contribution to human good.

The Church sees reconciliation as part of the salvific mission that it claims from Jesus Christ. It is part of a religious imperative to conform 'the earthly city. . .' to a constant truth, where human creation in the image and likeness of God assures all people an inherent dignity that can only be repeated and upheld in the public realm. Reconciliation draws together the Christological and the anthropological by locating Christ at the center of proper human relationships:

> Christian reconciliation is the drawing of persons to discover their humanity through forgiveness, repentance and reparation. It takes place inherently in the victim, and leads to forgiveness of the wrongdoer. Vulnerability is the condition for expressing the reconciling love of God. One is able to acknowledge and honor one's brokenness. One's personal story becomes integrated in the Christ narrative of passion, death and resurrection. It seeks repentance and forgiveness. It involves victims, wrongdoers, bystanders, the dead and future generations.[12]

Reconciliation's ultimate objective is the reordering of social values and relationships, which the Church sees in theological terms because values are the product of human conscience, ideally informed by 'the Grace of Jesus Christ in order to live and act as new creatures in the love of neighbor and in the effective search for justice.'[13]

Reconciliation reflects the role that memory plays in the human construction of the present. The past is recalled to suggest apology, atonement and relational justice. Its associated narratives have 'explicit and direct impact on national

11 Michael Phillips, 'Aboriginal Reconciliation as Religious Politics: Secularisation in Australia,' *Australian Journal of Political Science*, Vol 40 (2005), 111–124, 116.

12 Cyril Hally, 'Reconstructing the Moral Order of Society by Forgiveness and Reconciliation,' *Aboriginal Issues Newsletter*, No 2 (1998), 2.

13 Sacred Congregation for the Doctrine of the Faith, 'Instruction on Certain Aspects of the "Theology of Liberation",' Vatican City (1984) www.ewtn.com/library/CURIA/CDFLIBR1.HTM [accessed 10 January 2000], IV, 15.

identities'[14] which, in turn, influence how indigenous peoples experience and interpret the neo-colonial state's prevailing political arrangements and their own places in the national political community. Reconciliation's concern for just political relationships makes sense only with reference to the memory of injustice, and memory's public character is important because it is only through its public form that reconciliation counters the proposition that 'memory presents a threat to democratic community because it can undermine cohesion, increase the cost of cooperation, and cause moral damage to civil society by conflating political and ethnic or cultural boundaries.'[15] Instead, 'what matters for democracy's health is not social remembering *per se* but the way in which the past is called up and made present.'[16] 'Remembering is not a remedy for all problems. . . but open and reflexive public recollection can help make social life less alienating, autocratic, or dogmatic and more meaningful, decent, and creative.'[17] Reconciliation is a particular way of 'calling up' the past to ensure its presence. It is not couched in secular terms and is not proposed for liberal democracy's better functioning, but it does have that potential and it does illuminate for liberal democracy the importance of public memory to sustained relational justice.

In Australia, reconciliation has 'several distinctly Christian resonances and ambiguities, including the difficult relation of justice and forgiveness,'[18] and, since the early 1960s, shifts in public thinking have seen the Church's official teachings on just human relationships move from the margins to the broad, although still contested, mainstream of public thought on indigenous rights. In 1967 a referendum amended the Commonwealth Constitution to allow indigenous people to be counted in the national population census and to allow the Commonwealth, as well as the states, to pass laws for indigenous benefit. With his Anglican counterpart, Edward Doody, Bishop of Armidale, supported the amendments because removing 'any suggestion of race prejudice will demonstrate our real concern for the dark people who are fellow citizens.'[19] While the Australian bishops' expectations are yet to be fully met, the referendum allowed the Whitlam (1972–1975) and Fraser (1975–1983) governments to accord mainstream legitimacy to indigenous land rights which, by the late 1980s, had become the subject of important public policy measures. Public opinion on the merits of these policies was divided, but the policy environment provided a clear and concrete context for the Church to note an inescapable connection between religious rights and political means. By 1992 the High Court had rejected *terra nullius*, the

14 Elazar Barkan, 'Introduction: Historians and Historical Reconciliation,' *The American Historical Review*, Vol 114 (2009), 899–913, 900.

15 Barbara Misztal, 'Memory and Democracy,' *American Behavioral Scientist*, Vol 48 (2005), 1320–1338, 1320.

16 Ibid.

17 Ibid, 1336.

18 Phillips, 111.

19 Scott Bennett, *Aborigines and Political Power* (Sydney: Allen and Unwin, 1989), 11.

doctrine of British 'discovery' of 'unoccupied territory,' and held that British sovereignty did not, in and of itself, extinguish native title to land (*Mabo and Others* v *Queensland (No 2)*).[20] For John Bathersby, Archbishop of Brisbane, *Mabo* responded to Australia's 'evil' treatment of indigenous peoples, which ought to attract considerable public concern 'because we cannot really call ourselves a Christian nation until we have faced up to the problems squarely and engaged it with the energy and resources that it demands.'[21]

In 1991 the Hawke government (1983–1991) established a Council for Aboriginal Reconciliation to provide a 'lasting foundation for reconciliation' by the time of the centenary of Australia's federation in 2001. The council sought a 'document of reconciliation' to provide 'recognition and respect for the unique position of Aboriginal and Torres Strait Islander peoples as the indigenous peoples of Australia.'[22] By 1997 reconciliation still held particular indigenous policy influence and the 'Report of the National Inquiry into the Separation of Aboriginal and Torres Strait Islander Children from their Families' reinforced its significance. The Royal Commission recommended parliamentary apologies to removed children. While all state parliaments accepted the recommendation, it was not until 2008 when, after much debate and resistance, the federal parliament passed its own motion of apology.

Memory in political context

The Second Vatican Council's (1962–1965) reappraisal of the Church's relationship with the public realm prompted a greater awareness of connections between religious objectives and secular politics. It encouraged greater attentiveness to the Holy See's established teachings on the rights of indigenous peoples, and encouraged Catholic lay people to consider their participation in secular politics with particular reference to the Church's social doctrines. The shifting parameters of secular political debate influenced the Church's public memory of itself and the Holy See's consistent repudiation of racism came to influence, more systematically, the Church's understanding of itself as an ecclesial body '*in* but not *of* this world.' Faith could not be accepted just as a matter of private conscience. Instead, bearing witness to one's faith and accepting the 'discipleship of Christ' required public expression. It did not require uniformity of thought or suppression of individual conscience, but it did require the formation of conscience, according to an evaluation of 'the signs of the times' and attention to the public implications of human creation 'in the image and likeness of God.'

20 '*Mabo and Others v Queensland (No 2)*,' in *175 CLR 1 F.C. 92/014* (High Court of Australia, 1992).
21 John Bathersby, 'Address to Griffith University, 20 March 1992' (1992).
22 Council for Aboriginal Reconciliation (2003) www.austlii.edu.au/au/orgs/car/ [accessed 7 January 2003].

> The separation of faith from life has been resolved for those who really took the [Second Vatican] Council's message to heart. The Spirit is moving the Church in Oceania to discover new ways of telling the truth of Jesus Christ in a secular society.[23]

However, the choice to intervene is not always a simple one and the ease with which intervention occurs is a product of the political space that exists for certain ideas to be advanced. The contemporary Church has certainly taken advantage of the movement of its ideas on racial equality from the fringes of secular debate to the mainstream. The parameters of accepted public debate have broadened significantly, and even as racism remains an important part of the political landscape it is more overtly contested. There is significant scope for the alignment of common aspiration between ecclesial and secular actors interested in relational justice, as reconciliation's ultimate purpose. For the Australian Catholic Social Justice Council, relational justice for indigenous peoples stems from the right to self-determination. It

> follows from the belief that each person is unique, and created to the image and likeness of God. Each then reflects God's beauty, intelligence, power, freedom and love. We are all called to be free, autonomous, self determining masters of their own destiny responsible for our own decisions.[24]

From the right to self-determination arise rights to dignity, culture, religious freedom and a share in the common good. While the Church accepts that these goals require political realization, it sees them and advocates for them as a 'discipleship of Christ,'[25] which is not an abstract concept but one demanding practical expression in the immediate context of people's lives. For the Church to exercise its mission authentically and prophetically it must be alert to opportunities to give secular context to its wider aspirations for humanity.

Self-determination belongs first and foremost to individuals, but in Catholic teaching the human person is fundamentally social and exercises the rights and responsibilities of their human being in association with others. Self-determination must, then, logically extend to the cultural groups to which people belong and must imply the right to exist as preliminary to any further rights. In 1978 the Australian Catholic Social Justice Commission's discussion of racism as 'the most insidious and oppressive form of prejudice and discrimination'[26] preceded a series

23 The General Secretariat of the Synod of Bishops and Editrice Libreria, *Instrumentum Laboris, Synod of Bishops for Oceania. Jesus Christ and the Peoples of Oceania: Walking His Way, Telling His Truth and Living His Life* (Vatican: 1998), 23.

24 Australian Catholic Social Justice Council, 'Social Justice Council Marks National Sorry Day' (media release, 1998).

25 Matthew, 28: 19–20 *Good News Bible: Today's English Version* (London: 1981).

26 Australian Catholic Social Justice Council, 'Social Justice Sunday Statement' (1978), 4.

of Catholic interventions that showed the fuller possibilities of Leo XIII's injunction that:

> from God has the duty been assigned to the Church not only to interpose resistance, if at any time the State rule should run counter to religion, but, further, to make a strong endeavor that the power of the Gospel may pervade the law and institutions of the nations.[27]

The Church's post Vatican II teaching on the rights of indigenous peoples is itself a public memorialization of the past. Broad statements of religious principle provide a rationale for parliaments to say sorry and it is in response to public memory that the Church 'attempts not merely to proclaim principles of Christian social teaching and of the natural law. It also tries to apply these principles to real and oppressing social issues. . . .'[28] For example, in response to a 'Petition to John Paul II from the World's Oldest Living Culture' during a tour of Australia in 1986, the Pope drew on Polding's memory to confront the assimilationist narrative that questions reconciliation's legitimacy and utility.

> From the earliest times men like Archbishop Polding of Sydney opposed the legal fiction adopted by European settlers that this land was *terra nullius* – nobody's country. He strongly pleaded for the rights of the Aboriginal inhabitants to keep the traditional lands on which their whole society depended. The Church still supports you today. . . .
>
> Let it not be said that the fair and equitable recognition of Aboriginal rights to land is discrimination. To call for the acknowledgement of the land rights of people who have never surrendered those rights is not discrimination.[29]

The Pope encouraged indigenous peoples to pursue their human rights as a mark of inherent dignity and to show a new-found acceptance of the relationship between religious means and political ends.

John Paul II's insistence that the Church's social teaching 'be taught and implemented still more effectively' in the context of it being the 'Church's task to help indigenous cultures preserve their identities and maintain their traditions' was made alongside an unequivocal admission of the Church's own role in the disruption of indigenous cultures.

> In the past, some Christians in Oceania have. . . shared responsibility for political and social injustices. Not only individual Christians but also church

27 Leo XIII, 'Sapientiae Christiannae,' Vatican City (1890) www.ewtn.com/library/ENCYC/L13SAPIE.TXT [accessed 12 March 1998].

28 Australian Catholic Bishops' Conference, 'Aboriginal People' (Pastoral Letter, 1980).

29 John Paul II, 'Address to Aboriginal and Torres Strait Islanders,' in *Always the Same Spirit*, edited by Sandie Cornish (Homebush, NSW: St. Paul's, 1996).

> leaders have committed errors, approved un-Christian actions or been passive before injustices.[30]

This admission of moral failure allows the Church to recall the memory of earlier Australian Catholics such as Archbishop Polding, whose perspectives on just human relationships remain relevant in the modern era, and provide guidance on how Christians might contribute to policy debate and strengthen the Church's belief in public memory as an important contributor to justice.

Public memory, public reconciliation

The public reconciliation movement was compromised by the Howard government's (1996–2007) resolve to diminish the significance of judgments in *Mabo* and *Wik Peoples* v *the State of Queensland* and by the Prime Minister equating 'sorrow' with personal guilt and culpability. Howard's fear was, in fact, a deeper one and, theologically, there is no association between public apology and personal guilt.[31] The Prime Minister was concerned to avoid the commitments that follow from sorrow. His Aboriginal Affairs Minister, John Heron, presented the argument in this way:

> The government does not support an official national apology. Such an apology could imply the present generations are in some way responsible and accountable for the actions of earlier generations, actions that were sanctioned by the laws of the time, and that were believed to be in the best interests of the children concerned.[32]

Clearly the state parliaments that passed motions of apology did not share Heron's view and it is reasonable to conclude that, if a parliament is not bound by its predecessors, it can legitimately set aside and correct the consequences of a predecessor's legislation. In this sense, contemporary legislators can accept responsibility for addressing the consequences of the policies of another era's legislation. Indeed, governments do not, as a matter of course, deny compensation to people who have been disadvantaged or discriminated against through considered public policy. Additionally, the suggestion that apologies are not warranted simply because measures were legal at the time of their commission suggests that it is the law alone that determines right from wrong, rather than deeper moral principles.

30 John Paul II, 'Ecclesia in Oceania,' Vatican City (2001) www.vatican.va/holy_father/john_paul_ii/apost_exhortations/documents/hf_jp-ii_exh_20011122_ecclesia-in-oceania_en.html [accessed 13 December 2001], 28.

31 Christopher Prowse, 'Australia's Two Founding People's – Implications for Pastoral Directions,' *Australasian Catholic Record*, 74 (1997).

32 John Heron (Letter to Father Frank Brennan, SJ, 1996).

The policy merits of restitution and reparation have, in contrast, been accepted into New Zealand public policy discourse, where settlements for Crown breaches of the Treaty of Waitangi include apologies by Acts of Parliament. In 1995 the Waikato Raupatu Claims Settlement Act became the first of many acts of reconciliation with tribal communities. There was no argument about the merits of saying sorry; the instances of sorrow and the people to whom the apology was directed were clearly set out to show that 'the government led by a lay Catholic, Jim Bolger, accepted what the Howard government dismissed – that saying "sorry" is accompanied by a requirement to address the consequences of injustice.'[33] The apology was for what the Crown acknowledged as an 'invasion' in 1863, and sought 'on behalf of all New Zealanders to atone for these, acknowledged injustices, so far as that is now possible, and. . . to begin the process of healing and to enter a new age . . . of cooperation.'[34]

Further settlements acknowledged that the Crown 'acted unconscionably and in repeated breach of the Treaty of Waitangi,'[35] while settlement with the Tūhoe tribe, in 2014, again emphasized the significance of political relationships among memory, apology, restitution and relational justice. As the Minister for Treaty of Waitangi Negotiations explained:

> Through this apology and settlement the Crown hopes to honestly confront the past and seeks to atone for its wrongs. The Crown hopes to build afresh its relationship with Tūhoe and that this new relationship will endure for current and future generations. Let these words guide our way to a greenstone door – *tatau pounamu* – which looks back on the past and closes it, which looks forward to the future and opens it.[36]

Treaty settlements give practical political effect to reconciliation's theological imperatives. They make apologies but do not impose personal culpability on the descendants of those who commissioned the original transgression. Compensation is offered as both an act of atonement and restitution to support the economic foundation for stronger relationships between the *iwi* (tribe) and wider society. Yet Howard's 'practical reconciliation' avoided the possibility of financial recompense and is further understood with reference to the assimilationist narrative that distinguished his government's indigenous policy. For Howard, practical reconciliation was:

33 O'Sullivan, 73.

34 Waikato Raupatu Claims Settlement Act 1995, Part I, s 6 (6).

35 Ngai Tahu Claims Settlement Act 1988, www.legislation.govt.nz/browse_vw.asp?content-set=pal_statutes [accessed 2 June 2003].

36 Christopher Finlayson, 'Address to Tuhoe-Crown Settlement Day in Taneatua' (2014) www.beehive.govt.nz/speech/address-tuhoe-crown-settlement-day-taneatua [accessed 6 October 2014].

> more than recognition of the damaging impact on people's lives of the mistaken practices of the past. It also calls for a clear focus on the future. It calls for practical policy making that effectively addresses current indigenous disadvantage particularly in areas such as employment, health, education and housing.[37]

Although practical reconciliation can be substantively important it cannot, theologically, 'be fully appropriated without apology. Those who are in great pain cannot experience health until dignity has been restored.'[38] Apology's symbolism is accompanied by substantive recognition of human dignity, which means that apologies are not always and necessarily inconsistent with measures of practical value. Apology has, in fact, become 'a very powerful instrument of recognition . . . refusal to give one withholds that recognition with new sharpness.'[39] It is this consideration, and the connection it made between sorrow and substance, that made the Motion of Apology, moved by Kevin Rudd, the Australian Prime Minister, in the House of Representatives in February 2008 especially significant:

> The time has now come for the nation to turn a new page in Australia's history by righting the wrongs of the past and so moving forward with confidence to the future.
>
> We apologize for the laws and policies of successive parliaments and governments that have inflicted profound grief, suffering and loss on these our fellow Australians.
>
> We apologize especially for the removal of Aboriginal and Torres Strait Islander children from their families, their communities and their country.
>
> For the pain, suffering and hurt of these Stolen Generations, their descendants and for their families left behind, we say sorry.
>
> To the mothers and the fathers, the brothers and the sisters, for the breaking up of families and communities, we say sorry.
>
> And for the indignity and degradation thus inflicted on a proud people and a proud culture, we say sorry.
>
> Let us resolve over the next five years to have every indigenous four-year-old in a remote Aboriginal community enrolled and attending a proper early childhood education centre. . . and engaged in proper preliteracy and prenumeracy programs. . . . Let us resolve [also] to use this systemic approach. . . to provide proper primary and preventive health care for the same children, to begin the task of rolling back the obscenity that we find

37 Judith Brett, 'Relaxed and Comfortable: The Liberal Party's Australia,' in *The Australian Quarterly Essay* (Melbourne: Schwartz Publishing, 2005), 89.

38 Francis Carroll, *Catholic Leader* (2000).

39 M. Warner quoted in Misztal, 13.

today in infant mortality rates in remote indigenous communities – up to four times higher than in other communities.[40]

For Pope Benedict XVI the apology was 'courageous' and could complement 'concrete steps' towards reconciliation. That Benedict's intervention was not met with the same derision that distinguished some public responses to John Paul II's advocacy of land rights in 1986 suggests that, perhaps with reconciliation's influence, there has been a significant shift in public attitudes to indigenous rights and aspirations. However, with apology setting the context for relational justice there is still much to be achieved in practical policy outcomes, as measures to improve indigenous incomes, education, housing and life expectancy have enjoyed only partial success in the years following the apology. At the same time, measures to improve relative political equality are neither fully developed nor accepted.

Conclusion

Public memory, including the Catholic Church's memory of its own acquiescence with public policies of un-Christian intent, helped to bring reconciliation on to the Australian indigenous policy agenda. Reconciliation, with its focus on sorrow as the basis for substantive political recognition, makes sense of the present and the future with reference to the public memory of the past. While reconciliation is an instrument of practical contemporary politics, its rationale is very much based on the ways in which the past influences the present. It recalls the past to propose new forms of political relationships and, from a religious perspective, shows the relevance of secular politics to the realization of religious goals, including the recognition of religious, economic, cultural and land rights and the rights of the family to function as a primary social unit. The Church's public memory is the memory of an institution that allowed its own religious values to be set aside in favor of secular colonial objectives. There are both political and theological explanations, but what is especially significant is that, on balance, the memory is one of profound failure. Yet failure is a powerful inspiration to think and act differently and to recall the 'religious truths' that it claims might guide alternative human relationships, including those explicit in public apology and those that might give effect to policies of material significance.

40 Kevin Rudd, *Apology to Australia's Indigenous Peoples* (Dept. of Prime Minister and Cabinet, 2008).

12 A pastoral care for reconciliation?

Spanish Catholic bishops and historical memory during the Zapatero era (2004–2011)

Mireno Berrettini

The end of the 'transition consensus'

In 1936 a failed military *golpe* against the Spanish Second Republic government led to the civil war. The Catholic Church did not take part in the *putsch* but immediately took the rebel side.[1] In reaction to this some uncontrolled Republicans started burning churches and killing priests, until the official Republican government stopped them.[2] After three years of fighting the rebels – who called themselves Nationalists – won the war. In 1939 Spain did not reach peace, there was just victory of one side over the other. With the active and passive collaboration of some Catholic believers,[3] Francoists started a radical political repression.[4] For 40 years the dictatorship promoted its official memory and wrote its official history.[5] For 40 years the Catholic Church supported the regime, played a central role in the Spanish political system,[6] and celebrated those priests killed by Republicans during the years of the civil war. However, in 1975 the old dictator, Francisco Franco, died. The Spanish transition to democracy started, changing the *rules of the game.*

The transition has long been considered a model of peaceful change from authoritarian to democratic rule, particularly in comparison to other countries of

1 Alfonso Álvarez Bolado, *Para ganar la guerra, para ganar la paz: Iglesia y guerra civil: 1936–1939* (Madrid: Universidad Pontificia de Comillas, 1995).

2 José Luís Ledesma Vera, 'Total War Behind the Frontlines? An Inquiry into the Violence on the Republican Side in the Spanish Civil War,' in *If You Tolerate This. . . The Spanish Civil War in the Age of Total Wars*, edited by Martin Baumeister and Stefanie Schüler-Springorum (Frankfurt-New York: Campus, 2008), 154–168.

3 See: Gumersindo de Estella, *Fusilados en Zaragoza 1936–1939. Tres años de asistencia espiritual a los reos* (Zaragoza: Mira, 2015).

4 Javier Rodrigo, *Violencia durante la Guerra Civil y la dictadura franquista* (Madrid: Alianza, 2008).

5 Paloma Aguilar, *Memoria y olvido de la Guerra Civil española* (Madrid: Alianza, 1996).

6 Alfonso Botti, *Cielo y dinero. El nacionalcatolicismo en España (1881–1975)* (Madrid: Alianza, 1992).

the so-called 'Third Wave' of democratization.[7] Today Spain is a leading western democracy with stable political institutions and the rule of law. However, the transition did not resolve the issue of the collective memory of Spain's traumatic twentieth century. In the 1970s the civil war was stamped out from public discourse.[8] The Catholic Church actively contributed to this silence.[9] However, nearly 40 years after the end of the Franco regime the civil war has once again become a central issue in Spanish politics. From the mid-1990s civil society groups such as the Association for the Recovery of Historical Memory started to claim public recognition for the memory of the Republicans defeated in 1939, and the Spanish political class began a modest revaluation of the losers (*vencidos*).[10] Within this new framework we can find the genesis of the so-called *Ley de Memoria Histórica* or Law of Historical Memory (HML), proposed by the socialist government of José Luis Rodríguez Zapatero and approved by the *Cortes* in 2007.

Although HML is moderate and does not impose an official memory, some sectors of Spanish Catholicism saw it as the symbolic vengeance of the Socialist Party 60 years after the end of the civil war. In 2006, during the negotiations for the law, the *Conferencia Episcopal Española* (CEE), the assembly of bishops, issued '*Orientaciones morales ante la situación actual de España*' ('A moral guideline for the present Spanish situation'), a collective document that considered HML as a 'historical and civil regression that represents a clear risk in terms of tensions, discrimination and alterations to compromise the peaceful coexistence.' In the bishops' opinion the HML was reopening the 'old wounds of the civil war' that had been healed during the transition.[11]

This article analyzes the Spanish bishops' memorial narrative on the war. The Catholic bishops, believing that Spanish reconciliation was threatened, began to represent themselves as the true guardians of the memory constructed during the transition and developed a pastoral strategy which, although aiming at reconciliation, resulted in a multiplication of frictions among the Spaniards.

October 28 2007: new Catholic blessed in Zapatero's Spain

In the second half of the 1980s the Catholic Church began to follow a special path of victimization, if not martyrization. The first step occurred in Rome on

7 The concept in Samuel P. Huntington, *The Third Wave: Democratization in the Late Twentieth Century* (Norman: University of Oklahoma Press, 1991).

8 Santos Juliá, 'Echar al olvido. Memoria y amnistía en la transición,' *Claves de Razón Práctica*, Vol 129 (2003), 14–24.

9 Mireno Berrettini, 'La riconciliazione nel pensiero pastorale del Cardinal Tarancón,' *Storia e problemi contemporanei*, Vol 47 (2008), 81–90.

10 Francisco Sevillano, 'La construcción de la memoria y el olvido en la España democratic,' *Ayer*, Vol 52 (2003), 297–319.

11 Asamblea Plenaria de la Conferencia Episcopal Española, *Orientaciones morales antes la situación actual del España* (Madrid: Conferencia Episcopal Española, 2006), 4.

29 March 1987 when Pope John Paul II declared 'blessed'[12] the Carmelite of Guadalajara killed in 1936. Considering that during the post-conciliar years Pope Paul VI had decided to put a stop to the canonization and beatification process, Pope John Paul II's decision is all the more ground-breaking. Between 1987 and 1999 he beatified 227 martyrs of the Spanish Civil War. In 1999, for the first time, nine of the martyrs reached sainthood; while in 2001 the first mass celebration took place in which 233 new martyrs were declared. In total almost 500 martyrs were declared up to 2004, the year when Zapatero and his Partido Socialista Obrero Español (PSOE) won the elections in Spain. Despite the great controversy that this policy has generated,[13] the Catholic hierarchy has always rejected the accusation of complicity with the Nationalists during both the civil war and the subsequent political repression during the period of the Franco regime. The bishops represented the entire Church as 'passive and just a victim.'[14]

On 28 October 2007, under the direction of Pope Benedict XVI, 498 (new) victims of the civil war violence were beatified as martyrs during a spectacular ceremony in Rome. The Spanish prelates expressed their opinion on the matter both in pastoral letters and in public speeches and homilies.[15] This doctrinal production shares some common traits: the martyrs are represented as simple people, faithful innocents killed *in odium fidei* (hatred of the faith). The bishops highlighted the correct meaning of these beatifications and described the new blessed as not 'involved in the fight between brothers'[16] and 'above the factions or partizanship.'[17] According to the Catholic hierarchy the 'historical background' of the 1930s was 'marked by radical materialism of some triumphant political ideologies: Fascism and Communism.[18] But the martyrs 'neither sympathized with this or that ideology, nor were in the battlefield for one side or another in our civil war.'[19] All these positions are well summarized in the collective document entitled *Vosotros sois la luz del mundo* (You are the light of the world), a pastoral

12 In Catholicism a 'blessed' is a person who, after a special process, is recognized to have had in life exceptional virtues from the point of view of faith. After the official declaration ceremony a blessed becomes a reference point for believers. A blessed differs from a saint because the latter has a higher position in the theological and canonic hierarchy.

13 See: Hilari Raguer, 'Los martires de la Guerra Civil,' *Razon y Fe. Revista ispano-americana de cultura*, Vol 5 (1987), 883–892.

14 Juan G. Bedoya, 'Los Obispos insisten en que la Iglesia fue «sujeto paciente y víctima» de la Guerra Civil,' *El País*, 8 April 2000, 12.

15 See Mireno Berrettini, 'Spagna e nuovi beati. La Jerarquía tra riconciliazione e combate por la memoria,' *Studi e Ricerche di Storia Contemporanea*, Vol 70 (2008), 2–32.

16 José Sánchez González, *Beatificaciones en Roma el 28 de Octubre de 2007* (Sigüenza-Guadalajara: Obispado de Sigüenza-Guadalajara, 2007), 24.

17 Demetrio Fernández, 'Mártires de nuestro tiempo,' *Zenit*, 3 November 2011, 7.

18 Antonio M. Rouco Varela, 'San Rafael Arnáiz Barón: un santo de nuestro tiempo, Homilía en la Eucaristía de Acción de Gracias en honor de San Rafael Arnáiz Barón con motivo de su Canonización,' *Archimadrid*, 12 October 2009, 5.

19 Braulio Rodríguez Plaza, *Mártires* (Valladolid: Arzobispado de Valladolid, 2007), 2.

letter issued by the CEE in April 2007 that stated: 'the martyrs are above the tragic circumstances that led to their death.'[20] In a clear and explicit way the bishops represented the Catholic Church as a 'third space,' not involved in the war and victim of this conflict.

This narrative construction has many implications. First, the 'third space' position contributes to an axiological discrimination among the victims of the civil war. Also in 2007, another collective document '*Beatificación de 498 mártires del siglo XX en España*' ('Beatification of 498 martyrs of the twentieth century in Spain') explained that:

> Wars have *fallen* on one side and the other. Political repressions have *victims*. . . . Only the religious persecutions have *martyrs*.[21]

Therefore the dead are not all equal. The Catholic victims of Francoist violence are less important than those killed by the anti-clerical Republicans; they cannot be martyrs because they are ontologically different. This position resounded with the historiographical analysis of Vicente Cárcel Ortí, a Spanish priest, researcher and head of the Supreme Tribunal of the Apostolic Signatura in the Holy See. In 2008 he published '*Caídos, víctimas y mártires: La Iglesia y la hecatombe de 1936*' ('Fallen, victims and martyrs: The Church and the carnage of 1936') explaining that 'this is a substantial difference because the martyr is not involved in the war; the martyr was not killed for political reasons but for religious reasons.'[22]

The presence of Catholics killed by Francoists represents a logical anomaly within this argument. The bishops faced this problem with two discursive strategies: silence and flexibility. The first can be seen in July 2011 when the remains of a priest murdered by Francoists were found in a mass grave near Gumiel de Izán (in the province of Burgos).[23] No comments were released by the Catholic hierarchy. As an example of the second strategy we can consider '*Purificar la memoria, servir a la verdad, pedir perdón*' ('Purifying the memory, serving the truth, asking for forgiveness'), a collective document issued by the four bishops of the Basque dioceses in 2009. They officially recognized 'the dignity of those who have been forgotten or excluded and ease the pain of their families and friends.' Newspapers saw this document as the first public celebration by a Catholic authority of the victims of Francoist repression. However, a careful reading reveals that the bishops celebrated only the '14 [Basque] priests executed

20 Asamblea Plenaria de la Conferencia Episcopal Española, *Vosotros sois la luz del mundo (Mt 5,14). Mensaje con motivo de la beatificación de 498 mártires del siglo XX en España* (Madrid: Conferencia Episcopal Española, 2007), 2.

21 Oficina de Información de la Conferencia Episcopal Española, *Beatificación de 498 mártires del siglo XX en España* (Madrid: Conferencia Episcopal Española, 2007), 5.

22 Vicente Cárcel Ortí, *Caídos, víctimas y mártires: La Iglesia y la hecatombe de 1936* (Madrid: Espana-Calpe, 2008), 295.

23 L. Sierra, 'Aparece un religioso entre los restos de 50 fusilados en una fosa de Gumiel de Izán,' *El Norte de Castilla*, 6 July 2011, 8.

in 1936 and 1937 by the winner of that war.'[24] In this sense, their discourse reiterated the same argument of the CEE; the Catholic Church was still presented as a victim of the conflict. It was still presented as a 'third space,' not involved in the war. And, finally, the Basque hierarchy asked God's forgiveness for the sins of all Spain and did not request any forgiveness for the collaboration of the Church in the anti-Republican repression.[25]

Spanish 'martyrs of the twentieth century'

The Spanish Church has been using the expression 'martyrs of the twentieth century' since the transition in the 1970s. This formula shows the bishops' interpretation of the entire century as an age of destruction driven by humanity's repudiation of God. It is an updated version of the long-term post-French Revolution Catholic paradigm. However, it would be simplistic to consider the above-mentioned expression as a return to a remote past; rather, it as a flexible return to the path left momentarily during the transition, a new pastoral strategy that allows the Church to face the challenges of the present situation.

The expression 'martyrs of the twentieth century' is a vague formula, used to engraft the Spanish case onto a global-scale persecution that runs throughout the entire twentieth century, from the Mexican Revolution in the 1910s to present day Islamic fundamentalism. It follows the lines of two important books edited in the framework of the Great Jubilee of 2000: *The Catholic Martyrs of the Twentieth Century: A Comprehensive World History*, published by Robert Royal, president of the American Faith and Reason Institute,[26] and, most of all, Andrea Riccardi's *Il secolo del martirio* (*The Century of Martyrdom*), translated into Spanish in 2001 with the title *El siglo de los mártires*.[27] Riccardi, who is Professor of Contemporary History at Università degli Studi di Roma III, is the founder of the Comunità di Sant'Egidio, an international Catholic secular movement which had a great influence on the Church of John Paul II. Significantly, the Pope gave the Comunità di Sant'Egidio the direction of the 'New Martyrs Committee' and the pastoral care of the Basilica of St Bartholomew on Tiber Island, in Rome, which can be considered as the memorial to the 'witnesses of the faith of the twentieth century.' The Pope himself mentioned Riccardi's thesis in his homily during the ecumenical ceremony at the Coliseum on 7 May 2000:

24 Ricardo Blázquez, with Juan María Uriarte and others, 'Purificar la memoria, servir a la verdad, pedir perdón,' *Boletín Oficial del Obispado de Vitoria*, Vol 10 (2009), 646–648.

25 See: Mireno Berrettini, 'A settant'anni dalla Carta Collettiva dell'Episcopato spagnolo: Jerarquía, martirio, memoria collettiva,' in *Un conflitto che non passa. Storia, memoria e rimozioni della guerra civile spagnola*, edited by Enrico Acciai and Giulia Quaggio (Pistoia: ISRPT, 2012), 42–65.

26 Robert Royal, *The Catholic Martyrs of the Twentieth Century: A Comprehensive World History* (New York: Crossroad, 2000).

27 Andrea Riccardi, *El siglo de los mártires* (Barcelona: Plaza y Janés, 2001).

> The experience of the martyrs and the witnesses to the faith is not a characteristic only of the Church's beginnings but marks every epoch of its history. In the twentieth century, and maybe even more than in the first period of Christianity, there has been a vast number of men and women who bore witness to the faith through sufferings that were often heroic.[28]

One of the most important books written by a Spanish Catholic historian, Carcel Ortí's *La persecución religiosa en España durante la Segunda República, 1931–1939,* has been translated into Polish (*The Religious Persecution in Spain during the Second Republic, 1931–1939*).[29] Like Jorge López Teulón's *Los mártires de Hitler* (*The Martyrs of Hitler*),[30] this book is an example of an attempt by a Spanish Catholic writer to connect the martyrs of the Spanish Civil War to other international persecutions, such as those perpetrated by the Nazis and the Communists.

Moreover, according to Monseñor Carcel Ortí, the religious persecution in Spain began in 1931 with the official institution of the Second Republic (1931–1939), while during the civil war (1936–1939) the entire Church was in a 'third space' position between the two fighting parts. Significantly these kind of arguments were expressed in some books published before and during the Zapatero era: *La gran persecución: España, 1931–1939* (*The Great Persecution: Spain 1931–1939*) and *Pío XI entre la República y Franco: angustía del Papa entre la tragedia española* (*Pius XI between the Republic and Franco: Pope Anguish during the Spanish Tragedy*).[31] In its pastoral letters the Spanish hierarchy follows these positions. In this way bishops remove the responsibilities of the anti-Republican rebels (the Francoists) in the genesis of the religious persecution, since the historiography demonstrated that anti-clerical violence was indirectly triggered by Franco's coup.

The new narrative is an ideological legitimation of the rapprochement between Catholicism and the Spanish post-Francoist political party: the Partido Popular (PP). The PP shares the bishops' vision of the past,[32] and during the Zapatero

28 John Paul II, *Ecumenical Commemoration of the Witness of the Faith in the Twentieth Century.* 7 May 2000, 2.

29 Vicente Carcel Ortí, *La persecución religiosa en España durante la Segunda República, 1931–1939* (Madrid: Rialp, 1990) and *Mrok nad ołtarzem: prześladowanie Kościoła w Hiszpanii w latach 1931–1939* (Warszawa: Pax, 2003).

30 Jorge López Teulón, *Los mártires de Hitler. Víctor in Vínculis: altísimo Señor, bendice también a mis enemigos* (Talavera de la Reina: Trinidad, 1996).

31 Vicente Carcel Ortí, *La gran persecución: España, 1931–1939* (Barcelona: Planeta, 2000) and *Pío XI entre la República y Franco: angustía del Papa entre la tragedia española* (Madrid: Biblioteca de Autores Cristianos, 2008).

32 See Pedro C. González Cuevas, 'El retorno de la "tradición" liberal-conservadora. El "discurso" histórico-político de la nueva derecha española,' *Ayer*, Vol 22 (1996), 71–87; Xosé M. Núñez Seixas, 'Sobre la memoria historia reciente y el "discurso patriótico" español del siglo XXI,' *Historia del Presente*, Vol 3 (2004), 137–155.

governments the PP opposed passage of the HML, affirming that 'the compensation to victims has been done, past wounds were closed in the transition.'[33] It is not a coincidence, therefore, that between 2004 and 2011 the hierarchy supported the *populares* in every round of elections.[34] The Church acts as a 'strategic moral actor.'[35] The bishops are using martyrs to 'indicate an authentic social project,'[36] to convey political positions, to criticize abortion and to repair the 'degradation of the family.' In doing so they are triangulating with the PP initiatives. Both of them perceive Zapatero's policies (like same-sex marriage, so-called 'express' divorce and abortion) as proof of the crisis of western civilization, brought about by the extreme consequences of secularization and philosophical relativism.[37]

Martyrs are an example of a new model of citizenship that is not founded on fleeting and relativistic opinions but on a transcendental Truth defined and preserved by the Church. In the aforementioned *Vosotros sois la luz del mundo* we can read that martyrs 'testified a supreme Truth that sets us free,' and that this Truth is the 'biggest promoter of dignity and freedom of every person.'[38] This means that the bishops are proposing a religious foundation of human rights. These ones cannot be based solely on pure secular pillars.[39] For Spanish Catholic bishops, the final guarantor of human dignity, freedom and rights can be only God. If democracy does not have a transcendent reference it can easily turn into totalitarianism.[40]

The bishops are also proposing a religious foundation for Spanish democracy, updating an old paradigm. During the dictatorship the bishops spoke of the 'debt to the dead,' meaning the debt of the Spanish nation towards the victims of Republican anti-clerical persecution. Their blood allowed the re-establishment

33 These are the words of a PP politician, Manuel Atencia, see Pedro A. Navarro, 'Ley de Memoria Histórica ¿Insuficiente o innecesaria? Los rescoldos de la guerra aún queman,' *El siglo de Europa*, 721 (2006), 2.

34 See Mireno Berrettini, 'The Spanish Catholic Church from the Zapatero Era to the Rajoy Government,' in *Politics and Society in Contemporary Spain: From Zapatero to Rajoy*, edited by Bonnie Field and Alfonso Botti (New York: Palgrave, 2013), 161–178.

35 Paul C. Manuel and Margaret Mott, 'Una Messe est Possible. The Imbroglio of the Catholic Church in Contemporary Latin Europe,' *Center for European Studies Working Paper*, 113 (2004), 22.

36 Carlos Osoro, 'Homilía en el 75° aniversario de los Mártires de Turón. Parroquia de San Martín de Turón, 9 de octubre de 2009,' *Boletín Oficial del Arzobispado de Oviedo*, No 11 (2009), 607.

37 See: Vincenzo Ferrone, *Lo strano Illuminismo di Joseph Ratzinger* (Roma-Bari: Laterza, 2013).

38 Asamblea Plenaria de la Conferencia Episcopal Española, Vosotros sois la luz del mundo, 4.

39 See: the arguments of Benedetto XVI, *Discorso del Santo Padre Benedetto XVI. Reichstag di Berlino* 22 September 2011.

40 See: Daniele Menozzi, *Chiesa e diritti umani. Legge naturale e modernità politica dalla Rivoluzione francese ai nostri giorni* (Bologna: Il Mulino, 2012).

of peace and was the pillar of the Francoist state. Something similar is happening today when the bishops speak of the martyr's 'heroic forgiveness' as the pillar of 'the spirit of reconciliation.'[41] That is, the citizens of (the Spanish) democracy are now indebted to the martyrs. Their forgiveness has become the basis of the democratic present. The references are changed but the logic is the same: the religious foundation of common life. The bishops, through the martyrs' intercession, are actively asking for forgiveness for the sins of all the Spaniards. According to this construct the Church becomes a place of true reconciliation, a channel through which it is possible to overcome division among Spaniards. The forgiveness offered by the martyrs to their executioners is 'the true commitment to reconciliation in relation to conflicts that already belong to history and involves a determination to combine the forgiveness to the true.'[42] This is the reason why the celebration of the historical memory of the victims of Francoist repression, HML, reopens wounds while the celebration of the martyrs of Republican persecution helps reconciliation. This position strengthens the 'third space' model, making of the Church the place for reconciliation, the actor which seals the new foundation of Spanish society, and of the transition the new golden age of Spanish democracy.

The new citizen promoted by the bishops possesses the distinctive traits proper to the martyrs: orthodoxy to the commandments of the Church, austerity and self-discipline. These are also the main characteristics of the new believer. According to this logic the 'pastoral of memory' promoted by the Catholic hierarchy is a strategic move connected to the Church program for a 'new evangelization' of Spanish society.[43] The martyr figure provides a tactic to face the changes in Spanish religion, from Catholicism *à la carte*[44] to the crisis of institutional religions.[45] It is no coincidence that the celebrations of the martyrs tend to be huge mass events, where participants are mobilized at the irrational level.[46] The mass celebration of 2007 was not only a test of strength against the PSOE but a real pastoral tool: 71 Spanish bishops and 1,300 priests attended the event, and more than 50,000 pilgrims went to St Peter's Square in Rome. According to the CEE, more than 534,000 viewers watched the beatification ceremony and the mass of thanksgiving

41 Oficina de Información de la Conferencia Episcopal Española, Beatificación de 498 mártires del siglo XX en España, 8.

42 Agustín García-Gasco, 'Reconciliación,' *Paraula. Iglesia en Valencia*, 25 March 2007, 20.

43 The formula in John Paul II, *Santa messa nel santuario della Santa Croce. Omelia di Giovanni Paolo II*, 9 June 1979, 3.

44 The formula in Jean L. Schlegel, *Religions à al carte* (Paris: Hachette, 1995).

45 See José M. Mardones, *Postmodernidad y cristianismo. El desafio de la diferencia* (Santander: Sal Térrae, 1988) and Danièle Hervieu Léger, *Vers un nouveau christianisme. Introduction à la sociologie du christianisme occidental* (Paris: Cerf, 1986).

46 See Rafael Aguirre, 'Gestión de las tradiciones y crisis de la Iglesia,' *El Noticiero de las Ideas*, 24 (2005), 14–17.

broadcast live by the Vatican Television Center, Televisión Española (TVE), Popular TV and Intereconomía TV.[47]

Although the new martyrs are assigned a precise day in the calendar, with their collective feast being celebrated on 6 November, they are repeatedly commemorated on other occasions throughout the liturgical year: from 18 January, with the *memoria* of Manuel Barbal Cosán to 20 November with the celebration of Paula de San Antonio. The pastoral care construction of these holy figures is instrumental to structuring the believers' mind. Martyrs become their moral and religious point of reference thanks to the many prayers that have been written in 2007: the *Oración a los Mártires del Sagrado Corazón* (Prayer to the martyrs of the Holy Heart), or the *Memoria Obligatoria para los Martires de España del siglo XX* (Compulsory memory for the Spanish martyrs of the twentieth century). These connect the martyrs to the believer, giving him the 'integrity and constancy of faith,' helping him in the 'setbacks of life' and in facing 'the temptations of the world and the flesh.' The believer must be ready to follow the example set by the martyrs in 'not hesitating to die for you [God],' and in being 'strong in the confession of your [God] name.' In *Semillas de paz* (Seeds of peace), the anthem in honor of the martyrs written by José Luis Moreno, the Christian asks God for the strength 'to follow [the martyrs] along the way of the Lord, [as] faithful witness.' The liturgical guidelines issued by the Oficina para las Causas de los Santos de la Conferencia Episcopal Española (Office for the Causes of Saints of the Spanish Conference of Bishop (OCS)) explained that this orison 'indicated that they are an example to be followed today, torches of faith for our way, not mere historical memory, but a future program.'[48]

According to the bishops, the martyrs are 'our teacher of life.'[49] Through them the hierarchical Church is trying to construct the identity of the believer, clearly delimiting static boundaries; it is a monolithic identity clearly contrasting with the multi-dimensional post-modern religious self.[50] During the Zapatero era, in order to credit these positions, the CEE developed a real cultural offensive and its publishing house issued large numbers of books about the Spanish martyrs. Six of them were edited by María Encarnación González, Professor of Geography and History at the Instituto Egara in Sabadell-Tarrasa and since 2001 director of the OCS. Particularly relevant are the five editions of *Quienes son y de dónde vienen. 498 mártires del siglo XX en España* (*Who they are and where they come*

47 Among other things CEE issued a CD *con los Himnos en honor a los mártires del siglo XX en España* (Madrid: Edice, 2007) and a DVD *Beatificación de 498 mártires del siglo XX en España* (Madrid: Edice, 2008).

48 Oficina para las Causas de los Santos, *Partituras de los himnos en honor a los mártires del siglo XX en España* (Madrid: Edice, 2007), 24.

49 Fernando Sebastián Aguilar, 'Mártires en la vida de la Iglesia. La vida cristiana como vida martirial,' in *Mártires del siglo XX en España. Don y desafío*, ed. by María E. González Rodríguez (Madrid: Edice, 2008), 41.

50 Ulirch Beck, *Il Dio personale: La nascita della religiosità secolare* (Roma-Bari: Laterza, 2000).

from. 498 martyrs of the twentieth century in Spain), a hagiographic tome about the lives of the martyrs.[51] This pastoral strategy functions as a barrier to the crisis of the institutional systems of belief.[52] The new identity is attached to a new invented tradition, determined by the hierarchy that connects the Church of today with those persecuted by the Roman Empire.[53]

During the Zapatero governments the new pastoral on martyrs has been an instrument to fight a struggle for memory, which is still in progress and which is hampering the construction of a shared vision of Spain's traumatic twentieth century. The new narrative developed by the Catholic bishops does not call for the construction of a shared space of meanings, but rather leads to 'symbolic wars'[54] between 'communities of memory.'[55] This has given rise to many controversies, not only in 2007[56] but also in 2010 on the occasion of the inauguration of the *Santuario de los Beatos Mártires valencianos* (Sanctuary of the blessed martyrs of Valencia),[57] the parish dedicated to the new martyrs. In November 2011 the Comisión pola Recuperación da Memoria Histórica da Coruña (Commission for Historical Memory Recovery of Coruña) sent a public letter to Rouco Varela, Archbishop of Madrid, affirming that 'it is time that the Catholic Church asks for forgiveness for its role in the crimes against humanity and for its great sin to support a Fascist dictatorship.'[58] There was no response from the bishops. On the contrary, they opposed the government's proposal to transform the Valley of the Fallen, the Francoist monument located near Madrid, into a learning

51 María E. González Rodríguez (ed.), *El martirio cristiano. Testimonio y profecía* (Madrid: Edice, 2007); *Hablar hoy de martirio y de santidad* (Madrid: Edice, 2007); *Los Santos evangelizan* (Madrid: Edice, 2011); *La vida en el Espíritu. Ser santos por la práctica heroica de la virtud* (Madrid: Edice, 2010); *Mártires del siglo XX en España. Don y desafío. La Instrucción "Sanctorum Mater"* (Madrid: Edice, 2008); *Los primeros 479 santos y beatos mártires del siglo XX en España. Quienes son y de dónde vienen* (Madrid: Edice, 2008).

52 Danièle Hervieu Léger, *De la mission à a la protestation. L'évolution des étudiants chrétiens en France (1965–1970)* (Paris: Cerf, 1973).

53 See: Eric J. Hobsbawm and Terence O. Ranger, *The Invention of Tradition* (New York: Cambridge University Press, 1983).

54 The concept is taken from Anna L. Tota, *La memoria contesa. Studi sulla comunicazione sociale del passato* (Milano: Franco Angeli, 2001).

55 The concept is taken from Micheal Richards, 'El régimen de Franco y la política de memoria de la Guerra Civil española,' in *Guerra Civil. Mito y memoria*, edited by Julio Arostegui (Madrid: Marcial Pons, 2006), 167–200.

56 See: Manuel Montero, 'Otros "mártires" de la Guerra Civil,' *El País*, 6 May 2007, 38 and Julián Casanova, 'Franco, la Iglesia católica y sus mártires,' *El País*, 26 June 2007, 43.

57 See: Miquel Alberola, 'Una iglesia para los "mártires" del 36,' *El País*, 2 July 2007, 23.

58 Comisión pola Recuperación da Memoria Histórica, 'Carta aberta ao Sr. D. Antonio María Rouco Varela, presidente da Conferencia Episcopal Española,' www.memoriadacoruna.com [accessed 15 May 2014].

center on the atrocities of the dictatorship because the Benedictine basilica was a part of it.[59]

The new pastoral of memory promoted by the Catholic Church created political strains between the Church and the socialists, wide public controversy, and also led to tensions within Spanish Catholicism. On the one hand, there was no official recognition of martyrdom for those Catholic Republicans killed by Francoist repression. Stating that they were killed or harassed simply for political reasons is too simplistic: through it, Spanish Catholicism avoids critical reflections both on its own responsibilities in the genesis of violent Iberian anti-clericalism, and on the reasons for one of the most rapid and profound secularizations in western history (namely the one that followed democratization). On the other hand, the beatifications of the victims of Republican anti-clerical repression confused the part of the Catholic world that did not identify with the conservative turn, which started in Spain in 1982 with the change of leadership of the Church. It is not the case that the expression of dissent from the official CEE's narrative was isolated and (easily) neutralized. A few months after the ceremony of 2007 the Bishop of Bilbao, Ricardo Blázquez, said the Church had to 'ask for forgiveness. . ., recognize limitations, sins, need for a change of attitude and the purpose of the repair.'[60] Some segments of the same CEE did not waste time to restrict the scope of the speech: Juan Antonio Martínez Camino, the bishop's former spokesman and Secretary General of the CEE, declared that Blázquez's words had been 'taken out of context,'[61] while the former cardinal Carlos Amigo Vallejo, Archbishop of Seville, stated that the Bishop of Bilbao's opinion 'does not represent the entire Church.'[62]

The pastoral memory on the civil war promoted by the Catholic Church is not something given, or ahistorical, but something that has been constructed over time and in response to different issues: from the slowdown in the reforms of the Second Vatican Council to the secularization of Spanish society after the transition to democracy. Concerning the relations between socialists and the Catholic Church, the Zapatero era has often been considered among the most problematic in the post-transition period. However, the bishops' new memorialistic narrative was structured before 2004, during John Paul II's pontificate, as part of the process of the repoliticization of Spanish Catholicism.[63] In developing this new pastoral

59 Pedro Blasco, 'Los Benedictinos no participarán en las conversaciones del Valle de los Caídos,' *El Mundo*, 16 June 2011, 51.

60 Ricardo Blázquez, 'Discurso Inaugural del Excmo. y Rvmo. Sr. D. Ricardo Blázquez Pérez, Obispo de Bilbao Presidente de la Conferencia Episcopal Española,' www.conferenciaepiscopal.es/documentos/plenaria/XC_plenaria.html [accessed 15 May 2014].

61 'Mons. Martinez Camino: No pueden sacarse de contexto las palabras de perdón' de Mons. Blázquez,' *Aciprensa*, 24 November 2007, 44.

62 'Amigo afirma que el discurso del Blázquez no representa a la Iglesia,' *El País*, 21 November 2007, 31.

63 José M. Mardones, 'La desprivatización del catolicismo en los años ochenta,' *Sistema*, 97 (1990), 123–136.

memory the hierarchy has continued along the path undertaken in the second half of the 1980s. There were other options open to the Church. In 1986 all the bishops issued *Contructores de la paz* ('Builders of the peace'), a document in which they stated that the Church in the 1930s was not 'without error.' However, this path was not taken. They chose another one: to represent the clergy as the real victim of the conflict, and thereby detract from, rather than contribute to, a genuine reconciliation within Spanish society.

13 The Australian Christian churches and the Aboriginal reconciliation process

Public religion and its limitations

Michael Phillips

In 2008 the Australian Parliament apologized to Aboriginal Australians for historical wrongs committed against them by the State, including the removal of Aboriginal children from their families. The apology was a cathartic event in the life of the nation. But a nation does not 'come to terms with its past' in a single day. Australians have been debating, in one context or another, the morality of colonialism, its effect on Aboriginal Australians, and the moral quality of Australian history and the Australian state throughout the colonial period but with increasing intensity from the 1970s. In academic and popular history, in civil society associations, in the media and in government policy and political debate the 'public memory' of Australia has been profoundly reshaped. Nevertheless, the idea that Australia might 'resolve' these issues in a moral and political sense through an apology was in large part a construct of the quasi-theological framework applied to indigenous affairs policy in the 1990s: reconciliation.[1] Like assimilation and treaty politics before it, reconciliation as a framework offered a 'solution' to deep-seated political problems arising out of colonization itself. And like assimilation and treaty politics, reconciliation failed to resolve the underlying question arising out of the British settlement of Australia without the consent of indigenous peoples: what is due to Aboriginal Australians as a consequence of past wrongs and what is the proper shape of a democratic relationship between Aboriginal and non-Aboriginal Australia? This paper examines the intervention of the Australian Christian churches into these debates since the 1970s, a period of wide-ranging change within society. I argue that the decision of the churches to become advocates and practitioners of Australian 'reconciliation' is indicative of wider changes in the country's religious scene, and of changes in public norms regulating the participation of religious actors in Australian public life. However, the failure of the reconciliation process to resolve the underlying political and constitutional

1 See Michael Phillips, 'Aboriginal Reconciliation as Religious Politics: Secularisation in Australia,' *Australian Journal of Political Science*, Vol 40, No 1 (2005), 111–124.

questions facing Australia also reveals the limits of reconciliation processes that operate primarily at the level of public memory.

The Aboriginal reconciliation process

Government policy towards Aboriginal people has historically been deeply paternalistic, indeed racist. Brewer describes the impact of colonialism on Aborigines as one of 'cultural annihilation,' leaving a legacy of internally directed violence and community dysfunction.[2] Loos described the legacy of colonialism as a 'holocaust.'[3] Numerous government reports, including the 'Royal Commission into Aboriginal Deaths in Custody,' 'Bringing Them Home' and 'Little Children are Sacred,' have documented the contemporary effects of past policies on Aboriginal peoples. The annual 'Closing the Gap' report, established in 2008 to track progress in narrowing Aboriginal disadvantage across a range of socio-economic indicators, continues to show significant disparities in life expectancy and other matters.[4] Australia today remains a deeply unequal society that has not addressed the legacy of colonialism in either constitutional or socio-economic terms. This inequality persists despite very significant changes in government policy and the law (including with respect to native title), and in public awareness and understanding of the effects of colonialism and its implications for Australian history and the moral quality of the Australian State.

Between 1991 and 2000 the country undertook a formal process of reconciliation between indigenous and non-indigenous Australians. The political and legal framework for the reconciliation process was set out in the Council for Aboriginal Reconciliation Act 1991. The act established a Council for Aboriginal Reconciliation consisting of indigenous and non-indigenous appointees, chaired throughout the life of the council by an Aboriginal person, and charged with the task of improving community relations and developing a set of 'documents,' a deliberately vague word, of reconciliation. Beyond the task of community education the council did not have any legal powers or constitutional role. It did not provide Aboriginal people with a 'seat at the table' of national decision-making. Nor did it have the power to award reparations, conduct truth and reconciliation hearings or assign legal accountability for historical injustices.

The seeds of the Australian reconciliation process were sown in the failure of an earlier movement for political and constitutional reform of the country, called treaty politics.[5] As Short has argued, treaty politics was connected both to claims

2 John D. Brewer, *Peace Processes: A Sociological Approach* (Cambridge: Polity Press, 2010), 24

3 Noel Loos, *White Christ, Black Cross: the Emergence of a Black Church* (Canberra: Aboriginal Studies Press, 2007), 41.

4 Department of Prime Minister and Cabinet, 'Closing the Gap: Prime Minister's Report 2015,' Australian government, Canberra, www.dpmc.gov.au/sites/default/files/publications/Closing_the_Gap_2015_Report.pdf [accessed August 2015].

5 See: Damien Short, *Reconciliation and Colonial Power: Indigenous Rights in Australia* (Aldershot: Ashgate, 2008), 32–37.

for self-government and to claims for control of Aboriginal lands.[6] Unlike New Zealand, Canada and the United States, Australia does not have a treaty or treaties with its indigenous people. Rather, Australia was colonized as a *terra nullius*, a land belonging to no one. This principle was overturned in respect of native title (a property right enjoyed by indigenous peoples based on prior occupation and customary law) by the High Court of Australia in the *Mabo* case in 1992.[7] However, the *Mabo* case also affirmed that *terra nullius* continues, in effect, to apply in respect of sovereignty because the British acquisition of sovereignty over Australia is not 'justiciable' (i.e. capable of being heard and determined) by an Australian domestic court. The result of this ruling is that it is not possible to bring a claim based on the sovereignty of indigenous peoples in an Australian court.

Beyond the law courts, treaty politics was also a cultural and symbolic critique of contemporary Australian society. Treaty politics was part of the revision of Australian history that occurred during the 1970s and 1980s, and it came to a peak of controversy during the 1988 bicentenary of the landing of the First Fleet in Sydney Harbour in 1788. While the Australian government planned a jubilant national celebration, Aboriginal activists claimed that the bicentenary celebrated the 200th anniversary of 'invasion day.' These Aboriginal activists were calling into question the legitimacy of the national celebration and, by extension, the legitimacy of the State and the moral character of Australian history. In 1988, in response to the 'Burunga Statement' issued by the Central and Northern Land Councils, the Prime Minister and the Aboriginal Affairs Minister signed a statement that 'the government affirms that it is committed to work for a negotiated treaty with Aboriginal people.'[8] However, treaty politics was extremely controversial, was bitterly opposed by the Liberal-National conservative parties, and never took the form of a program of government action. The Labor government abandoned its proposal for a treaty with Aboriginal Australians, having reached a political impasse.

In the late 1980s a number of Australian churches were cooperating in an attempt to promote a formal reconciliation process between Aboriginal and non-Aboriginal Australia, and to advance national progress on Aboriginal affairs policy more generally. In 1988 the Catholic Commission for Justice and Peace, the Uniting Church Social Responsibility and Justice Committee and the Australian Council of Churches Commission for Church and Society jointly published 'A Just and Proper Settlement,' intended to guide public discussions by Australians during the bicentenary of British settlement. In February 1988, at a service to

6 See: John Gardiner-Garden, 'From Dispossession to Reconciliation,' Commonwealth Parliament Library and Information Services, Research Paper No 27 (1998–1999), www.aph.gov.au/binaries/library/pubs/rp/1998-99/99rp27.pdf; Short, 31–65; Tim Rowse, *Obliged to be Difficult: Nugget Coombs' Legacy in Indigenous Affairs* (Melbourne: Cambridge University Press, 2000), 174–187.

7 *Mabo v Queensland (No 2)* (1992) 175 CLR 1.

8 Short, 35.

celebrate the bicentenary of the first Christian church service in Australia, the Anglican Primate, Archbishop Sir John Grindrod, apologized to Aboriginal people for past mistreatment. Arthur Malcolm, Australia's first Aboriginal bishop, accepted the apology on behalf of Aboriginal members of the Anglican community.[9] In the same year the heads of 14 churches issued a document entitled 'Towards Reconciliation in Australian Society,' calling on the Commonwealth Parliament to pass a motion of reconciliation.[10] The Australian Catholic bishops sent Father Frank Brennan SJ to Canberra to lobby parliamentarians to support the motion.[11] Gary Johns, a minister in the Keating Labor government, later wrote that 'a grateful Labor government ran with [the churches' proposal for a motion of reconciliation] as a means of keeping the constituency occupied, knowing that no Australian government would ever accept the breach of sovereignty that a treaty implies.'[12] Bob Hawke, the Prime Minister, moved the motion, modified to accommodate Opposition concerns relating to references to Aboriginal self-determination, as the first order of business in the newly built Parliament House in Canberra. The resolution acknowledged that 'Aborigines and Torres Strait Islanders suffered dispossession and dispersal upon acquisition of their traditional lands by the British Crown [and were] denied full citizenship rights of the Commonwealth of Australia prior to the 1967 referendum.' The Parliament considered it 'desirable that the Commonwealth further promote reconciliation with Aboriginal and Torres Strait Islander citizens, providing recognition of their special place in the Commonwealth of Australia.'[13]

However, the formal reconciliation process was not established until after the Royal Commission into Aboriginal Deaths in Custody recommended, in 1991, that 'reconciliation between the Aboriginal and non-Aboriginal communities in Australia must be achieved if community division, discord and injustice to Aboriginal people are to be avoided.'[14] As in 1988, the leading Christian churches offered their support for reconciliation. The Royal Commission reported expressions of support from the senior clergy, including the President of the

9 Alison Longworth, 'Churches and Aboriginal Issues,' in *Encyclopaedia of Religion in Australia*, edited by James Jupp (Melbourne: Cambridge University Press, 2009), 106–115, 111.

10 Gardiner-Garden, 16. The Australian sociologist C.D. Rowley had also written in the 1970s that Australia should undertake a 'patient attempt at reconciliation and negotiation' with Aboriginal Australians, and make 'an admission of colonial guilt.' C.D. Rowley, 'From Humbug to Politics: Aboriginal Affairs and the Academy Project,'1972, in Ramola Yardi and Geoffrey Stokes, 'Foundations for Reconciliation in Social Science: The Political Thought of C.D. Rowley,' *Melbourne Journal of Politics*, Vol 25, No 1 (1998), 45–61, 45.

11 Brennan gave his own account of the passage of the motion: 'Waiting for the Resolution,' *Australian Quarterly*, Vol 61, No 2 (1989), 242–250.

12 Gary Johns, 'Reconciliation: Read the Fine Print,' *Quadrant*, November 1999, 16.

13 Robert (Bob) Hawke (Prime Minister), *House Hansard*, 23 August 1988, 137.

14 Royal Commission into Aboriginal Deaths in Custody (1991), *National Report*, Vol 5 (1991), Canberra: Australian Government Publishing Service, 38.

Uniting Church, the Roman Catholic Archbishop of Sydney, the Moderator-General of the Presbyterian Church and the Primate of the Anglican Church of Australia.[15] The Labor government responded to the recommendation by proposing the establishment of the Council for Aboriginal Reconciliation.

In the period between and immediately after the High Court's decisions in *Mabo* (1992) and *Wik* (1996), the issue of native title dominated the reconciliation process.[16] These decisions revived the older debates relating to Aboriginal sovereignty and self-determination that had animated treaty politics, and brought the character of Australian history and the moral quality of the State into question. In *Mabo*, Justices Deane and Guadron stated that Australian colonial history had left a 'national legacy of unutterable shame.'[17] Following the *Mabo* decision, Paul Keating, Prime Minister, at Redfern in Sydney, made an historic acknowledgement of the responsibility of non-Aboriginal Australians for the catastrophic effects of colonialism:

> We took the traditional lands and smashed the traditional way of life. We brought the diseases. The alcohol. We committed the murders. We took the children from their mothers. We practiced discrimination and exclusion. It was our ignorance and our prejudice.[18]

The Keating government legislated to protect native title in the Native Title Act 1993 in the face of bitter conservative opposition and widespread public controversy. The churches participated in these debates, taking the side of Aboriginal Australians. For example, in 1992 John Bathersby, Archbishop of Brisbane, described Australia's treatment of indigenous peoples as 'evil' and urged Australia to face up to its past.[19] The Catholic Church also entered the public sphere to argue for fair treatment of Aboriginal peoples after the *Wik* decision in 1996.[20]

The conservative Liberal-National government of John Howard, elected in 1996, was hostile to both native title and the larger symbolic program of reconciliation. Its policies were consistent with earlier critiques of treaty politics and Aboriginal self-determination. It adopted a policy of 'practical reconciliation' which was ostensibly focused on practical improvements in social welfare but which

15 Ibid.

16 *Mabo* v *Queensland (No 2)* (1992) 175 CLR 1 established that native title existed in Australia, and found that native title had not been extinguished in the Torres Strait. In *Wik* (1996) 187 CLR 1 the High Court held that native title had not been extinguished by grant of a pastoral lease on the mainland of Australia.

17 *Mabo (No 2)* (1992), 104.

18 As quoted in John Gardiner-Garden, '*From Dispossession to Reconciliation*,' Canberra Department of the Parliamentary Library, Australian Parliament House, 2000, 17.

19 Dominic O'Sullivan, *Faith, Politics and Reconciliation: Catholicism and the Politics of Indigeniety* (Wellington: Huia Publishers, 2005), 101.

20 Ibid, 104–109.

many Aboriginal people found insulting. Geoff Clark, Chair of the Aboriginal and Torres Strait Islander Commission, argued that practical reconciliation was demeaning because it was limited to the provision of those rights to which Aboriginal people were already entitled to as citizens, but failed to recognize the political rights of indigenous peoples.[21] The 1996 election also saw the emergence of Pauline Hanson and, later, her One Nation party. Hanson was implacably opposed to any special treatment for Aboriginal people, arguing that 'reconciliation is everyone recognizing and treating each other as equals. . . That is why I am calling for the Aboriginal and Torres Strait Islander Commission to be abolished.'[22]

In 1996 the Human Rights and Equal Opportunity Commission (HREOC) released the 'Bringing Them Home' report into the removal of Aboriginal children from their families by successive Australian governments. The commission concluded that the practice constituted genocide under the 1948 United Nations Convention on the Prevention and Punishment of the Crime of Genocide and stated that:

> Official policy and legislation for indigenous families and children was contrary to accepted legal principle imported into Australia as British common law and, from late 1946, constituted a crime against humanity. It offended accepted standards of the time and was the subject of dissent and resistance. The implementation of the legislation was marked by breaches of fundamental obligations on the part of officials and others to the detriment of vulnerable and dependent children whose parents were powerless to know their whereabouts and protect them from exploitation and abuse.[23]

The commission's conclusion that the child removal policy was genocidal, together with its recommendation that there be a national apology, produced a backlash that obscured rather than clarified the impact of the child removal policy on Aboriginal people.[24] The genocide finding and the apology question became part of the 'history wars' (so-called in pale imitation of the American culture wars) that marked Australia in the first decade of the twenty-first century. These debates were brought to a tentative and perhaps provisional conclusion by the 2008 national apology. A number of Christian churches and welfare agencies offered apologies to members of the Stolen Generations for their role in the child

21 Geoff Clark, 'Not Much Progress,' in *Essays on Australian Reconciliation*, edited by Michelle Grattan (Melbourne: Bookman, 2000), 228–235.

22 Pauline Hanson, *House Hansard*, 10 September 1996, 3861.

23 Human Rights and Equal Opportunity Commission, 'Bringing Them Home: Report of the National Inquiry into the Separation of Aboriginal and Torres Strait Islander Children from Their Families' (Canberra: Commonwealth of Australia, 1997), Chapter 13, www.humanrights.gov.au/publications/bringing-them-home-chapter-13.

24 See Short, 100–104 and Robert Manne, 'In Denial: the Stolen Generations and the Right,' *Quarterly Essay*, (2001), No 1.

removal policies. The Chair of the Bishops Committee for Social Welfare, the Chair of the National Aboriginal and Torres Strait Islander Catholic Council and the National Director of the Australian Catholic Social Welfare Commission made a joint submission: 'On behalf of our constituent national groups we sincerely and deeply regret any involvement Church agencies had in any injustices that have been visited upon Aboriginal and Torres Strait Islander families.'[25] The Catholic welfare organization, Centacare, said that it 'deeply regrets the enormous suffering.' The Anglican Church Social Responsibilities Commission and the Kimberly Sisters of St John also apologized in their submissions to the inquiry.[26] The Uniting Church issued an apology,[27] as did various para-church organizations such as the Australian Conference of Leaders of Religious Institutes.[28]

Over and above their apologies for historic wrong-doing associated with church missions, their *ad hoc* interventions into various public debates, and their efforts at parish level and in civil society, the major contribution of the churches to the Aboriginal reconciliation process was the idea of reconciliation itself. As I have argued elsewhere, the idea of reconciliation, although vague and flexible in the hands of politicians, does have a distinctive Christian background and shape. This was evident in the Australian context in the latter period of the reconciliation process, which was heavily focused on questions of guilt, apology and forgiveness. There was also a Christian rationale for combining reconciliation with social justice derived from Christian teaching on the link between reconciliation and penitential works. Overwhelmingly, though, the dominant image of reconciliation was of a united Australia. Yet one of the ironies of the reconciliation process was that it was anything but peaceful or unified. From the *Mabo* decision to the mass Bridge Walk for Reconciliation over the Sydney Harbour Bridge in 2000, the Aboriginal reconciliation process was marked by an atmosphere that at times bordered on venomous. The conservative Liberal-National government was opposed, on point of principle, to the symbolic apparatus of treaty politics that it saw, rightly or wrongly, as contained within a reconciliation Trojan horse. Those Aboriginal people who had greeted the process as a sell-out would themselves contribute their own, often radical, definitions of reconciliation. The process of reconciliation, which was supposed to bring Australia together, produced a politics of difficult moral analysis – of guilt and of shame as much as apology and redemption – and of unexpected political controversy. There was a tension between the hopeful, aspirational unity of reconciliation politics and the difficulties faced by a settler democracy confronting its colonial past, which was not easy to resolve – and was not resolved.

Philpott, Shah and Toft's study of religion and democratization processes identifies two factors affecting the propensity of religious actors to participate in transitional justice processes, particularly democratization processes: institutional

25 HREOC, 31.
26 HREOC, 40–41.
27 Council for Aboriginal Reconciliation. Annual Report, 1994–95.
28 Council for Aboriginal Reconciliation, media release, 11 June 1997.

independence and a democratic political theology.[29] The question remains, though, why do some churches develop the kind of political theology that is both broadly supportive of democratic change and which motivates religious actors to involve themselves in transitional justice processes? Particular religious traditions do not automatically or naturally tend towards democratic, authoritarian or any other particular form of political system. Catholicism, for example, has produced apologists for a wide variety of political regimes. In twentieth-century Europe, Catholic thinkers were supportive of the Franco regime in Spain and the Vichy government in France, as well as Christian Democracy.[30] Religious ideas are symbolically complex and require interpretation before they can be applied to social and political problems. Religious ideas must therefore be activated through the conscious choice of religious actors operating within their particular religious traditions, the wider social and political context, and within the constraints of their own authority. These choices should be understood as the result of a reflective process, which incorporates not only theological reflection and prayer but an element of strategic calculation, which is in turn related to church mission (the church's understanding of the social and political role of that church within a given society) as well as to developments in the wider socio-religious context. I have elsewhere described the theological dimensions of the Australian Christian churches' commitment to 'reconciliation,' and others have explored the link between Christianity and reconciliation.[31] In the next two sections of this paper I describe the changes in the Australian political environment and religious scene that had a significant impact on the later development of the politics of reconciliation and on the churches' role in that process.

The advent of 'self-determination'

Beginning in the 1960s and continuing through the 1970s there were significant changes in public norms regarding the treatment of Aboriginal Australians. The 'Aboriginal turn' in Australian history contributed to significant changes in the

29 Daniel Philpott, Timothy Samuel Shah, and Monica Duffy Toft, *God's Century: Resurgent Religion and Global Politics* (New York: W.W. Norton & Co, 2011). See also John D. Brewer, Gareth I. Higgins, and Francis Teeney, *Religion, Civil Society and Peace in Northern Ireland* (Oxford: Oxford University Press, 2011). Their analysis of religious involvement in peace processes identifies the matrix of church-civil society-state relations as a key factor, arguing, for example, that minority status churches are better placed to play a constructive role in peace processes than majority status churches; see: 10, 148–171.

30 See: Emile Perreau-Saussine, *Catholicism and Democracy: an Essay in the History of Political Thought* (Princeton: Princeton University Press, 2012).

31 Daniel Philpott, 'What Religion Brings to the Politics of Transitional Justice,' *Journal of International Affairs*, Vol 6, No 1 (2007), 93–110. More generally, see R. Scott Appleby, *The Ambivalence of the Sacred* (Lanham: Rowman and Littlefield, 2000) and Megan Shore, *Religion and Conflict Resolution: Christianity and South Africa's Truth and Reconciliation Commission* (London: Ashgate, 2009).

public understanding of the history of colonialism and its effect on current generations of indigenous people. As Attwood notes:

> the turn to Aboriginal history revealed the revolutionary nature of the nation. Once it was acknowledged that Aborigines were here prior to the British and in place, the British were rendered out of place, so their colonization of the country could be seen more clearly as an act of invasion rather than settlement.[32]

This new way of understanding Australian history uncovered the moral shortcomings of the State. Attwood describes how:

> many settler Australians came to believe that Australia faced a critical moral problem because its historical foundations were mired in the crimes committed against its first peoples. They saw this as original sin, a problem of guilt or a shameful past, which had to be atoned for the sake of the nation. . . . This was regarded, in other words, as a crisis for the whole culture – a moment of instability as the country's colonial legacy came to haunt settler Australian identity.'[33]

In addition to these broader changes in the national culture there were also significant changes in public policy regarding Aboriginal affairs. In the 1950s and 1960s Australian policy was that Aboriginal people would be 'assimilated' into the general population and would cease to exist as Aboriginal people *per se*. After the election of the Whitlam Labor government in 1972 Australian policy moved away from assimilation towards 'self-determination.' Current debates have highlighted the shortcomings of government policies conducted under the self-determination framework. It is not my intention to enter these debates in this paper. What is important for my argument is that, from the 1970s to the 1990s, the churches were operating within a wider political context in which certain old practices became unacceptable and new solutions had to be found.

Reacting to these changes in the wider political environment, a number of churches sought to decolonize their internal relationships with Aboriginal people. Through the nineteenth and twentieth centuries a number of churches had been deeply involved in the establishment and management of missions for Aboriginal people.[34] In this role the churches had become participants in State policies for

32 See: Bain Attwood, *Telling the Truth About Aboriginal History* (Sydney: Allen & Unwin, 2005), 19.

33 Ibid, 25.

34 See: Noel Loos, *White Christ, Black Cross: the Emergence of a Black Church* (Canberra: Aboriginal Studies Press, 2007); Peter Lewis, *Acting in Solidarity: the Church's Journey with the Indigenous Peoples of Australia* (Melbourne: Uniting Academic Press, 2010); Anna Pattel-Gray, *The Great White Flood: Racism in Australia* (Oxford: Oxford University Press, 1998); Anna Haebich, *Broken Circles: Fragmenting Indigenous Families 1800–2000* (Freemantle: Fremantle Arts Centre Press, 2000).

the removal of Aboriginal children from their families (the 'Stolen Generations'). From the 1960s the churches came under pressure to close the missions as paternalist norms gave way to rights-based arguments for Aboriginal control of their lands. In 1963 the Aboriginal communities of Cape York presented the Yirkalla Bark Petition to the Australian government, and conducted litigation to obtain legal recognition of native title to their lands. Although the case was unsuccessful, it prompted a rethink of Aboriginal affairs policy within the churches. In 1965 the Australian Council of Churches rejected assimilation as a goal of public policy in a pamphlet 'Land Rights for Australian Aborigines.' In 1969 the Methodist Board of Mission advocated land rights for Aboriginal communities, including mineral rights. The Anglican, Presbyterian and Congregationalist churches followed soon after.[35] In 1979 the General Assembly of the Uniting Church handed church lands back to Aboriginal communities, and the Catholic and Anglican churches soon followed.[36] In 1981 the Catholic Commission for Justice and Peace, which had been established by the Australian Church following the Second Vatican Council, began advocating for land rights for Aboriginal people (notably provoking a conservative Catholic reaction which contributed to the commission's abolition in 1987).[37] Seen in this context, the churches' 1988 intervention into the wider politics of Aboriginal affairs with the publication of the pamphlet 'Towards Reconciliation in Australian Society' can be seen as the culmination of a period of relatively rapid social change in the country, and as a continuation of earlier developments within church thinking and practice with respect to Aboriginal Australians.

The changed role of religion in Australian public life

In addition to changes in the specific context of Aboriginal affairs policy described above, the period from the 1970s to the 1990s also witnessed significant changes in the Australian religious scene that had implications for the public role of the churches. The Australian churches have historically taken an active role in the public sphere. According to Maddox, 'many [Australian] clergy have regarded an active, even controversial, role in Australian public debate to be part of their core responsibility for almost as long as they have been here.'[38] Overall these contributions have tended to be conservative rather than progressive or leftist (although there are some notable exceptions, such as the Uniting Church). Melleuish notes that Australia in the nineteenth century developed 'a distinctive form of Protestant politics that was associated with the causes of moral improvement, such as temperance, anti-gambling and Sabbatarianism. This is what has traditionally been

35 Roger C. Thompson, *Religion in Australia: a History* (Melbourne: Oxford University Press, Melbourne, 2002), 129.

36 Ibid.

37 Ibid, 126.

38 Marion Maddox, God, Caesar and Alexander, AQ Magazine (Sept-Oct 2003), 4–10, 9.

known as 'wowserism' in Australia.'[39] Attempts to establish a 'Protestant moral order' had a significant role well into the twentieth century, contributing to the 'quiet Sunday' seen in big Australian cities, the closed pubs and censored films described by Thompson in his *Religion in Australia: A History*. The other significant fact of Australian religious life was Catholic–Protestant sectarianism, which occurred in waves from the 1830s to the 1960s. Prior to the 1960s, Australian society 'comprised two distinct communities: one was British in origin and Protestant in faith, the other Irish and Catholic. . . . Catholics were mostly Irish by birth or descent, the Irish were mostly Catholics, and Irish Catholics were mostly on the lowest rungs of the socio-economic ladder.'[40]

Today Catholic–Protestant sectarianism and the old role of religion as Australia's moral policeman have collapsed or, in the latter case, nearly so. Part of this is due to a decline in overall patterns of church attendance and religiosity. The mainline Protestant churches have suffered particularly large falls in religious observance. The Catholic Church, where attendance has held up best overall, has also faced difficulties.[41] There have been significant demographic shifts, caused by changes in immigration policy, which have produced a more diverse population, with implications for the churches. For example, the Catholic Church, historically largely Irish, underwent significant changes in its demographic make-up as a result of immigration from Italy, Malta, the Netherlands, Germany, Croatia, Hungary and the Ukraine.[42] There has also been significant growth in non-Christian religions and in the number of Australians who have no religion.[43]

At a very broad level the changes in Australian religion since the 1960s are a familiar story of decline, on a western European model. Australian political scientist Gregory Melleuish writes that 'during the 1990s and in the early years of this century one might have characterized Australia as a typical western country in the European mold. Religious observance in the traditional denominations had declined; those who did attend church were aging. The churches, and religion, appeared to be a declining influence on Australian political life.'[44] David Martin, the eminent sociologist of religion, has described Australia, in common with New Zealand and Canada, as a relatively and increasingly secularised western country:

39 Gregory Melleuish, 'Religion and Politics in Australia,' *Political Theology*, Vol 11, No 6 (2010), 909–927, 911.

40 Jeff Kildea, 'Sectarianism: Politics and Australia's Catholics,' *The Sydney Papers* (Sydney: The Sydney Institute, 2002), 162.

41 Patrick O'Farrell, *The Catholic Church and Community: An Australian History* (Sydney: New South Wales University Press, 2002), 432, 446.

42 Trever Batrouney, 'Some Patterns in Religious Settlement of Religious Communities in Australia,' in *Many Religions, All Australian: Religious Settlement, Identity and Cultural Formation,* edited by Garry Bouma (Melbourne: Christian Research Association, 1996).

43 Australian Bureau of Statistics, *Losing My Religion?* www.abs.gov.au/ausstats/abs@.nsf/Lookup/4102.0Main+Features30Nov+2013 [accessed September 2016].

44 Melleuish, 913.

> the underlying trend affecting the sister societies of Britain (rather than their American cousin) is one it shares with western Europe as a whole. Established religion gently collapses as the supports provided by ecclesiastical control of welfare, education, media and so on finally give way.[45]

Melleuish points to the uncertainty that the collapse of the old patterns of religious participation has meant for the public role of the Christian churches. Although he identifies a religious revival in the 2000s, the new patterns of religious participation are quite different to those that previously applied:

> A smaller, but in some ways more committed, group has been identified, and has identified itself, as a 'Christian community' that operates as part of an essentially secular society. It has become an interest group in a pluralist society that tends to focus on issues that could be described as 'religious issues' and which are largely of a moral nature.[46]

Melleuish's analysis is suggestive of a type of interest group politics whereby religious actors attempt to set or influence policy on matters of morality and censorship. That may very well be occurring in Australia today, but that is not the concern of this chapter. What I would like to draw out of the above discussion is that the participation of the Australian churches in the Aboriginal reconciliation process points to a second type of public religion and a broader and potentially more socially beneficial role for religion in the public sphere. Australian religion lacks the dynamism and vitality of that in the US, but there is nevertheless a limited, although important, sense in which the Australian religious scene now reflects elements of a denominationalist model of public religious expression which is in some respects similar to that described by Jose Casanova in his classic work *Public Religions in the Modern World*. According to Casanova, in a secularized society (i.e. one in which the political and religious spheres are independent and where citizens are entitled to the free exercise of religion) the primary form of religious organization is the denomination rather than the church. In this analysis 'church' is a universal, compulsory association, whereas the primary characteristic of denominationalism is voluntarism, the idea that membership of a religious association should be based on the free choice of the individual. An implication of denominationalism is the idea that religious life should be pluralistic.[47] A denominationalist or voluntarist model therefore implies certain limits on interventions by religious actors into the public sphere, and these limits shape norms regarding the public practice of religion. These norms are broadly

45 David Martin, *Pentecostalism: The World Their Parish* (Oxford: Blackwell, 2002), 43–44.

46 Melleuish, 925.

47 Jose Casanova, *Public Religion in the Modern World* (Chicago: University of Chicago Press, 1994), 52.

accommodating of religious actors who enter the public sphere to defend the interests of marginalized communities. For example, Casanova argues that religion plays a legitimate 'public role' in modern, pluralist societies where it seeks to:

1. protect not only its own freedom but a broad set of democratic rights, to be enjoyed by all;
2. challenge the secular state or the capitalist economy on moral or ethical grounds; and;
3. protect the 'traditional life world' from state interference.[48]

Bouma's analysis of changes in the Australian religious scene echoes, to a degree, Casanova's analysis of the US. Bouma observed in 1996 that:

> there has been a. . . loss of a single 'normal' within the various denominations of the Christian churches in Australia which, like Australian society, has become multicultural. . . . Denominations have become plural churches in a plural society.[49]

According to Bouma, by the 1990s Australia had become a 'nation of denominations . . . in which there is a wide range of ways of being religious, a nation with many religious organizations which are seen as a legitimate part of the religious landscape.'[50] Bouma concluded that, in a religiously diverse society, religious actors may participate in the public sphere as religious actors only if they accept the right of other religions actors to participate in the same way: 'the acceptance of plurality is a precondition to achieving the ends of a particular group. ecoming one among others is the first critical lesson.'[51] By the time the Aboriginal reconciliation process began, the Christian churches could no longer behave, and no longer sought to behave, in the public sphere in the same way they had previously; that is as representatives of two conflicting cultural formations or as the moral police force of Australian society. However, the churches could, and did, intervene in the public sphere to raise questions of broad national importance relating to the country's widely unequal treatment of Aboriginal Australians, and to challenge the nation to overcome the legacy of colonialism. This type of 'prophetic' religion works best not in connection with detailed policy analysis and formation but primarily on the level of public memory, and as a contribution to wider civil society efforts to both recall and reimagine the past so that it can form the basis for a new political settlement in the present. This was particularly true of the churches' intervention into the apology debate following the release of the

48 Casanova, 57–58.

49 Gary Bouma, 'Religion and Plurality in Australia,' in *Sociology of Religion*, Vol 56, No 3 (1995), 285–302, 297.

50 Ibid,106.

51 Ibid,105.

'Bringing Them Home' report. In that context the churches enacted reconciliation in their own interventions, offering apologies and making redress for historical wrongs. Australian political culture may no longer accept religious leaders as moral policemen, but Australian democracy has space for religion as a voice for the disadvantaged and as an interlocutor on questions of national historical importance.

The limits of public religion in transitional justice processes

Notwithstanding the contribution of the churches at the level of public memory and their contribution to the achievement of the national apology in 2008, the Aboriginal reconciliation process did not resolve the underlying justice claims raised by Aboriginal Australians. Reconciliation was also corrupted as an idiom for thinking about Aboriginal affairs policy by a crude concept of equality that positioned Aboriginal Australians as privileged and by the Howard government's policy of 'practical reconciliation.' These failures tell us something important about the limits of religious participation in transitional justice processes in modern, secularized democracies. Whilst religious actors can enter the public sphere to challenge the dominant political assumptions giving rise to injustices, whether those issues are taken up and resolved remains a matter for democratic political deliberation and action. These matters are outside the control of religious actors but they can contribute to their realization through involvement in civil society coalitions, or through concrete measures to provide redress to Aboriginal communities.[52]

A more troubling problem for the churches is that their interventions may be ineffective and potentially harmful to the groups they intend to represent. Brewer, writing in relation to church involvement in peace processes where the underlying conflict is related to religion itself, argues that church leaders may end up stoking the underlying sectarian identities which animate the conflict. According to Brewer, this was the case in Northern Ireland: the Northern Irish churches desired 'to continue to reproduce themselves as collective religions' and maintained an 'enduring loyalty to ethno-religious "groupness".'[53] The churches 'rarely transcended the sectarian divide in Northern Ireland and ended up reproducing sectarian identities.'[54]

Where the underlying conflict is not a religious one, as in Australia, religious actors face a different danger: the temptation to play the role of a neutral umpire

52 Maddison, for example, argues that the Australian Christian churches could make a 'more concrete contribution to the reconciliation process [by] returning land or paying appropriate compensation for loss of land to Aboriginal communities.' Sarah Maddison, *Conflict Transformation and Reconciliation: Multi-Level Challenges in Deeply Divided Societies* (Oxford: Routledge, 2015), 200.

53 Brewer, Higgins and Teeney, 228.

54 Brewer, Higgins and Teeney, 27.

sitting above the conflicting groups. This role is appropriate and helpful in 'symmetrical' conflicts, where there is some kind of parity between the contending parties and where they each bear a degree of blame. It is not necessarily appropriate, and may be harmful, in 'asymmetrical' conflicts, i.e. conflicts where a dominant group has committed wrongs against a minority. Transitional justice processes in the settler democracies of Australia, New Zealand, Canada and the US are all of this kind. The danger here is that churches, by playing the role of umpire or 'peacemaker,' may undermine their own ability to be an advocate for the minority group. In the Australian context, the churches attempted to play both roles – to be advocates for justice for Aboriginal Australians but also for a broader, national reconciliation that would unify the country. By adopting both roles, as advocate and umpire, arguably the churches made it more difficult for themselves to be advocates for Aboriginal people.

Damien Short, in his powerful critique of reconciliation politics in Australia, argues that 'far from providing the basis for nation to nation treaty negotiations with indigenous peoples on equal terms,' the process 'positively promoted an overt nation building agenda which aimed to cosmetically legitimize the settler state.'[55] To be clear, Short does not impute these motives to the churches, and for my part I do not think that there was any lack of sincerity there. The churches were moved by a deep theological and moral conviction that there is something fundamentally wrong in Australia's treatment of Aboriginal people. However, I agree with Short to the extent that the reconciliation framework, which lent itself strongly to discussion of apology, forgiveness and national unity, and was effective at the level of public memory, was less effective as a language for advancing a clear view on what should be done at the level of practical politics. I do not fault the churches for this result, but it does indicate that a reconciliation process that operates at the level of public memory alone, and which has significant effects on public understanding of historical injustices, may not by itself lead to any changes in the underlying political and constitutional structures that generate contemporary injustices.

55 Short, 177.

Conclusion

Varosha, a memorial to conflict

Mertkan Hamit and John Strawson

There is a Facebook group called 'Αμμόχωστος – Η Πολη μας,' which means 'Our City – Famagusta.'[1] In its description the administrators claim that this group was formed in order to unite the ex-residents of Famagusta who had fled their homes and became refugees after the Turkish invasion of Cyprus in 1974. There are now a thousand members of the group and the page is dominated with old pictures of Famagusta in general and, in particular, of Varosha. The majority of comments underline the good old days in the town and the desire to return.

Varosha is a neighborhood of Famagusta and until 1974 it had a population of 39,000 Greek Cypriots. It had been a lively part of the city and home to 50 per cent of hotels in Cyprus. Its long sandy beach attracted thousands of tourists each year. Now its abandoned buildings, surrounded by barbed-wire, have been left to crumble and it is often referred to as a 'ghost town.' More accurately it should be called a memorial to the Cyprus conflict.[2] It is special type of performance art which nourishes the memory of injustice among both Greek and Turkish Cypriot communities. As Kayim comments, it is 'a haunted place dense with memories and a powerful symbol of the Cyprus dispute.' 'The suburb has been left to rot,' she continues, 'an intentional reminder of the pain and presence of an irresolvable conflict. It languishes, slowly decaying in the sun.'[3]

The 'Our City' group demonstrates that the loss of place can move from an individual to a shared remembrance. Once shared on Facebook it becomes a new means for the transmission of memory from the displaced generation to future generations. It helps spark the images of a lost, warm home, a living community

1 www.facebook.com/groups/205964922756784/ [accessed 15 November 2016].

2 Before 1974 the population of Cyprus was composed of 79 per cent Greek Cypriots, 18 per cent Turkish Cypriots, with other minorities, including Armenians and Maronites, making up the remainder. For the legal aspects of the conflict see: Kypros Chrysostomides, *The Republic of Cyprus: A Study in International Law* (The Hague: Kluwer Law International, 2000) and Zaim M Necatgil, *The Cyprus Question and the Turkish position in International Law* (Oxford: Oxford University Press, 2001).

3 Gulgun Kayim, 'Crossing boundaries in Cyprus: landscapes of memory in the demilitarized zone,' in *Walls, Borders, Boundaries: Spatial and Cultural Practices in Europe*, edited by Marc Sliberman, Karen E. Till and Janet Ward (Oxford: Berghahn Books, 2012), 211–233, 216.

with all its joys, the smell of jasmine, the music and *jouissance*. The fading photographs of life past refresh the memory of those who lived in Varosha and enter the consciousness of those who did not. As Bryant puts it, the 'struggle requires a constant mobilization of memory.'[4]

The mobilization of memory has become a contemporary feature of the Cypriot narrative. In Bryant's terms 'memory has been institutionalized as a wound, visible in the rupture of partition as well as in politicized personal suffering.'[5] A Greek Cypriot resident of Varosha until 1974 demonstrates that, for the individual, there is a particular point at which the wound is inflicted, saying in an interview: 'I had only good memories until the day of the Turkish invasion.'[6] For Greek Cypriots, on the whole, it is the 1974 invasion that transformed their outlook. Until then their lives had been happy and relations with Turkish Cypriots were good.[7] For them it was intervention from the outside, by Turkey, that destroyed not merely Greek Cypriot existence in the north but Cyprus itself. Although the Turkish invasion was a violent moment that led to the internal displacement of about 200,000 Greek Cypriots, including the inhabitants of Varosha,[8] the point Bryant is making is that the loss of an image of the entire country was in some ways greater than the dispossession of property and community. In place of the harmonious nation came partition and separation between Greek and Turkish Cypriots.

Greek Cypriots tend to silence the memory of the inter-communal conflict and separation that existed before 1974. The British had inherited the Ottoman millet system when they took power in 1878. Greek Christian and Turkish Muslim communities were administered separately with their own system of personal status law, imprinting differences on the two communities. Equally the rise of Greek nationalism in the nineteenth century and of Turkish nationalism in the twentieth century constructed two rival nationalisms on the island, with different visions of the future. As British rule came to end in the 1950s these visions transformed into violent conflict as Greek Cypriots sought *Enosis*, or union with Greece, for the whole island whereas the Turkish Cypriots sought *Taksim*, or partition. In 1955 EOKA (the National Organization of Cypriot Fighters) was formed to pursue *Enosis* and the TMT (Turkish Resistance Organization) was created to defend

4 Rebecca Bryant, 'Partitions of Memory: wounds and witnessing in Cyprus,' *Comparative Studies in Society and History*, Vol 54, Issue 2 (2012), 332–360, 337.

5 Ibid, 340.

6 Asla Hoşçakal Demedik Varosha (We Never Said Goodbye to Varosha). Dir. Sertaç Yıldız, 25 January 2014. www.youtube.com/watch?v=co_dB6FKDdI [accessed 19 November 2016].

7 These sentiments also receive reinforcement in the works of the key Greek Cypriot historians of post-1974, see: Mete Hatay and Yiannis Papadakis, 'A Critical Comparison of Greek Cypriot and Turkish Cypriot Official Historiographies (1940s to the present),' in *Cyprus and the Politics of Memory: History, Community and Conflict*, edited by Rebecca Bryant and Yiannis Papadakis (London: I. B. Tauris, 2012), 37–40.

8 The results of the invasion also saw 51,000 Turkish Cypriots flee from homes in the south to the north. See: Pierre Oberling, *The Road to Bellapais: The Turkish Cypriot Exodus to Northern Cyprus* (Boulder: Social Science Monographs, 1982).

Turkish Cypriot communities, with open hostiles between the two breaking out in 1957. In 1960, in a compromise that neither side wanted, the unitary independent Republic of Cyprus was created with a power-sharing government. However, by 1963 this broke down and inter-communal violence erupted, leading to the deaths of 364 Turkish and 174 Greek Cypriots in a few months. The violence spurred increasing separation of the communities. In 1931, 36 per cent of villages had been ethnically mixed but by 1960 this figure had fallen to 18 per cent and by the end of the 1960s the figure was just 10 per cent. The crisis of 1963 also affected Famagusta, which saw atrocities such as the deaths of 32 Turkish Cypriots in one incident. The city became increasingly segregated; it is this history that Greek Cypriot memory has erased.[9]

As a consequence there is a marked naivety about the way in which Greek Cypriots reconstruct events. For example, one person remembers 'people like me – 16, 17 or 18 – were also members of EOKA and I was a member too. I was supporting the idea of *Enosis* but we never thought that Turkish Cypriots were annoyed with this.'[10] The reconstruction of the Turkish Cypriots as by-standers in the struggle against the British also silences the Turkish Cypriot narrative. Self-determination became the responsibility of the Greek Cypriots – they become the Cypriots. In a sense this reproduces the dominant discourse of the original *Enosis* program. The Turkish Cypriots become the unrecognized 'other.' In this account, Turkish Cypriots may have rights but only as individuals; as Muslims and as Turkish speakers, but not as a nation. Their program, Taksim, is seen as a veto on liberation; as a minority vision it needs to know its place. It was only when conflict erupted between EOKA and the TMT that it became evident the Turkish Cypriots were committed to their communal vision as much as the Greek Cypriots were. But this reality of the 1950s and the 1960s is partially forgotten in the Greek Cypriot memory of a Cyprus past.

Another Greek Cypriot waxes lyrically about his mother's garden. At the center of his account is the way in which jasmine plants frame the memory of the lost home. 'Every time my mother talks about the jasmine outside her veranda. . . . You know jasmine? She never went back to see her jasmine, she died.'[11] The narrative on jasmine is very evocative for both communities in Cyprus.[12] The plant is also connected with Cypriot identity in popular discourse; its strong smell wafts

9 Due to the conflict in the 1950s, Vasrosha had become entirely Greek Cypriot by 1958.

10 Mertkan Hamit, 'Memories on Varosha.' Interview conducted 2 May 2013 (records retained by the author).

11 Asla Hoşçakal Demedik Varosha (We Never Said Goodbye to Varosha). Dir. Sertaç Yıldız, 25 January 2014. www.youtube.com/watch?v=co_dB6FKDdI [accessed 19 November 2016].

12 The Jasmine Movement was an umbrella organization that participated in the Turkish Cypriot elections in 2009. The political motto of the organization was 'reclaiming our jasmines.' See also: Mete Hatay, 'The Problem of Pigeons: Orientalism, Xenophobia and a Rhetoric of the "Local" in North Cyprus,' *The Cyprus Review*, Vol 20, No 2 (2009), 145–171.

across ethnic divisions, offering the possibility of unity. But like all scent, however powerful, it can be transient and elusive. Too often the scented evening has been replaced by a harsh morning.

In narrating memories of Varosha it is significant that the scent of flowers and fruit are prominent. One former resident records 'We were growing oranges. We know and we made very good oranges. I remember my orange grove and . . . I want to cry. When I smell orange trees that are blossoming I remember mine . . . My orange grows and I miss it. Now there is nothing, they let it dry and nobody watered it.'[13] This image of the luscious fruit of memory compared with the barren present offers significant insights about the way in which dispossession is far more complex than the violence of forced displacement. It literally hangs in the air. Memory is very much a thing of the present.

There are also the fixed images of the past. The photographs that have survived the trek from Varosha assume an iconic role. This means for one family that 'Famagusta is everywhere in my house. There are photographs of our past life. Famagusta, at least for my family, definitely is not a forgotten city.'[14] At one and the same time the photographs constitute a record of what has been lost and create a longing to return. A particularly striking comment by a former resident is that: 'Nobody said goodbye when we were leaving and I think it is a sign.'[15] The ritualization of memory comes across strongly in the accounts of those who left. A son remembers that 'every year on the major holidays my father would raise his glass and say let's hope that next year we go to Varosha and celebrate in Varosha. Every year and every year. Then he died.'[16]

These glimpses into the attitudes of people connected to Varosha are typical of those who have been displaced. 'Nobody said goodbye,' is a sentiment that perhaps should be emphasized. The past is awaiting the present to address it. In a very formal sense this has occurred with United Nations Security Council Resolution 550 (1984). Although the resolution's main purpose was to condemn Ankara's exchange of ambassadors with the Turkish Republic of Northern Cyprus, it contained two clear references to Varosha. In the key part of the resolution, article 5 reads that the Security Council 'considers attempts to settle any part of Varosha by people other than its inhabitants as inadmissible and calls for the transfer of that area to the administration of the United Nations.' While Varosha has not been resettled by the authorities in Northern Cyprus, the area has not been handed to the UN. Decades later the displaced people of Varosha and their descendants await a resolution of their situation. That resolution is complex; the

13 Asla Hoşçakal Demedik Varosha (We Never Said Goodbye to Varosha). Dir. Sertaç Yıldız, 25 January 2014. www.youtube.com/watch?v=co_dB6FKDdI [accessed 19 November 2016].

14 Ibid.

15 Ibid.

16 Ibid.

desire to return to the place pictured in the photographs is understandable but, like the orange groves and the jasmine plants, it no longer exists.

The former Varosha residents and their descendants face the challenge of finding ways in which a satisfactory resolution can be achieved. While they might not have said 'good-bye,' there is no going back. The experience of dispossession and the anxiety caused by loss of property is compounded by the loss of place. The disorientation of suffering haunts its victims. It is this disorientation that makes the search for justice particularly elusive. Legal justice offers narrow possibilities in terms of restitution and compensation. Judgments of the European Court of Human Rights provide the solace of recognition but can only deliver dry words. The finding in the landmark *Loizidou* v *Turkey* case, that Turkey is in effect in control of the north of Cyprus and therefore can be held responsible for breaches of article 1 of protocol 1 of the European Convention of Human Rights, which confers the right to own and enjoy property, has great significance to law students taking an examination in human rights but less to the applicant.[17] In a later case the court itself expressed the problem encountered by applicants:

> Thus, the Court finds itself faced with cases burdened with a political, historical and factual complexity flowing from a problem that should have been resolved by all parties assuming full responsibility for finding a solution on a political level.[18]

In other words, legal justice can only follow a political resolution of the conflict. This underlines the lifelessness of law. Unless it exists in a health political environment, law has little to offer. Of course the court in question is a human rights court and it is human rights that seem to offer victims of injustice a location from which to frame their claims in a wider context. However, as Stephen Hopgood has commented, human rights 'survive as parts of a grand narrative that gives an ideological alibi to a global system whose governance structures sustain persistent unfairness and blatant injustice.'[19] The ability of all sides to appeal to human rights – and to do so in a convincing manner – reveals the weak point of faith in human rights.

In this volume we have encountered many other situations where there is 'blatant injustice.' As we have seen, such injustice is seared into the memory of those affected. In most cases it is the memory of injustice that in part constitutes the identity of the victim. As with the people from Varosha there are various ways in which the injustice is refreshed through different forms of memorialization;

17 *Loizidou* v *Turkey*, European Court of Human Rights (1531|89) 1996.

18 *Demopoulis and Others* v *Turkey*, European Court of Human Rights (46113/99, 3843/02,13751/02, 13466/03, 102 (I00/04, 14163/04, 19993/04, 21819/040) 2001.

19 Stephen Hopgood, *The Endtimes of Human Rights* (Ithaca and London: Cornell University Press, 2013), 2.

from monuments to the social media. The appeal to justice is highly complex. Legal justice can be too narrow while political apologies can be too meager. However, hovering over the issues that have been raised here is the incommensurable character of loss, the inability to erase trauma. Injustice is perhaps best seen as bereavement. There is no way back, however serious the apology or professional the court. The lesson from this collection is not so much the development of mechanisms for dealing with the past as a commitment to address the present.

Index

For Product Safety Concerns and Information please contact our EU representative GPSR@taylorandfrancis.com
Taylor & Francis Verlag GmbH, Kaufingerstraße 24, 80331 München, Germany

www.ingramcontent.com/pod-product-compliance
Ingram Content Group UK Ltd.
Pitfield, Milton Keynes, MK11 3LW, UK
UKHW011004180926
475701UK00004B/554
* 9 7 8 0 3 6 7 2 6 7 0 4 9 *